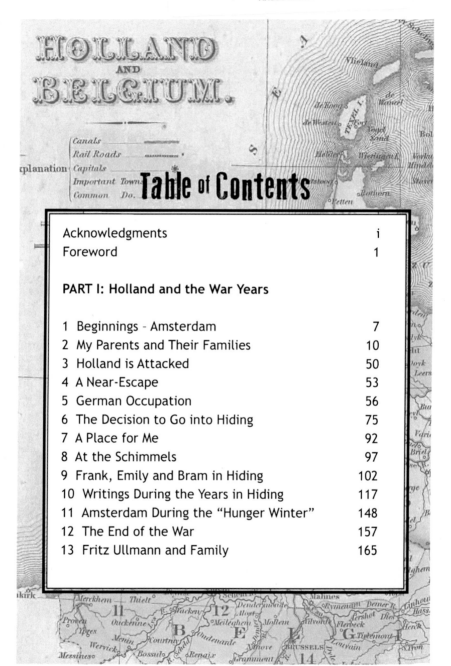

Table of Contents

Table of Contents (cont'd)

Acknowledgments

Most sincere thanks to:

Victoria Giambrone, my long-time valued assistant and associate, for transcribing and reviewing the first 16 chapters, and helping with all of the second edition (letting me know with raised eyebrows and an occasional smirk when my thoughts were inappropriate, or, God forbid, stupid), and, Jon Pevzner, for preparing the balance of the text as well as the initial photo and graphic image pages.

Lena Lopez who succeeded "Vikki" Giambrone and continued to slave on this second version with nary a peep.

My brother and friend, Henk (Dutch spelling), and his wife, Kathy, for reviewing the materials and helping me with the true facts and some photos.

Our son Frank, for helping with photos and reading the materials with useful comments.

Daughters Susan Ullman, Laura Schwartz and Valerie Taylor for reading the early draft with some thoughtful suggestions, and, where appropriate, no comments.

Son-in-law Arik Levinson and granddaughter Kira Ullman for their early encouragement and even a couple of tears.

Donald L. Webb Jr., the designated (by himself) "Cousriarch" of Kay Ullman's Lott family clan, for helping with the initial genealogy of my forebears (none of whom are in fact known to him).

Marjon Ullmann, daughter of cousin Joost and Anke Ullmann, for agreeing to dust off her German, and helping to discover the life of her grandfather and my dad in Cologne.

Juliemarthe Cohen, daughter of cousin Dorothy and Paul Cohen, for helping research a number of historical facts; she is also a fine curator at the Jewish Historical Museum in Amsterdam.

Hans (H.C.S.) Warendorf, first cousin extraordinaire, as further indicated in the text and footnotes, lawyer (retired), philanthropist, repository of much family lore, and the (well-balanced all-together) person I'd like to be when I grow up. We celebrated his 80th birthday recently with a 50-year vintage Magnum of Chateau Margaux, and he actually toasted this book.

Kay Ullman, extraordinary spouse, for reading the draft, tempering some comments, saying she liked it and letting me do it (provided I make no further comments about her personal trainer or golf game).

Lotte Warendorf, grandaughter of Hans (H.C.S.) Warendorf, located the relatives of Piet Hogenboom, Sr., whose involvement was critical to our family's survival.

Michelle Shain, who quickly saw that my original title and cover were ridiculous as well as the appearance of most other pages, brought to bear a remarkable artistic vision and insight, while remaining poised and focused amidst endless requests.

Gail Rosenthal, director of the Holocaust Resource Center at the Richard Stockton College of New Jersey for almost incomprehensible enthusiasm for this work and for her work.

Rob Huberman, the publisher (he is ComteQ), introduced to me by Gail Rosenthal, an incredible bulldog, growling and barking, while never letting go until this volume was done (to be added to the other 50 or so earlier published Holocaust titles bearing his imprimatur).

Our wonderful parents, Frank and Emily (Frans and Lotje, in Dutch, sometimes combined as "Frotje" to save money in a telegram), who in addition to giving us life and love, guidance and standards to try to uphold, left us with tons of photo books with millions of photos going back to the twenties, with all sorts of people, and, regrettably, at this point, no clue who they are.

Finally, above all, those beautiful people, my "war family" (the family who cared for me as their "hidden child" for 796 days), the relatives, friends, teachers and others, mentioned in the text, who touched, even saved, our lives in such critical and truly indescribable times. We were blessed and they are greatly loved and missed.

Foreword

The original intent of these pages was to scriven some thoughts on my experience as a "hidden child" in World War II in preparation for a talk I was asked to give in January 2013 at my old prep school, Phillips Academy, Andover, Massachusetts, ("Andover"), and also in response to requests (not too many) received to "tell my story" about those difficult times.

It seemed especially useful and perhaps even interesting to do so, as I am the only person alive at this point who knows very much about my particular matters and circumstances. It's also important in my view to continue to publish, in the widest sense, the story of the Holocaust as part of an overriding mandate to focus on intolerance and injustice.

The target audience, if any, of this effort is primarily the next two generations in our family. Thus, while they may have heard snippets, this, hopefully, will supply some further context. This has resulted in the creation of a new category of grandchildren, to wit, "favorite grandchild" available to any and all of our 7 grandchildren who read this tome. The youngest, Kevin Taylor, age 9 at the time, earnestly wants to be included and has undertaken voluntarily to read it "next year."

It should be noted that my Mom has written about her experience in short vignettes which she prepared for a writing class and which my father collected in a small book, *Stories by Emily Ullman*. Both parents also wrote a *Story of Survival* for my brother Henk and me on the occasion of their 40th wedding anniversary, in response to incessant nagging by us. A number of the photos (and statements which I assume to be facts, as well as some unsolicited and unsupported opinions) were taken from that (unpublished) book (and many of the photos were taken from albums prepared and kept by my father). A video of their story (and to a much lesser extent, mine) was recorded for Steven Spielberg's Shoah Foundation. Yet there are certain remaining inconsistencies and incomplete links which may never be solved.

In deciding to do this, I have also been very much aware of my own mortality (not that I'm facing the end quite yet) and the erosion of memory (which I am definitely facing), as factors in favor of recording some thoughts and memories while I am still able to do so. At this point there are, regrettably, very few of us left who can report firsthand on being a "hidden child" during the Holocaust.

References have been made to many extra-nuclear family members; others have not been mentioned even once. In such references (or omissions), it has been, I hope understandably, impossible to provide perceived fair and equal coverage to everyone, including the (very partial) genealogy at the end of the book. This does not mean I love or value any of them any less.

The story has been extended initially to two phases beyond the Holocaust years. First, there's considerable material about my parents and about people and places in our town, Port Washington, New York, and their respective influences on those early years of my life. This work thus became, intentionally, to a large extent a story about

"Mom" and "Pop" (and they were truly extraordinary people), as well as certain other close family members and their War stories, rather than just about me. It is also about our town, which, too, is quite special, certainly to us.

The final part of this story, and I don't intend to go beyond it, is a minimalist recounting of my two years at Phillips Academy, Andover, a very special school, which holds a place of substantial significance in my heart and my life in opening up a world of opportunities.

In writing and illustrating the materials, I have necessarily drawn on references to events and times much later than my 17th year in order to place in context, and hopefully to create more interest in, the earlier story.

A further note: I will refer many times to "the War," which is intended, of course, to refer to World War II. I am aware, especially as an American, that there have been other wars, before and since. However, for Europeans, and certainly Dutch persons who have survived it, WWII is still "the War." At least in Holland this is evidenced by two special national days every year, May 4th, Remembrance Day, to honor the War dead, and May 5th, Liberation Day, to celebrate Freedom from the horrors of the German occupation. Similarly, I refer to "America" which, of course, is the United States of America.

A final (preliminary) note: I will refer in the text frequently and fairly interchangeably to "Nazis" and Germans. I am, of course, fully aware that "Nazis" refer generally to adherents to certain political thoughts and policies (and members of National Socialist Parties during the period here involved), while Germans generally constitute persons from, or having origins in, Germany, a country of enormous cultural history and gifts to the world. Yet during "the War," to those of us in Holland, overrun and occupied by Germans and governed largely by Nazis, they were, for us, at least during those difficult days, one and the same.

After distributing some 350 copies and then running out of the self-published first edition (each personalized with a flourish), and facing demand for at least 2, possibly 3, more copies, I thought it appropriate to revise the book in fundamental respects, to eliminate much of the personal story dealing with our lives beyond initially emigrating from Holland and settling in Port Washington.

On further reflection and introspection, I have come to the inevitable conclusion that the expanded timeline of the first version of this book would be of interest, if at all, primarily to family and local friends. Thus, while the first edition devoted fully half the text on my life in the Port Washington schools, our friends in town, various musical pursuits, a summer in Amsterdam and two years at Andover, this "second edition" provides only fleeting reference thereto. The intent is therefore to focus in this second edition on the early years as a "hidden child" in Amsterdam, the plight of my parents, as well as other close family members during the War, and the beginnings of our new life in America.

This edition also corrects untold numbers of errors in the first edition, some of which were just embarrassing and could easily have been fact-checked, and others that were graciously (and sometimes not so graciously) pointed out to me by family and friends. I have also attempted to add some further historical context, as well as other photos, letters and documents (many with my inexpert translations), reflecting the events taking place during those days in Amsterdam, impacting our lives. Any remaining inaccuracies and misperceptions are certainly not intended and are, of course, my own.

PART I:

Holland and the War Years

Chapter 1

Beginnings — Amsterdam

The story begins in Amsterdam, the Netherlands. The country, the land mass of which is roughly 1½ times the size of Massachusetts, is often referred to (herein as well) as Holland, but, in fact, the term Holland referred historically to the largest and most populous province of the Netherlands. In 1840 the Province of Holland was divided into two provinces; i.e., Noord (North) Holland (which includes the city of Amsterdam) and Zuid (South) Holland (which includes both The Hague and Rotterdam). There are now 12 provinces of what is now the Netherlands; the last, Flevoland, was established in 1986 and consists largely of reclaimed land from what was once the Zuiderzee.

Both the country and Amsterdam, its cultural and financial center, date back to 1275. The seat of Government is in The Hague, but the Queen's official palace is in Amsterdam. Referred to as the "Venice of the North," Amsterdam's remarkable inner city template of canals, fed by the Amstel River, was built in the 17th century, at which time Amsterdam was known as the "wealthiest city in the world." The city's oldest building is the "Old Church" built in the early thirteen hundreds, and rebuilt a few times since. The city even features a wooden building or two from the 1400s.

The population of Amsterdam within the city limits, both in 1940 and today, is in the order of 800,000. Rotterdam, the principal port city, is somewhat larger in terms of the greater metropolitan area with a population of some 1.3 million, including an estimated majority of immigrants. The country, at approximately 12,900 square miles, is densely populated today with some 16.6 million residents; in 1940, the population numbered approximately 9 million.

The city and country have long been known for their religious tolerance. A law passed all the way back in 1579, for example, prohibited persecution based on faith.

Many Jews, including the human rights philosopher Spinoza, came to Holland and Amsterdam from the Iberian Peninsula in the mid-1600's after the "80-year War" with Spain. The involvement of Jews in Dutch economic and social life during the "Golden Age" of Holland in the 17th century was extraordinary compared to other countries, and, unlike other countries, there was never a ghetto, as such, in Amsterdam or elsewhere in the Netherlands. Nor was there the type of virulent anti-Semitism in Holland as there was in Germany or Austria, for example. René Descartes, the French philosopher, reportedly asked at some point during that century, "In what other country can one enjoy such complete freedom; where else can one go to sleep without fear?"

Starting in the early Napoleonic era (1796), Jews were allowed in all professions in Holland; this does not mean, however, that they were in fact welcome in all. It's fair to say that Jews historically have generally, with very limited exceptions, not reached senior levels of management in many of the country's large commercial banks and financial institutions (ABN, AMRO, ING), nor the largest industrial companies (Philips, Shell). Prior to World War II, few Jews served in the Government. This changed noticeably in recent years, as Amsterdam has had at least 4 recent Jewish mayors.

The Jewish population of Holland was approximately 140,000 as of January 1940. So-called "half Jews" (a Jew married to a non-Jew) numbered an additional 20,000. In all, the Jewish population was thus less than 2% of the country's total population. Approximately 60% of the Dutch Jews lived in Amsterdam. There was statistically very little inter-marriage of Jews with non-Jews. In general, it is believed that most of the Jewish population went to a synagogue primarily on Jewish holidays and rarely otherwise, but most observed the Sabbath on Saturdays. There were basically two synagogues in Amsterdam, the very large and imposing Portuguese (Sephardic) synagogue built in 1671-1675 and the synagogue complex of the High German (Ashkenazi) Jews, consisting of two large and two small synagogues also dating back originally to 1671.[1]

One area of commercial life in Amsterdam that has been particularly identified with the Jewish population, especially from the beginning of the 20th century through the start of WW II, has been the diamond industry. In fact, that industry can be traced back to the 16th century, and by the middle of the next century was already dominated by the Portuguese Sephardic Community. Of the estimated 80,000 Jews in Amsterdam as of 1940 nearly 30% were employed in the diamond industry and in general lived well. However, a large part of the Jewish population was seriously impoverished, living in the densely populated *Jodenbuurt* (Jewish Quarter) near the two synagogues.

---

[1] *The four buildings of the High German Jewish community together represent one of the largest Jewish structures in Europe. The four buildings, which were ravaged during the War, were extensively renovated and combined architecturally, re-opening as the Jewish Historical Museum of Amsterdam's new location in 1987. Those buildings together with the Portuguese Synagogue and several Holocaust-related sites further described herein are now all controlled and administered by the Jewish Historical Museum of Amsterdam.*

Chapter 2

My Parents and Their Families

My mother, Emily ("Lotje") Konijn (hereinafter generally "Mom"), grew up in a relatively well-to-do family in Amsterdam. While born Jewish, the family was extremely well-integrated into Dutch upper society and they observed little other than important holy days. Her father, Salomon Konijn, owned (together with his brother Soesman Konijn) a diamond cutting business (Gebroeders S. & S. Konijn) at a time when Amsterdam was the world's leader in diamond cutting. Mom's father married her mother, Bertha Konijn-Prins (hereinafter often referred to as "Grootmoeder") in a pre-arranged wedding through a "chatchen" (a marriage broker). In fact theirs was a double wedding with two sisters (Bertha and Julie Prins) marrying two brothers (Salomon and Soesman Konijn). Grootmoeder, attempted to propagate the story that her husband noticed her when she was crossing a bridge over one of the canals in Amsterdam and doffed his hat. This more glamorous fictional version of their meeting did not survive family scrutiny.

Grootmoeder's family, named Prins, has its roots primarily in the small town of Dinxperlo on the German border.[2] Grootmoeder herself

---

[2] *In the 1930's many Jewish German refugees crossed the border in Dinxperlo until the border was sealed in 1938.*

in her early years had been a bookkeeper in the Prins family carpet business. Maurits Philip Prins, born in Arnhem in 1840, moved his large family to Dinxperlo from Deventer in 1882 and continued there the carpet manufacturing business which his father had started in 1853. The factory continued under the control of two cousins, Maurits Prins (known as "Kleine (Little) Mau") and Maurits Philip Prins (known as "Lange (Tall) Mau") both born in 1898.

Grootmoeder (who adjusted from a small town girl to head of household with maid service) and Salomon Konijn, and their 4 children, of whom Mom, born on May 5, 1913, was the youngest (her sister Margaretha (Margaret) was the oldest (born on April 27, 1904); her brother, Abraham Salomon (Bram), born April 29, 1905, was the second oldest and died in 1922 at age 17 of leukemia; her other (older) sister, Julie Martha (Juliemarthe), was born on February 19, 1912), lived in an elegant large home, with maids, near the Rijksmuseum. Mom was chauffeured to school in super automobiles which embarrassed her greatly. She always insisted on walking the last couple of blocks to school. When her father died,[3] Grootmoeder and Mom moved into an apartment in Amsterdam. The year was 1932.

Mom was smart, funny and fun, quite attractive, physically active in horseback riding, skiing, etc. and, while at the University of Amsterdam, was immensely devoted to her sorority life and her sorority sisters (her popular and well-known sorority, Arktos, was fully integrated).

My father, Frans (also "Franz," Americanized as "Frank," or sometimes on U.S. documents, "Francis") Ullmann (hereinafter generally "Pop"), was born and raised in Cologne, Germany, where he was the

---

[3] Mom's father was a "Parnas" (Trustee) of the Jewish community and was thus buried in a special reserved section of the Muiderberg (Orthodox) Jewish cemetery (where women are not allowed).

son of Salomon ("Sally") Ullmann (hereinafter often referred to as "Opa Sally") and Annemarie ("Aenni") Ullmann-Loeb (hereinafter often referred to as "Oma Aenni").

Sally was a merchant in laces and had a small manufacturing facility where he made silk handkerchiefs, scarves and blouses. The Ullmann side of the family can be comfortably traced back to 1742, to Philip Summann (Ullmann), born in 1742, who married Sophie Abraham. They begat Abraham Ullmann in 1786. Abraham married Sibilla Ahrens (Weinberg), who then begat Phillipp Jacob Ullmann in 1833, who in turn married Melane Ehrlich. It is they who gave birth to my grandfather, Salomon Ullmann, who married Pop's mother, Annemarie Loeb.

Aenni was a Dutch woman whose family came originally from Germany. Her father, Leopold Leib, married Sibilla Gumpertz (my great-grandmother, later known as "Oma Munchen-Mum"). Leopold's discharge papers from the German military in 1898 refer to his last name as Loeb (no longer Leib). He subsequently moved to Utrecht and founded a general retail and furniture store.

Pop never went to college, though he became well-educated, possessing an incredible breadth of knowledge on a remarkable array of subjects. He graduated high school (*Real Gymnasium*) in Cologne, on February 17, 1932 and in March arrived in Utrecht, Holland, where his mother's family lived. He thus left at the beginning of the Hitler era in Germany.

Pop obtained a job and started working on April 1, 1932 in De Bijenkorf, the largest department store chain in Holland, which was in fact owned by in-laws of Oma Aenni's brother, Herbert ("Harry") Loeb. Pop worked in the flagship Amsterdam store of De Bijenkorf until January 1935 at which time he was assigned to the Rotterdam store, where he worked until April 15, 1937. In the meantime, he moved from Utrecht to Amsterdam in January 1935, and commuted to work.

In 1935, Pop obtained a German passport from the German consulate in Amsterdam which added the middle name "Israel" to his name, as Frans Leopold "Israel" Ullmann.

He met my mother through Mom's (double) cousin, Willem ("Wim") Konijn, who was also working at De Bijenkorf.[4] Wim introduced Mom to Pop as someone at the University who could help him with his Dutch. Mom at the time taught Dutch to impecunious immigrants.[5]

At the time he met Mom, she was engaged to a young man, Mark Rozelaar, of whom the family generally approved, although reportedly without great enthusiasm. One day, my maternal grandmother caught Mom sitting on my father's lap during his Dutch lesson. Pop probably appealed to her because he was intelligent, very good looking, over 6 feet tall, and a very good swimmer, playing on championship water polo teams.

This did not bode well for Mom's engagement to young Mr. Rozelaar, which was soon terminated by Mom (her family, reportedly was also not especially thrilled by Pop as suitor). Not too long thereafter, in 1936 at age 23, my parents were married in a synagogue in Ams-

---

[4] Wim Konijn (later known to me as "Uncle Bill") was a son of Soesman and Julie Konijn.

[5] In all, some 34,000-40,000 Jewish persons were estimated to have emigrated to Holland from Germany in the years 1936-1940. The Dutch Government was not especially anxious to house and retain the influx of German Jews and in fact formally closed its border with Germany in 1938, limiting permitted immigrants at that point to only 7,000 Jews, but, with financing from the Jewish community, placed many of such immigrants in a "model village" (which was in fact demeaning to the German Jews, many of whom had wealth) at Westerbork, which was opened in October 1939, and which later became a transit camp for deportation of Dutch Jews to German concentration/death camps. Note that the move to close the border was supported in part as a means of combatting an increase in anti-semitism. The order to close the border with Germany was issued by the Prime Minister, Frederikus Colijn, whose son, Geert Jan Colijn, a valued friend, recently retired as professor and the Dean of General Studies at the Richard Stockton College of New Jersey. He is the author of several books on the Holocaust, and a founder of the Holocaust Resource Center at that college.

terdam, which is now part of the Jewish Historical Museum of Amsterdam. Mr. Rozelaar ultimately married someone else and moved to Israel. He wrote to my Mom, as far as I know, only once, to congratulate her on her 75th birthday in 1988.

Their wedding was equal to Jewish elegance, with high hats, tails, chauffeured limos, etc. They combined their honeymoon with business traineeships in London and Stockholm, and then in the U.S.

Thus, on behalf of De Bijenkorf, Mom and Pop spent time in a number of U.S. cities where Pop served as a trainee at major U.S. department stores, including Macy's, Gimbels, Filene's, Bullocks, Rich's, Wanamaker's and others. He was joined on this U.S. traineeship tour by Mom's cousin, Wim Konijn.

My father's specialty at De Bijenkorf had been purchasing rugs and household furniture. As he was leaving for the U.S., he was advised in a letter from De Bijenkorf's CEO that he should not expect to learn much about furniture in the U.S. because the U.S. was behind Europe in design, but that he might be able to learn something about marketing from the various U.S. stores.

In late-1938, Mom became pregnant (with me) and more-or-less at the same time, Hitler commenced his expansive invasions on the eastern front of Europe, annexing Austria in 1938 and invading Czechoslovakia in March 1939. At that time, my parents decided to return to Amsterdam to be with their family.[6] In returning to Holland, they always assumed that, as was the case in WW I, Holland would remain neutral and that such neutrality would be respected by Germany, effectively exempting Holland from the ravages of war. Holland in the meantime had little military defense, relying in part on that historic neutrality.

---

[6] *Wim Konijn, however did not return. He stayed in the U.S. and wound up in Manhasset, New York.*

Shortly after they returned, Leopold Salomon Ullmann (the author) was born on July 14, 1939.

Leopold and Salomon, names which I came subsequently to hate (I thought, especially at daily roll calls while in the U.S. Marine Corps, that it was like a boy named "Sue") were the names of my great-grandfather (Leopold) and two grandfathers (Salomon).

I apparently had a relatively small "wine spot" on my shoulder, which could conceivably grow and spread to my neck and face. My parents arranged to remove that spot immediately after my birth, leaving a noticeable scar but a happy ending with no further damage (to date, to the best of my knowledge).

In April 1940, Pop applied for Dutch citizenship. That application was never acted upon because of superseding events occurring just weeks thereafter.

Auszug

aus den Personenstands-Registern der Bürgermeisterei: *Münstereifel*

(1)

№ 93.   **Geburts-Urkunde.**

Gemeinde *Münstereifel* — Kreis *Rheinbach* — Regierungsbezirk Köln.

Geburt
des Leopold Leib zu Münstereifel

Im Jahre tausend achthundert *sechs und fünfzig* den *fünften* des Monats *Juni,* — *Nach* mittags *fünf* Uhr, erschien vor mir *Wilhelm Lorbach, Beigeordneter als* Bürgermeister als *Delegirten* — Beamten des Personenstandes der Bürgermeisterei *Münstereifel.*

Salomon Leib, ein und dreißig Jahre alt, Standes *Handelsmann,* wohnhaft zu *Münstereifel* und erklärte, daß — von der *Maria Alma Levy, fünf und zwanzig* Jahre alt, Standes *ohne Gewerb,* wohnhaft zu *Münstereifel,* — verheirathet *mit dem Declaranten*

am *fünften Juni dieses* — Jahres *Morgens fünf* Uhr zu *Münstereifel* — ein Kind *männ*lichen Geschlechts geboren sei, welchem Kinde d*er* Vorname *Leopold* beigelegt wurde. —

Diese von mir aufgenommene Erklärung ist geschehen in Anwesenheit der beiden Zeugen als nämlich: —

1) *Carl Sommer, ein und zwanzig* Jahre alt, Standes *ohne Gewerb* wohnhaft zu *Münstereifel,*

2) *Peter Joseph Nelles, vier und fünfzig* Jahre alt, Standes *Tagammacher* wohnhaft zu *Münstereifel.*

Nach geschehener Vorlesung und Genehmigung wurde diese Urkunde unterschrieben von mir dem Personenstandsbeamten *dem Declaran-*
ten und den Zeugen.
Salomon Leib, Karl Sommer, Peter Jos.
Nelles. —
W. Lorbach —

Für die Richtigkeit dieses Auszuges.

Münstereifel den *1* ten *Mai* — 190*5*

Gebühren *50* Pfg.   Der Standesbeamte.

Birth Certificate of paternal great-grandfather Leopold Leib, born 1856 in Munstereifel, Germany (extract dated 1905).

Birth Certificate of great-grandmother Sibilla Gumpertz ("Oma München-Mum"), daughter of Leiser Gumpertz and Sophia Ehrlich; 1858.

Heirathsurkunde.

5 A

Nr. *4*

Aldenhoven am *dreizehn* ten *April* tausend acht hundert *achtzig und zwei*

Vor dem unterzeichneten Standesbeamten erschienen heute zum Zwecke der Eheschließung:

1. der *Kaufmann Leopold Leib*

der Persönlichkeit nach *bekannt*, *jüdischer* Religion, geboren den *fünften Juni* des Jahres tausend acht hundert *sechs und fünfzig* zu *Münstereifel*, wohnhaft zu *Düren*

Sohn des *Pferdehändler Salomon Leib* und *dessen verstorbenen Ehefrau Maria Anna* geb. *Levy* wohnhaft zu *Düren*

2. die *gewerblos Sibilla Gumpertz*

der Persönlichkeit nach *bekannt*, *jüdischer* Religion, geboren den *eilften Januar* des Jahres tausend acht hundert *acht und fünfzig* zu *Aldenhoven*, wohnhaft zu *Aldenhoven*

Tochter des *verstorbenen Metzger Leiser Gumpertz und dessen Ehefrau Sophia geb. Ehrlich* wohnhaft zu *Aldenhoven*

Marriage Certificate of paternal great-grandfather Leopold Leib and Sibilla Gumpertz in 1895 in Aldenhoven, Germany.

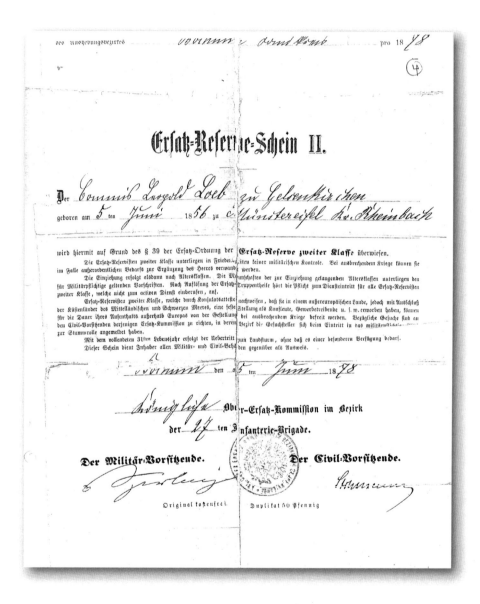

Certificate that my paternal great-grandfather Leopold Loeb, residing in Gelsenkirchen, has been discharged from the German military in 1898.

Paternal great-grandfather Leopold Loeb (formerly Leib) in his German
military uniform.

(above) The home (the left part only) on Jan Luijkenstraat where Mom grew up in Amsterdam.

(right) Pop's family home at Volksgartenstr. 18, Cologne, Germany.

(l to r) Bertha Konijn-Prins, Julie Konijn-Prins, Soesman Konijn, and Salomon Konijn.

My maternal grandfather, Salomon Konijn, with Mom (on the left) and her sister Juliemarthe (on the right).

My maternal grandmother, Bertha Konijn-Prins, also referred to by me as "Grootmoeder," was sometimes referred to, behind her back, of course, as "Her Majesty."

Meeting of the Dutch Jewish Poverty Aid Board – my maternal grandfather, Salomon Konijn, is 2nd from the right in the back row.

Maternal grandfather Salomon Konijn with my cousin Dorothy.

Paternal grandfather Salomon ("Opa Sally") Ullmann with me.

(l) **Paternal great-grandfather Leopold Loeb.** (r) His store, "All Sorts of Goods." The store was in the *"Ganzemarkt"* ("Geese Market") in Utrecht. Its advertising slogan was, *"spreek met Loeb, en het komt in orde"* ("speak to Loeb, and it will be taken care of").

Paternal grandmother Anne Marie ("Oma Aenni") Ullmann-Loeb and grandfather Salomon ("Opa Sally") Ullmann.

Paternal grandmother "Oma Aenni" Ullmann-Loeb with siblings
Fritz, Otto and Herbert Loeb.

(L-R) Fritz Loeb, grandmother ("Oma Aenni") Ullmann-Loeb, great-
grandmother ("Oma Munchen-Mum") Sibilla Gumpertz, great-grandfather
Leopold Loeb, Herbert ("Uncle Harry") Loeb, and Otto Loeb.

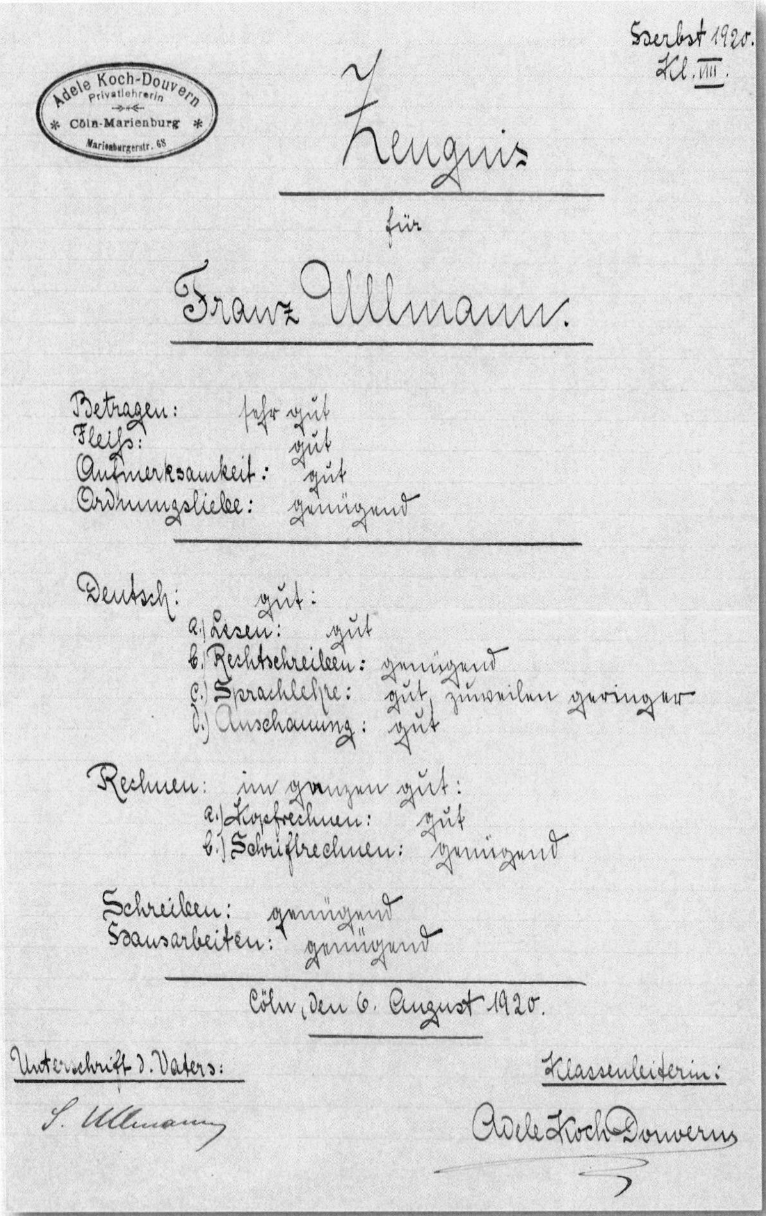

Adele Koch-Douvern
Privatlehrerin
Cöln-Marienburg
Marienburgerstr. 68

Herbst 1920.
Kl. VIII.

Zeugnis
für
Franz Ullmann.

Betragen: sehr gut
Fleiß: gut
Aufmerksamkeit: gut
Ordnungsliebe: genügend

Deutsch: gut:
a.) Lesen: gut
b.) Rechtschreiben: genügend
c.) Sprachlehre: gut, zuweilen geringer
d.) Anschauung: gut

Rechnen: im ganzen gut:
a.) Kopfrechnen: gut
b.) Schriftrechnen: genügend

Schreiben: genügend
Hausarbeiten: genügend

Cöln, den 6. August 1920.

Unterschrift d. Vaters: S. Ullmann

Klassenleiterin: Adele Koch-Douvern

Pop's report card for second grade in Germany (1920).

**Städtisches Gymnasium und Realgymnasium
in der Kreuzgasse, Köln**

ZEUGNIS

über den _2_ Abschnitt des Schuljahres 19 _31 /32_

für den Schüler

Ullmann   Franz der Klasse _6z1_

Urteile : Für Betragen: 1 = Sehr gut, 2 = Gut, 3 = Im ganzen gut, 4 = Nicht ohne Tadel, 5 = Tadelnswert.
Für die Leistungen: 1 = Sehr gut, 2 = Gut, 3 = Genügend, 4 = Mangelhaft, 5 = Nicht genügend.

Betragen: —		Ordnungsliebe: _gut_
Aufmerksamkeit: —		Handschrift: _genügend_
Religion: _gut_	Geschichte: _gut_ Staatsbürgerkunde	Musik: _genügend_ Singen
Deutsch: _genügend_	Erdkunde: _genügend_	Leibesübungen: _gut_ Schwimmen
Lateinisch: _gut_	Mathematik: _gut_ Rechnen	**Wahlfreie Fächer:**
Griechisch: —	Physik: _gut_	Englisch: am Gymnasium
	Chemie: _genügend_	Hebräisch: /
Französisch: _genügend_	Biologie: —	Spanisch:
Englisch: _genügend_	Zeichnen: _genügend_	Kurzschrift:
		Werkarbeit:

Schulbesuch: —

Bemerkungen: ....

Datum des Beschlusses über die Versetzung der Schüler: Konferenz vom ....
Nach § 5 der Versetzungsbestimmungen kann verfügt werden, daß ein Schüler nach erfolglosem zweijährigen Besuch derselben Klasse die Schule verlassen muß.

Köln, den _5 Dez._ 19 _31_

Der Direktor:

Dr. Niederländer

Der Klassenleiter:

Dr. Ernst Dornfeld
S. Ullmann

Unterschrift des Vaters oder seines Stellvertreters: ....

Pop's report card for his last year in secondary school in Cologne, Germany.
(1932)

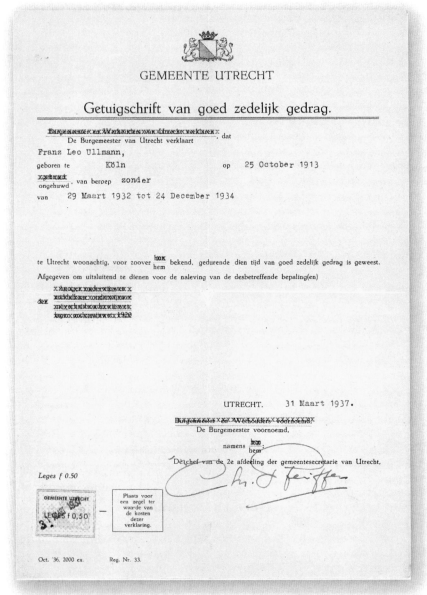

Certificate of "good conduct" by Pop while living in Utrecht from 3/32 to 12/34 (permitting him to move to Amsterdam).

Pop's German passport issued in 1935 (with added middle name, "Israel," as required of all male Jews).

No. 407

Het Kerkbestuur der Nederlandsch-Israëlietische Hoofdsynagoge alhier, verklaart uit legale bescheiden te hebben gezien, dat de

KERKELIJKE HUWELIJKS-INZEGENING

van Frans Leo Ullmann

met Emily Konijn

op den 25 Marcheswan 5697 / 10 November 1936 heeft plaats gehad.

Amsterdam, 15 November 1936.

Het Kerkbestuur voornoemd:

A.S. Vedy *Voorzitter.*

de Secretaris,

My parents' (religious) Wedding Certificate: "The Board of Directors of the Netherlands Israeli Chief Synagogue certifies…that the (religious) wedding took place on November 16, 1936."

Mom and Pop's Wedding (1936). The three youngsters are cousins Otto Loeb, Dorothy Warendorf and Herman Jacobs.

The newlyweds

Pop (left) and his brother Fritz
played water polo.

Mom

Mom on horseback;
this activity did not
rub off on her spouse
or sons.

(left to right) Mom's siblings – Margaret, Emily (Mom), Abraham Salomon and Juliemarthe Konijn.

Mom and Pop

Hierboven moet een legesstempel van *f* 1.— staan.

BURGERLIJKE STAND

Arrondissement
AMSTERDAM

Gemeente
AMSTERDAM

Reg. __10__ Fo. __65__

Uittreksel

uit het Geboortenregister.

Op __veertien juli negentienhonderd negenendertig__ - - - - - -

is in de gemeente Amsterdam geboren een kind van het __mannelijk__ geslacht, genaamd:

__Ullmann, Leopold Salomon__ - - - - - -

Vader: __Ullmann, Franz Leo__ - - - - - - -

Moeder: __Konijn, Emily__ - - - - - - - - -

Coll.:

Dit uittreksel stemt overeen met de toestand op het ogenblik van de afgifte.

AMSTERDAM, __31__ januari 195 __7__.

De Ambtenaar van de Burgerlijke Stand,

Zegel *f* 2.—
Leges . 1.—
_____
  f 3.—

My (Leopold Salomon Ullmann's) birth certificate.
(Inset) Leo as a (very cute) baby.

Mom with me at the Milletstraat apartment.

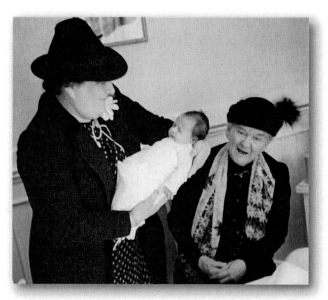

Paternal great-grandmother ("Oma Munchen-Mum")
at right and grandmother ("Oma Aenni") with me.

DE JOODSCHE INVALIDE
Goedgek. bij Koninkl. Besl. 13 Maart 1918 No. 540
Eere-Voorzitter Dr. W. DE VLUGT
Burgemeester van Amsterdam
———   Le.
WEESPERPLEIN 1
Telefoon Nos. 50248 & 53362
Postgiro 10260 - Gem. Giro V 1026

AMSTERDAM, 18 Juli 1939.

        Den Weledelen Heer en Mevrouw
        F.L. Ullmann-Konijn,

                            AMSTERDAM,
                            Milletstraat 37.

Weledele Heer en Mevrouw,

        Door dezen betuigen wij U onzen hartelijken

dank voor de hoeveelheid kersen, welke U ons ge-

zonden hebt ten behoeve van onze verpleegden en

personeel ter gelegenheid van de geboorte van Uw

zoon.

        Wij zijn U voor dit blijk van sympathie je-

gens onze Vereeniging ten zeerste erkentelijk en

geven U de verzekering, dat onze patiënten heerlijk

gesmuld hebben.

        Onze Stichting ook voor de toekomst in Uw

belangstelling aanbevelend, verblijven wij,

                            HOOGACHTEND,

                    V O O R   D E   V E R E E N:

                    "DE JOODSCHE INVALIDE"

        Ambtenaar in alg. Dienst.   Administrateur.

A note to Mom and Pop thanking them for donating a large amount of cherries to this Jewish hospital in honor of my birth, four days after the blessed event, and assuring Mom and Pop that the patients greatly enjoyed them.

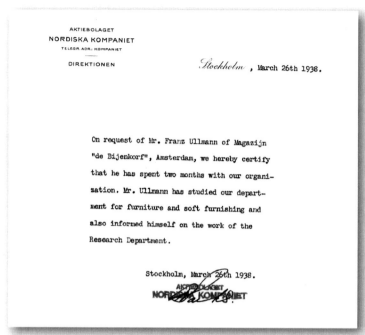

Pop as trainee in Sweden.

German passport issued in May 1940 (after commencement of German occupation of Holland) to Pop, again with (required) middle name, "Israel."

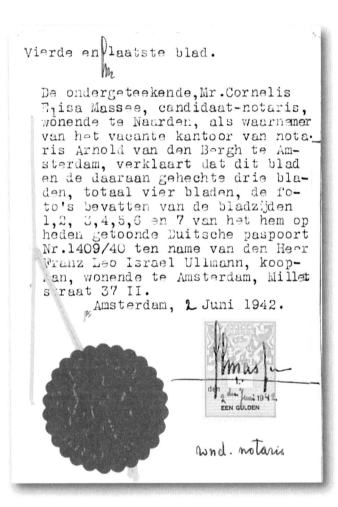

Vierde en laatste blad.

De ondergeteekende,Mr.Cornelis
Elisa Massee, candidaat-notaris,
wonende te Naarden, als waarnemer
van het vacante kantoor van notaris Arnold van den Bergh te Amsterdam, verklaart dat dit blad
en de daaraan gehechte drie bladen, totaal vier bladen, de foto's bevatten van de bladzijden
1,2, 3,4,5,6 en 7 van het hem op
heden getoonde Duitsche paspoort
Nr.1409/40 ten name van den Heer
Franz Leo Israel Ullmann, koop-
man, wonende te Amsterdam, Millet
straat 37 II.
        Amsterdam, 2 Juni 1942.

Certificate of Dutch Notary issued in June 1942 as to
validity of Pop's German passport.

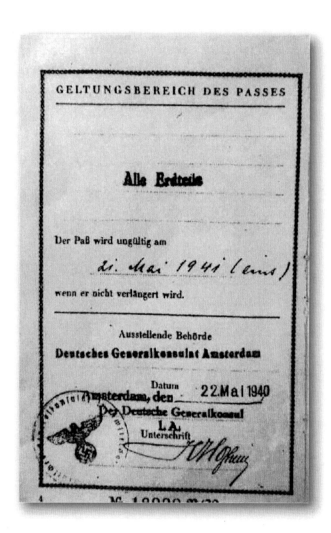

Permit for Pop to stay in Amsterdam for a one-year period commencing 5/22/40 through 5/21/41, issued by the German Consulate in Amsterdam shortly after commencement of German occupation.

2663

360

BURGEMEESTER EN WETHOUDERS DER GEMEENTE AMSTERDAM

verklaren, dat   Franz Leo ULLMANN

van beroep   ass.inkoopleider Bijenkorf
geboren te   Keulen
den   vijf-en-twintigsten October negentienhonderd dertien.
zoon van   --------

geboren te   --------   den   -------
thans woonachtig alhier   Milletstraat 37,II
sedert   den 24.12.1934 komende van Utrecht tot den 31.10.1935 toen
hij werd afgeschreven naar Rotterdam en van den 14.4.1937
komende van Rotterdam tot op den datum van afgifte dezer verklaring, --

binnen deze Gemeente heeft gewoond, en wel gedurende de laatste vijf jaren aan de volgende
adressen :

     van 24.12.1934 tot 31.10.1935 Willemsparkweg 131
     van 14. 4.1937 tot 13.11.1937 Minervaplein 3
     van 13.11.1937 tot 22. 1.1938 Koninginneweg 33
     van 22. 1.1938 tot 7.12.1938 Minervaplein 3
     van 7.12.1938 tot h e d e n Milletstraat 37

Hij is gehuwd met   Emily KONIJN
geboren te   Amsterdam   den 9.5.1913

eerder gescheiden/weduwnaar van --------

Kinderen :   Leopold Salomom ULLMANN geboren 14.7.1939 te Amsterdam

AMSTERDAM, den   10 Februari   19 40

coll.

Burgemeester en Wethouders voornoemd,

Weth.

De Secretaris,

Extract from Civil Registry.
(translation on next page)

```
                        (My translation)


The Mayor and Council Members of the Municipality of Ams-
                         terdam
              declare that Franz Leo ULLMANN
occupation Assistant Purchasing Director Bijenkorf
born in     Cologne
on          25th of October, 1913
son of      -----------
born in     -----------
currently residing at       Milletstraat 37, 2nd fl.
since       12/24/1934 coming from Utrecht to 10/31/1935
            when he
            exited to Rotterdam and from 4/14/1937 coming
            from
            Rotterdam until the date of execution of this
            declaration.
has resided in this Municipality and during the last five
years at the
following addresses:
            from 12.24.1934 to 10.31.1935 Willemsparkweg
            131
            from 4.14.1937 to 11.13.1937 Minervaplein 3
            from 11.13.1937 to 1.22.1938 Koninginneweg 33
            from 1.22.1938 to 12.7.1938 Minervaplein 3
            from 12.7.1938 to date Milletstraat 37
he is married to    Emily KONIJN
born in        Amsterdam on 5.9.1913
earlier
divorced from
widowed
children: Leopold Salomon ULLMANN born 7.14.1939 Amster-
          dam
                         AMSTERDAM the 10th February 1940
```

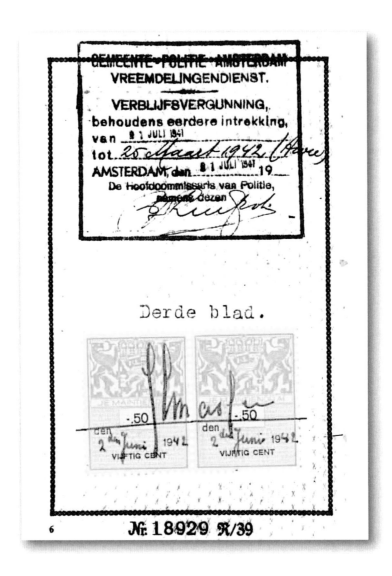

Permit issued by Dutch Immigration Service for Pop to stay in Amsterdam from 7/21/41 to 3/25/42.

Visa in the passport of Sientje Konijn (sister of my grandfather Salomon Konijn), one of perhaps as many as 30,000 issued and signed, without his government's authorization, by the heroic Portuguese Consul-General, Aristides de Sousa Mendes.

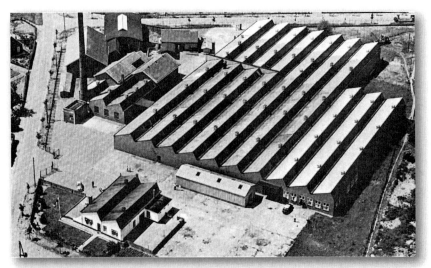

The Maurits Prins Rug Factory in Dinxperlo, the Netherlands as of 1940.

The Maurits Prins rug factory, workers and townsfolk in Dinxperlo.

The reverse side of a small area rug manufactured by the Maurits Prins Rug Factory in Dinxperlo.

Mosaic plaquette in the town-hall of Dinxperlo in memory of the two cousins
Prins.

(translation on next page)

**In memory
of the partners
of
"De Deventer Tapijtfabriek
(The Deventer Carpet Factory)
Maurits Prins"
Dinxperlo**

Maurits Philip Prins	**Maurits Prins**
12 December 1898	**11 January 1898**

**and their employees
1. Menist
W.B. Nyland
Th. Veerbeek**

**Who died as victims
Of Nazi Terror**

Once the Germans conquered Holland, the two cousins Prins both made arrangements to go into hiding. Maurits Philip Prins (Tall Mau) arranged to go into hiding in the town of Veenendaal, while Maurits Prins (Little Mau) intended to escape to Switzerland. Toward that end, he had arranged to purchase fake ID's (at 325 florins, or $1,312 in current U.S. dollars) from an underground / illegal printer in Amsterdam on October 17, 1942. At the moment that the false ID's were delivered, two policemen arrested Little Mau. All of the Prins families from Dinxperlo were then deported by the Nazis to Auschwitz-Birkenau, where they were killed.

Chapter 3

Holland is Attacked

On May 10, 1940, German tanks invaded Holland "falling in unannounced" early in the morning without declaring war. This was less than nine months after Hitler "guaranteed" the neutrality of the Netherlands (also after the Dutch government itself declared its neutrality). There was some vigorous resistance by the Dutch military for four days, but then, on May 14, the Germans bombed the City of Rotterdam, which was then, and still is now, one of the world's most important ports, to smithereens, causing more than 1,000 casualties.

At the same time, the dikes were compromised in large measure by the Dutch, to slow the German advance. This caused a large part of Holland to be flooded and, to the extent it held back German ground troops, resulted in history's first parachute operations, effected by the Germans in response thereto. The German military threatened to embark on similar intensive and extensive bombing of Amsterdam and The Hague unless the Dutch capitulated, which they did on May 15th. The Queen and her family left Holland for England on May 13th by a British warship, to carry on the fight against the Germans from there, but also to protect Dutch interests in their East and West Indian colonies. The Dutch cabinet followed, transferring authority to General A.C. Winkelman, who signed the surrender documents.[7]

This, of course, was a terrible psychological blow for the Dutch people, and a particular shock and horror for the Jews of Holland. In fact there were many reported suicides and an estimated 700 suicide attempts by Dutch Jews. Many Dutch Jews, from the moment of the German invasion, and thereafter, carried a cyanide pill or two in their pockets in contemplation of suicide. No one, as indicated, had expected the Germans to attack Holland, and in a matter of days, the Germans occupied and controlled the country, and installed a military government. Amsterdam was thus basically left free of bombing attacks and the famous inner part of the city with its canals and houses from the 1400s on, largely remained intact. Yet, in the meantime, there were air raid signals and people like my parents had no idea how to protect themselves. They literally walked around with copper and aluminum pans on their heads.

---

[7] General Winkelman, although his military defense against the Germans lasted only 4 days, nevertheless remained a highly-regarded figure in Dutch history.

20 foot-high bronze sculpture created by the Russian/French sculptor Ossip Zadkine named *"De Verwoeste Stad"* ("The Destroyed City") unveiled in May 1953 and designated a Netherlands National Monument. The sculpture is situated in the square, Plein 1940, in front of the Maritime Museum in Rotterdam. It is intended to commemorate the destruction of the heart of the city of Rotterdam by German bombardment on May 14, 1940. In the words of the sculptor, it represents "a cry of horror against the brutality of this act of tyranny." The statue, which has a large hole where the heart would be, was commissioned and donated to the city (with the condition that it never be moved) by the owners and directors of De Bijenkorf (of which "Aunt Nellie's" father was co-founder, and where my father worked before, during (until discharged) and after the War).

Chapter 4

A Near-Escape

Once the Germans completed their bombardment of Rotterdam and seized control of the country, there were still several days before the borders were sealed.[8] Jewish people desperate to leave, including several of our relatives, were able to escape the country. Thus, for example, Pop's uncle, Herbert ("Harry") Loeb and his wife ("Aunt Nellie," whose father co-founded De Bijenkorf), Mom's sister, Juliemarthe, and her husband, Joost Jacobs, among others, were able to go to fishing ports, principally IJmuiden[9] and Scheveningen, and pay for passage to England, (but only if they had sufficient currency in silver coins, as paper currency had immediately become basically worthless), from which, in turn, they were generally able to obtain passage to Canada or the U.S. Uncle Harry and Aunt Nellie, with their sons, Otto and Arthur, wound up in Philadelphia and later in Cambridge, Massachusetts. Juliemarthe and Joost, with their kids, Herman, Bertien and Emily, wound up in Port Washington, New York.

---

[8] *It is interesting to note that much of the diamond inventory was smuggled out of Holland during those first days of German occupation in May 1940 to the U.K. on a U.K destroyer. Diamonds, of course, were a major actual and potential source of "hard" currency.*

[9] *Note that the letters I and J together (and therefore both capitalized in this instance) are treated as a single letter in the Dutch language equivalent to, and pronounced like, a "Y" in English.*

We, too, contemplated going to England on a fishing boat. My parents were urged to do so by Uncle Harry and Aunt Nellie, and, in fact my parents, together with me, and my maternal grandmother, (Grootmoeder), went to IJmuiden, one of the fishing ports where they had decided to use this escape route. The scenes at the fishing ports were apparently chaotic. There were false rumors of large Dutch ships taking passengers out of the country. Many citizens arrived and sought desperately to fight their way onto the few boats.[10]

My father had bought a bag of *rijksdaalders* (2½ guilder silver coins) to pay for passage, and the 3 adults brought 3 suitcases. However, Grootmoeder and I had toothaches and earaches, respectively, the boat was not there yet, and my parents did not have valid passports, so they decided that we should go back to Amsterdam and leave when we were in better health and everything was in order. Mom, moreover, was very reluctant at the time, because I was not even a year old.

Hans and Margaret Warendorf (Mom's sister and brother-in-law) and their three children also tried to escape by boat at the port of IJmuiden and were unable to do so. Their story is further chronicled in a later chapter.

Of course, within a few days thereafter, the ports and borders were sealed and they (and I) were never again able to escape.

---

[10] *It is estimated that not more than 1,600 in all were able to escape in those first days in this manner by boat, including an estimated 74 German and Jewish children who had been taken to orphanages in Holland by Kindertransports. The last vessel to leave was the 5,600 ton cargo vessel, Bodegraven, which actually took several hundred persons. The other vessels were small boats; one canoe even made it.*

Cousins Emily, Herman and Bertien Jacobs
in Holland before emigrating to the U.S.

Mom's sister Juliemarthe and her husband Joost Jacobs, who escaped with
their children, Herman, Bertien, and Emily, when the Germans attacked
Holland in 1940, and who settled in Port Washington, New York.

Chapter 5

German Occupation

Shortly after taking military control of the country, the Germans installed, on May 29, 1940, an Austrian governor, Arthur Seyss-Inquart, who was designated as *Reichskommissar* of the Occupied Territories. Seyss-Inquart, a vicious anti-Semite and Hitler loyalist, had been Chancellor of Austria for 2 days (11-13 March 1938), at which time he "invited" the Germans to take over Austria, thus creating a colorable legal fiction to support the invasion.

At the same time, Hanns Albin Rauter, another Austrian, who, like Seyss-Inquart, had served in the Austrian army, was named *General-Kommissar Fur das Sicherheitswesen en Höhere SS-und Polizeifuhrer* in Holland, effectively in charge of Nazi terror and the apparatus for persecution of Jews through "Rauter's Police."

Among other things, when Seyss-Inquart took over in Holland, he quickly dissolved the Parliament and forbade any display of posters, photos or other images of the Dutch Queen. The designation of any entity as "Royal," such as the "Royal" Airline Company (KLM) was terminated. As to relations with Jews and the Dutch in general, Seyss-Inquart announced on his first day in office that he would not "force an alien ideology" on the Netherlands. Unlike the history of many countries annexed by Hitler, Dutch civil servants and leaders were generally not replaced, but, rather, slotted in with the German administration. Dutch law also remained in effect.

At first, during the occupation, extending over a period of approximately 1½ to 2 years, life in Amsterdam remained with some degree of normalcy and grudgingly tolerable, although increasingly difficult for the Jewish population, as the Germans attempted to woo the Dutch gently to their side. My parents, with friends, relatives and me, in fact went on several vacations to seaside beaches and parkland woods within the country as late as the fall of 1942, even though by a decree of September 1941, departure outside Amsterdam by Jews for a period of more than two days was strictly forbidden without a permit. Until May 1942, when the granting of permits was largely stopped, some 340,000 permits had been granted.

There were, however, during those first 1½ to 2 years, many edicts published by the Nazis in newspapers and post offices, seemingly on almost a daily basis, the administration of which became increasingly harsh and oppressive for Dutch Jews. The very first edict, which essentially had little effect, but was issued as early as July 1940, prohibited ritual slaughter of animals.

The more severe decrees, designed to isolate Jews and to deprive them of any economic, cultural or public life, and those that ultimately doomed Jews in Holland to deportation and death, started with the requirement in October and December 1940 of special yellow identification cards for Jews over the age of 14, with photos and fingerprints.[11] Male Jews were required to use "Israel" as a middle name and female Jews the name "Sarah." A January 1941 decree required Dutch Jews to register with the Civil Registry, which resulted in a reported 140,552 (true) Jews, 15,549 "Half-Jews" and 5,719 "Quarter-Jews." Jews were also required to report their assets in such filing; few refused to do so.

In July 1942, all Dutch Jews were required to move to Amsterdam.

---

[11] A Jew was defined by decree as follows: (1) persons whose grandparents included three or more full Jews by race; (2) persons with only two fully Jewish grandparents if they either (a) belonged to the Jewish religious community on 9 May 1940 (or subsequently joined it); or (b) married to a Jew on or after 9 May 1940; and (3) a grandparent was deemed a full Jew if he or she was at any time a member of the Jewish religious community.

Poorer Dutch Jews who arrived from towns and cities outside Amsterdam were forced into areas known as the Jewish quarter, occupied by many lower income Jews. In February 1941, a group of Dutch Nazis attacked Jews in the Jewish quarter and one Nazi was killed. In retaliation, the Germans cordoned-off the Jewish quarter with barbed wire.

Pop's parents, his grandmother, his sister-in-law, Riet, and her son Joost, in accordance with the decree, all moved from Utrecht to my parents' two bedroom duplex apartment at Milletstraat 37 in Amsterdam. This was, of course, an uncomfortable arrangement which lasted more than a year. Pop's brother, Fritz, however, refused. He stayed in Utrecht and was soon picked up and sent to Westerbork (from which, with the help of Aunt Riet's father, himself a notorious Nazi sympathizer, he was soon released). (Fritz Ullmann's story is further detailed in Chapter 13 hereof).

Among the innumerable decrees and circulars issued by the Germans during those early years were the following, which had the effect of a continuing tightening vise:

- *As of October 1940, all civil servants, numbering some 200,000, were required to file an "ancestry form" stating the religion of their parents and grandparents; one month later all Jewish civil servants were dismissed.*
- *Persons of Jewish blood had to give up any "honorary positions."*
- *Jewish teachers at non-Jewish schools and Jewish professors at universities were terminated.*
- *Jewish employees of non-Jewish enterprises were terminated.*
- *Jewish members of orchestras (including the famous Concertgebouw Orchestra), theater groups and ballet troops were terminated.*
- *Non-Jewish orchestras were prohibited from playing the music of Mendelsohn, Mahler and other Jewish composers.*
- *Jewish newspapers were banned as of September 1940 (but commencing in March 1941 Het Joodsche Weekblad ("The Jewish Weekly") was published under German control).*

- *Jewish doctors, dentists, midwives, etc. could not work for non-Jews.*
- *Jews could not belong to bridge etc. clubs, fraternities or sororities or other social organizations (note that the sorority involvement by Mom in fact saved my life).*
- *Jews were not allowed to attend or participate in any outdoor sports, including football (soccer to us), tennis, sailing, swimming, rowing, fishing, etc.*
- *After July 1942, Jews could no longer have, or use, telephones.*
- *Jewish children could only attend Jewish schools.*
- *Jewish families could only have Jewish maids.*
- *There were separate hospitals for Jews.*
- *Jews were not allowed to give blood.*
- *Jews were allowed to shop only between the hours of 3 p.m. and 5 p.m. (after Gentiles had had their "pick") and only three days a week, and subsequently only in certain designated Jewish stores.*
- *Jews were subject to an 8 pm curfew.*
- *They were required to give up all forms of transportation, including automobiles and bicycles, and were prohibited from using public transportation.*
- *In fact they were not allowed to travel at all.*
- *Jews were barred from theaters (other than the Jewish Theater), cinemas, libraries, hotels, restaurants, cafes, public beaches, baths, swimming pools and parks; all such buildings and places had to have signs marked, "No Jews."*
- *Jews were prohibited from observing Jewish holidays.*
- *Jews were barred from the stock exchanges.*
- *English and American movies were forbidden.*
- *Even streets named after famous Dutch Jews, such as Sarphatistraat, had to be renamed.*

In April 1941 pursuant to an order of the new German boss at De Bijenkorf, Pop lost his job. He managed, however, to become a courier (with a bike) for the hated Amsterdam Jewish Council (further described below).

As of April 29, 1942, in an effort to visualize the demons, all Jews above the age of 6 were required to wear at all times, sewn on their clothing (pins were strictly prohibited), the yellow Jewish star with the word, "Jood" in Dutch or "Jude" in German ("Jew") on it. Adding additional insult, such stars had to be purchased from the Nazis (for 4 Dutch cents each).

Many non-Jewish Dutchmen at the outset wore the stars to show solidarity, but this, by ordinance, became a serious crime potentially punishable by death.

Once Jews were required to wear the Star of David, non-Jews were ordered not to socialize with them. In fact, with the Jewish star, our family and others were often greeted with the creed, "Dirty Jew." Yet, many persons also expressed sympathy.

At least one Jew took the position that he didn't mind wearing the star, as with his shuffling gait and long nose, you could tell he was a Jew from a kilometer away, even without the star.

A male Jew, later in the War, could avoid having to wear the Jewish star if he agreed to be sterilized and obtained a doctor's certificate thereof. It is estimated that some 2,500 Dutch Jewish males were sterilized. Jews in mixed marriages were required to be sterilized or they'd be deported. Some heroic and sympathetic doctors signed such certificates without effecting the required sterilization.

- *All businesses owned by Jews, or having one or more Jewish partners or directors, having Jewish capital or Jewish shareholders or "under Jewish influence" had to register and were prohibited from employing non-Jews (and were thereafter taken over by Germans).*

- *A decree of August 11, 1941, required that all real estate owned by Jews be registered and transferred to the Nazis. In September all agricultural businesses had to be turned over to German Verwalters (Supervisors).*

- *By decree of August 8, 1941, Jews had to surrender their gold, silver, jewelry, precious metals, art, bank accounts, deposits, stocks and bonds, all of which had to be turned over to a Dutch bank in Amsterdam, Lippmann-Rosenthal & Co., which was generally known as LIRO, and administered by the German authorities. The irony, of course, is that prior to Nazi con-*

trol, this had been a reputable Jewish investment banking firm. Jews could keep only (i) their wedding rings; (ii) personal silver wristwatches; (iii) table silver up to four pieces per person; and (iv) gold and platinum teeth.

- *By decree of February 1942 Jews had to give up all material goods, collections and "objects d' art."*

The stocks and bonds, incidentally, were subsequently sold during the War on the Amsterdam Stock Exchange, generating hundreds of millions of guilders, all with the knowledge of members of the Exchange and of Dutch brokers who enjoyed the benefits of commissions on such sales. There were many inquests and studies after the War as to the myth and reality of Dutch help for the Jews, versus cooperation with the Nazis, and this was one area of focus for such inquiries.

It is estimated that as a result of this program of systematic looting, more than 90% of the possessions of the Dutch Jewish population were stolen by the Nazis or Dutchmen, with a value at that time of perhaps 1 billion guilders, amounting to perhaps U.S. $10 billion currently.

Jews also had to pay a special tax on, and subsequently to give up, their radios, which my father, and an estimated 25% of the owners, did not do. In fact in 1943 all Dutchmen had to turn in their radios and more than one million radios were confiscated by the Nazis. He and others secretly listened to Winston Churchill's powerful speeches on the BBC, as well as those of Wilhelmina, Queen of the Netherlands, on *Radio Oranje*, from exile in London. Churchill throughout the War was the voice of hope, and the belief by almost all Dutchmen in the ultimate defeat of the Germans.[12]

It is interesting to note that one of the very few trades which for the most part exempted many Jewish employees from being terminated and sent off to forced labor camps and even concentration

---

[12] *The Dutch government broadcasts, remarkably, with the limited exception of a broadcast in October 1942 by the Queen where she stated that she was personally affected by the "systematic extermination of the Dutch Jewish population," were basically completely indifferent to the plight of the Jews and their deportation.*

camps, at least during the early years of occupation, was the diamond business.[13] The Germans coveted that business as part of the expanded Germany, which they contemplated to include Holland, after the War, and an important source of hard currency.

Pop, after being dismissed from employment with De Bijenkorf department store, found work as an apprentice carpenter with Simon Krieks, a skilled Jewish carpenter. Pop learned his trade well and, among other things, he and his colleagues made a beautiful dining room table, at the office. A handsome sideboard also made by him and colleagues at the Krieks firm sits at our daughter Laura's home.

Pop also became a (bicycle) courier for The Amsterdam Jewish Council ("Joodsche Raad"). The Amsterdam Jewish Council was created by the Germans largely in response to the Resistance in the Jewish quarter further described below. It had some 19 members who were prominent in the Jewish community and was headed by a well-known history professor, David Cohen, and by Abraham Asscher, who, like my grandfather, was head of a diamond cutting business (the Asscher business, unlike ours, still exists today).[14]

The Council had the power to issue a *"Sperre"* stamp, which certified that you need not be deported. The text of the stamp read *"Inhaber dieses Ausweises ist bis auf Weiteres vom Arbeitseinsatz Freigestellt"* (*"The holder of this certificate is exempt from labor facilities."*) This included as many as 17,500 people who at one time had a job with the Council (including Pop as a bicycle courier).

The ultimate horrible and critical activity of the Council was to

---

[13] *By 1944, however, the Germans had decided on the Entjudung ("Aryanization") of even the diamond business, and started the deportation of diamond workers, some of whom were permitted to remain in Holland for a period of up to 6 or 8 weeks if they paid the equivalent of 50,000 Swiss francs (approximately equivalent to $118,000 in current U.S. dollars).*

[14] *In fact when the Asscher firm moved to larger quarters prior to the War, the business of my grandfather and Soesman Konijn took over the former Asscher building (believed to have been on Valkenburgerstraat in the old Jewish quarter). Subsequently, Asscher took over the Konijn brothers' business.*

prepare lists of persons to be deported. The Council was thus a witting instrument of Nazi genocide pursuits and its members were complacent in the annihilation of its own (Jewish) people. Seyss-Inquart referred to the *Joodsche Raad* as a "body for transmission of orders." Some referred to the *Joodsche Raad* as the *"Joodsche Verraad"* (Jewish Treason).

The Council, and specifically David Cohen and Abraham Asscher, were accused after the War of attempting to save the Jewish elite from those lists. In the end, Cohen and Asscher were themselves deported in September 1943 to Theresienstadt (Terezin) and Bergen-Belsen, respectively.[15]

There was an incident at an ice cream parlor in February 1941 where Nazis fought against local Jews; the Nazis were sprayed with ammonia gas and one Nazi was killed. In response, 425 young Jewish men were rounded up, beaten and taken away to prisons, and ultimately sent to Mauthausen from which only one returned. After a call by the (already illegal) Communist Party for a strike in support of Dutch Jews on February 25th and 26th, 1941, the Dutch dockworkers (longshoremen) and other, primarily socialist, municipal labor unions led a sympathy strike, involving as many as 40,000-50,000 strikers, in support of the Dutch Jewish people, shutting down all transportation and effectively all commercial activity in Amsterdam and other cities. This, while incredibly brave, ultimately caused unbelievable harm, and in effect, death sentences, to a large part of the Jewish population. This Dutch general strike, the only such general strike in support of the Jews in any occupied country in WWII, was effectively stopped by the

---

[15] *Both Cohen and Asscher survived, but charges of complicity with the Nazis in the deportation and killing of Jews were brought against them by both the Dutch government and the Dutch Jewish community. The charges were ultimately dropped by both. Among the claims made in their defense was that they were not aware that the deportations, ostensibly to German forced labor camps, were in fact generally to concentration/killing camps and a death sentence. It is hard to imagine that they did not know of, or suspect such killings, when Anne Frank, while in hiding, wrote in her Diary in October 1942 that "The English radio says they're being gassed."*

Jewish Council, who, under orders from the Nazi rulers, contacted the unions and urged them to cease the protests for fear it might hurt, rather than help, the Jews.[16] Of course, after the strikes, railroad workers continued to efficiently send train transports on time with Jewish deports to Germany.

That strike effectively ended German efforts to quietly win over the Dutch populace. The Nazi rulers were so incensed by those sympathy strikes, that immediately after they were stopped, they executed on March 3, 1941 three strikers and 15 members of a Resistance group in the dunes. The Germans, as was their rule, widely published the names of all the persons whom they executed for their "misdeeds." Subsequently, 450 more "leaders of the strike" were executed. Seyss-Inquart, together with the notorious SS'er, *Obersturmfuhrer* Ferdinand Aus der Fünten, who was Commander of the German Security Police,[17] were determined brutally to crush all opposition and resistance within a matter of days, through roundups, killings and deportations. It is estimated that in all, as many as 2,000 Dutchmen were ultimately executed under Seyss-Inquart's direction. He also extracted an enormous monetary fine from the Dutch population, equivalent to tens of billions in current U.S. dollars.

There were other strikes in support of the Jews in 1943 and 1944. They included the April-May 1943 "Milk Strikes" when farmers refused to deliver milk to the factories and allowed private citizens to pick up as much milk at the farms as they wanted. However, at that point a preponderance of Jews had been deported.

---

[16] *The strikers and their unions were honored collectively many years later by Yad Vashem. A statue of a Dutch dockworker was erected on the square, Jonas Daniel Meijerplein, in 1952 in front of the Portuguese Synagogue to commemorate the strike. Every year, on the 25th of February, a very large group of people gather at the Monument to honor the Resistance.(See page 74.)*
[17]*Aus der Fünten, described generally as the ultimate killer of Jews, was tried and convicted by the Dutch Government and given a death sentence, which was later commuted to a life sentence. Ultimately, in 1989, he was granted amnesty and released over the protest of many war victims. He died a few months later.*

The wholesale deportation of Dutch Jews took place most intensively during the 15-month period from July 1942 through September 1943. As early as December 5 (Saint Nicholas – Santa Claus day), 1941, a decree called for all non-Dutch Jews to report for "voluntary emigration." This presumably included my father. Very few persons heeded that call.

The first major call-up notice, for all Jewish men and women between the ages of 16 and 40, was issued on July 5, 1942.[18] A few days later, on July 14 (my birthday), 1942, 700 Jews were summarily arrested in the streets and held hostage at the main Amsterdam police headquarters until the Jewish Council helped round up 4,000 Jews for "forced labor camps" in Germany. If the Council failed in this effort, the "hostages" were to be sent to such "work" or concentration camps. In the meantime, the Jewish Council was able to extricate members of the Council who were being held hostage.

On August 9, 1942 the Germans demanded 2,000 more. Starting the following month, hundreds of Jews were collected every night, usually in raids after midnight. All those Jews who were rounded up were first brought to the *Hollandsche Schouwburg* (the "Dutch Theater," later renamed "the Jewish Theater") used as a "holding pen" where they spent days, weeks, even months until they were transferred to Westerbork in the north of the country, for ultimate transit to the concentration camps. The trains left the *Hollandsche Schouwburg* twice a week; it is estimated that at least 15,000 of the Jews deported from Amsterdam passed through the *Hollandsche Schouwburg* before it was closed in late September 1943.[19] As a result of the required registration of Jews, the Nazis were able to develop and display large detailed maps of Amsterdam, for example, show-

[18] *One of such notices was received by Anne Frank's sister Margot.*
[19] *The* Hollandsche Schouwburg *has been designated as the principal building monument in the newly-designated Netherlands National Holocaust Museum, administered by the Jewish Historical Museum of Amsterdam.*

ing virtually every house with Jewish occupants.[20]

The deportations and killings were primarily at the hands of the Nazis but, to a not insignificant extent, also of Dutch collaborators, including especially Dutch Nazis. Thus there was a Dutch National Socialist Movement (*Nationaal Socialistische Beweging–NSB*), a Nazi party which had already, in the general elections of 1937, received 4.2% of the popular vote and several seats in the Lower House of Parliament.

The rise of the NSB in the 1930's was attributed in large part to massive unemployment in the Netherlands. As a counter party to the NSB, the *Nederlandsche Unie* was founded in 1940 and soon had 800,000 members, the most of any party ever in the Netherlands. However, it was banned by the Germans in December 1941. Anton Mussert, head of the NSB, was named "Leader of Dutch People" by Hitler in December 1942, which, however, was of little functional significance.

It should be noted that there were approximately 140,000 Jews left in Holland in late 1941-early 1942, a little more than 1.5% of the population, but nearly 10% of the population of Amsterdam. Of those, approximately 107,000 were deported to concentration camps via Westerbork, and of those deported, approximately 102,000 were gassed, died of starvation or disease, or were otherwise murdered. Of the Dutch Jews who were deported, an estimated 8,000-9,000 were discovered and delivered to the German Nazis by Dutch collaborators for a bounty.[21]

Ultimately, the percentage of Jews who survived after the War who had lived in Holland before the War, at an estimated rate of less than 20%, was far less than the rates of survival of Jews in any other country in Western Europe.

---

[21] *An estimated 80 bounty hunters were active in Holland during the War searching for Jews. The bounties paid at the outset were 5 guilders (roughly a week's pay for an unskilled laborer), later increased to 40 guilders, for each Jew turned in by the bounty hunter. The bounty hunters were organized under the leadership of Willem Henneicke and Willem Briedé, and were known as the Henneicke Column. Henneicke was murdered by the Dutch Resistance in 1944; Briedé, who fled to Germany at the end of the War, was tried in absentia in Holland, sentenced to death, but lived in Germany as a free man until he died in 1962.*

Paternal great-grandmother ("Oma Munchen-Mum") and Pop at the apartment on Milletstraat.

Beach hotel in Zandvoort where we vacationed in 1942.

DER VERWALTER
der Firmen
N.V. Magazijn „De Bijenkorf", Amsterdam,
N.V. Hollandsche Eenhexdsprijzen Mij „Hema",
Amsterdam

Amsterdam, den 9. April 1941.

EINGESCHRIEBEN

Herrn Ullmann,
Xilletstraat 37,
AMSTERDAM.

Als Verwalter der obengenannten Betriebe bestellt
von Herrn Reichskommissar für die besetzten niederländischen Gebiete, Generalkommissar für Finanz und Wirtschaft, durch Verfügung vom 27. Februar 1941 - habe
ich Ihnen mitzuteilen, dass Sie mit sofortiger Wirkung
bis auf weiteres von Ihren bisherigen Funktionen in
der Firma N.V. Magazijn "De Bijenkorf" freigestellt sind
und sich als beurlaubt zu betrachten haben. Wegen der
Regelung Ihrer Bezüge ergeht noch nähere Mitteilung.

(Dr. Brandt)

Notice (in German) from the new German directorate of De Bijenkorf
that my father's employment was being terminated pursuant to regulations
promulgated by the Commissioner for Finance and Commerce for the
Occupied Territory of the Netherlands.

GENOOTSCHAP
LIEFDADIGHEID NAAR VERMOGEN
OPGERICHT 1871

TELEFOON No. 44521, 40995 EN 46470
POSTGIRO-REKENING .... No. 14905
GEMEENTEGIRO-REKENING B No. 545

ONDERWERP:

AMSTERDAM, **30 October 1941**
RAAMGRACHT No. 4

Mevrouw B. KONIJN -PRINS.
Minervaplein 3 I.
AMSTERDAM.

Mevrouw,

De onlangs verschenen verordering No.199/1941 heeft
tot ons groot leedwezen tengevolge, dat U Uw werkzaamheid
voor ons Genootschap met ingang van 1 November a.s. zult
moeten staken.-

Wij willen niet nalaten bij dezen uiting te geven
aan onze erkentelijkheid voor Uwe met veel toewijding en ij-
ver verleende medewerking sedert 28 April 1936, zoomede voor
hetgeen door U is gedaan in ons distrikt 77 ten behoeve van
de aan U toevertrouwde gezinnen.-

Wij vertrouwen, dat U met voldoening zult kunnen te-
rugzien op Uw arbeid voor L.N.V. en teekenen inmiddels

Hoogachtend,
BESTUURDEREN VAN HET GENOOTSCHAP
LIEFDADIGHEID NAAR VERMOGEN

Voorzitter.

Termination of employment of maternal grandmother Bertha Konijn-Prins
(Grootmoeder) with a Dutch charity as of 11/1/41, based on a then-recently-
issued ordinance.

Pop's Jewish star

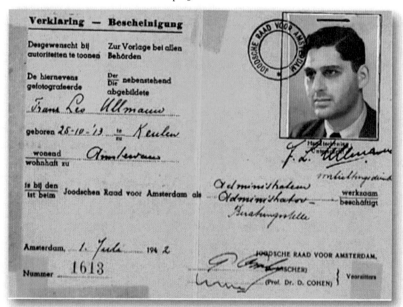

Pop's ID card issued by the Amsterdam Jewish Council.

Certificate issued in 1942 to the effect that maternal grandmother Bertha Konijn-Prins (Grootmoeder) was then employed as director of the named school and "must be considered as irreplaceable" (and therefore not terminable even though Jewish).

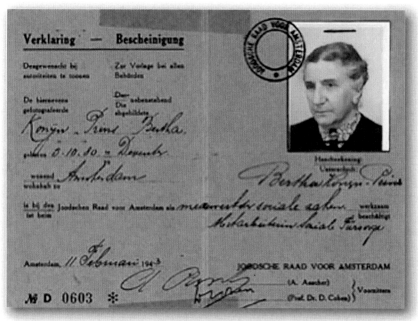

Maternal grandmother Bertha Konijn-Prins' (Grootmoeder) ID card issued by the Amsterdam Jewish Council.

JOODSCHE RAAD VOOR AMSTERDAM

VOORZITTERS { A. ASSCHER
            { Prof. Dr. D. COHEN
POSTGIRO 41.7242

Amsterdam-C., ...12 Febr.'43
Nieuwe Keizersgracht 58
Tel. 55003, 551 36, 54970

Bij Uw antwoord te vermelden :
AFD...IV/Pers.B..
REF...LPS/SE...

De Joodsche Raad voor Amsterdam verklaart, dat

    BERTHA KONIJN-PRINS
   Geb. 5-10-1880 = Minervaplein 3(I)

werkzaam is bij de Afd. Sociale Zaken van
de Joodsche Raad voor Amsterdam.

    NAMENS DE JOODSCHE RAAD VOOR
      AMSTERDAM

    (Meijer de Vries)
  Voorzitter Personeel-Commissie

Verzoeke aangeteekende brieven te zenden aan het postkantoor Keizersgracht

MODEL 331-ALG.-50.000-2254-K 262

Declaration in February 1943 that maternal grandmother Bertha Konijn-Prins
(Grootmoeder) was then employed by the Social Welfare Division of the Jewish
Council of Amsterdam.

P.B 125709

De Burgemeester van UTRECHT verklaart, dat
_____ Bertha Prins weduwe Kramer _____
geb. 15 Oct 1880 _____, wonende Nassaupark 42 M:
voor een EERSTE DISTRIBUTIESTAMKAART in aanmerking
zou komen, indien deze kaart nog mocht worden uit-
gereikt.

Utrecht, 19 Juli 1944.

De Burgemeester /AA,

Gemeente-
stempel

The Mayor of Utrecht here certifies in July 1944 that maternal grandmother Bertha Prins (the name "Konijn" intentionally omitted, as the name "Prins" is not necessarily a Jewish name), "widow of Kramer" (this, of course, is false), residing in Utrecht(!) (where she was in hiding) is eligible for a first "distribution master card" (for food coupons, etc.) "if such card may still be issued."

Hollandsche Schouwburg (Dutch Theater)
Image Bank WW2-Collection NIOD. Photo: Lydia van Nobelen-Riezouw.

Dockworkers Monument
The inscription on the monument
(translation) reads:

February Strike 1941
Act of Resistance of the Citizenry
Against Oppression of Jews by
The German Occupiers

Chapter 6

The Decision to Go Into Hiding

By 1942, the transport of Dutch Jews to concentration camps had started. As earlier indicated, Pop received a notice in July 1942 to report to the *Hollandsche Schouwburg* ultimately for transport to "work camps" in Germany. At first he and others thought that they could go to such camps and survive. The Germans had even established an Advice Group to promote the benefits of going to German work camps (an estimated 500,000 Dutchmen wound up working in Germany). He and Mom even prepared rucksacks with work boots and heavy clothing to get ready for an eventual work camp. The Germans, together with the Jewish Council, prepared a list of what they were to bring:

- rucksack or suitcase	- towels	- socks or stockings
- gloves	- pajamas	- food for 3 days
- warm clothing	- toiletry articles	- sweater or vest
- hat and shawl	- underwear	- raincoat or winter coat
- blankets	- plate, cup, spoon & fork	

My parents, and indeed most Dutchmen, always believed the War would not last long and that they could survive a work camp, if necessary. However, Pop saw the trains, consisting in large part of cargo and cattle cars, with not just able-bodied young Dutch men, but, in fact, many older people and children, being pushed into these cars and the doors locked behind them as they left for Germany. He turned back and determined never to go on those trains. While my parents believed that there were forced labor camps, they could not imagine or believe in the murder of millions in those camps.

By early 1942 there were daily *Razzias* (raids) of Jewish homes with police vans and German army vehicles to pick up the Jewish residents. As there were fewer than 200 German police in Amsterdam, and never more than 2,000 German civil servants, most of the raids were in fact conducted by Dutch police against their own Dutch Jewish citizens. Raids were followed shortly by a moving van which carried the name of the Amsterdam family who owned the business, A. Puls, to remove furniture and belongings. This gave rise to the concept, when asking about the status of a Jewish family, that they had been "Pulsed." Even before a house was "Pulsed," neighbors and hoodlums often grabbed anything of value.

Jewish-owned "hebraica," "judaica" and private book collections were separately carted away to Germany, intended to be housed in a special museum after the country had been cleansed of any Jewish presence.

The last three major citywide raids were held on May 25-26, June 20 and September 29, 1943. For those raids, the Jewish Council was required to submit lists of 7,500 for deportation in May and 5,500 for June. Jewish hospitals were also emptied by late August 1943. The September list included everyone still working for the Jewish Council, all of whom were in fact deported. At that time, Holland was declared *Judenrein* ("free of Jews"), the first European country to so qualify, thus achieving Hitler's goal of putting Holland in a position, as originally envisioned because of its largely Germanic background, to be part of the desired Aryan German commonwealth.

The Nazi *Grüne Polizei* (Green Police), so-called because they wore green uniforms, as well as Dutch collaborators and policemen trained by the Nazis, who wore black uniforms and were thus called *zwarten* (blacks), actually came to the apartment at Milletstraat to pick up Pop's parents. Plying them with whiskey and gifts saved for the occasion, they were able to persuade the officers to return on another day.

It was then that Mom and Pop made the decision that they had to go into hiding and to do so quickly. They were 29 years old.

It is not really known how many Jews in Holland actually went into hiding. It is estimated that 20,000 to 25,000 Jews went into hiding, of whom an estimated 12,000 to 16,000 were saved. In no other country of Europe did as many persons go into hiding as in Holland. Yet, there is still some bitterness that not more Dutch non-Jews stepped-up to prevent more than 100,000 Jews from being deported and killed.

Moreover, It was not just Jews that went into hiding. Ultimately, an estimated 300,000 or more persons went into hiding, including, in addition to Jews, former soldiers, and young men otherwise eligible for work camps.

Mom always said that the decision to go into hiding was extremely difficult for her because it essentially meant that they had decided to become "illegal" (they referred to it as "living like rats"), whereas they had always been law-abiding, upstanding, socially responsible, citizens.

Through a policeman in Utrecht, Piet Hoogenboom, a friend of Pop's Uncle, Fritz Loeb, our family was able to obtain, not only false ID cards (made by Piet, Jr.), but also hiding places for Mom's mother, Pop's grandmother, and Pop's parents, all in Utrecht and surroundings. All of them had been living in Mom and Pop's apartment.[22]

---

[22] *Piet Hoogenboom, who did so much to save our family, received payments from my maternal grandmother for the rent for his (modest) apartment in Utrecht during the remainder of her life.*

The false ID cards became terribly important in my parents' case. The difference between the false and the regular ID cards was the absence of the letter "J" affixed to the picture and the card, denoting a "Jew," as well as a false (Christian) name and address (often of a deceased person). They thus had obtained "clean" identity cards without the "J," but still with their own photo, which ultimately permitted them to obtain food stamps.[23] It is estimated that as many as 3,000 Dutch Resistance workers were involved in furnishing false ID papers, food coupons, money and hiding places for Jews in Holland.

The first to leave the apartment with Mr. Hoogenboom in his car to depart for a hiding place was Pop's grandmother, Oma Munchen-Mum. She was 83 years old, frail and nearly blind. She always wore a wig in observance of her Jewish beliefs and hooped skirts. I apparently gave her great joy playing with little toy cars in and around, perhaps even under, her hooped skirts.

She had great difficulty getting down the stairs and finally made it into Hoogenboom's car. She died just a few weeks later; no one had heard from her, and she was presumably buried somewhere, no one knows where, under her false identity.

Pop's parents were taken-in initially by the Hoogenbooms themselves in their home on Minnebroederstraat in Utrecht.

People who took in Jews, like most Dutchmen, assumed that the War would not last long, and that their hosting would also not have to last long. However, weeks turned into months and even years. Many Jews in hiding had to move several times for various reasons, including problems with their hosts and vice versa, and, of course, for safety concerns. Some families took in Jews with the

---

[23] *The original requirement of ID cards for Jews was issued in October 1940. The requirement that they be stamped with the letter "J" was added in June 1941.*

thought that it potentially represented cheap labor (as in the farms) or maid service. It is estimated that the average Jewish person in hiding had to change addresses up to four times. Unlike many countries in Europe, Holland generally lacked woods and forests where people could create their own shelters. The common creed of persons going into hiding was "anything is better than Poland."

My parents had to deal with their, at that time, 3 year old son (me), who could not be expected to grow up soundlessly in a hiding place. The decision to arrange a separate hiding place for me and to "give me up" (they referred to it as making me "disappear"), greatly upset Pop's parents. They thought this was unforgivable and when they left for Utrecht for their placement via Piet Hoogenboom, they did so without a word to my parents. Their anger at this decision and resolve of my parents, of course, upset my parents greatly.

Through Mom's sorority sister and best friend, Aleida Schot, my parents made a contact with the Minister of the Dutch Reformed Church in nearby Haarlem, who had been able to place a number of Jewish children in hiding places throughout the country.

Over a period of several weeks, my parents then consciously weaned me away from themselves so that they could ultimately place me elsewhere apart from their own hiding place. This was arranged, primarily with sorority sisters from Mom's sorority, Arktos[24], throughout the country for days at a time so that I would be relatively comfortable away from my parents. I assume my placement was effected

---

[24] *The Arktos bond with many of those women remained strong throughout Mom's life. The Arktos sorority held a 90th-year celebration in 2007. Isabel Ullmann, daughter of my cousin Eric Ullmann, M.D., and his wife Elsbeth, became a member of Arktos while a student at the University of Amsterdam. On the occasion of their special celebration I contributed a photo of Mom with some of her sorority sisters. Arktos included in the book, published for the event, a group photo of all the current members without their clothes. Mom would have been horrified. Arktos left the student fraternity/sorority organization ASC/AVS and effectively disbanded as of August 2010. Isabel maintains that it was because the student groups were all about partying and misbehaving, whereas Arktos always had a history of inviting young women who were strong, well spoken, intellectual, ambitious and passionate.*

several days before the others went into hiding.

Aleida Schot lived nearby in the Beethovenstraat (in a 4th floor walk-up) and later became a professor especially famous for translating into Dutch the works of leading Russian authors, like Dostoevsky, Pushkin, Tolstoy, etc., whose works pre-dated the Russian Revolution; she herself never visited Russia. During the War, in addition to her role in the Resistance, she gave English lessons.[25]

Mom in the meantime was able to arrange a hiding place in the heart of Amsterdam with a welfare client family, the Peysters, whom she came to know as a result of her social work while at the University; she brought them food stamps and money on a weekly basis. The Peysters lived above a shoe store on the Ceintuurbaan, one of the principal shopping streets in Amsterdam. The Peyster family consisted of Gerard, the father, who was mildly disabled, a mother ("Ma") and two daughters, Riet and Ellie. Gerard's mother, according to Mom, sold herself in the "red light district."

I've learned little about Ma Peyster except that she stayed home to care for Gerard, and when Gerard's mother was gravely ill, but still alive, Ma and her two teenage daughters borrowed a transport bike with a flatbed and took all her belongings, furniture, bedding etc., ostensibly so the government wouldn't take them to satisfy welfare claims.

The Peysters had space in the attic available to my parents, while they also rented out an apartment between the attic and their own apartment above the shoe store. They agreed to hide Mom and Pop in the attic in exchange for certain rental payments.

---

[25] *After her death, a prize named the Aleida Schot Prize, was awarded every two years for translation of Slavic languages. A foundation in her honor was created under her will but languished until infused with funding, and care, by my cousin H.C.S. ("Hans") Warendorf, who, through that foundation and otherwise, arranged translators for immigrants caught up in Dutch legal proceedings. Hans, incidentally, has published, among other things, a translation of the Dutch Civil Code into English.*

Preparing to go into hiding, my parents gave away many of their worldly goods; their larger furniture items and belongings were picked up and stored by a delivery man who worked at De Bijenkorf, and they buried their silverware in the backyard of one of Mom's sorority sisters. They carefully hid the silver chest under a tree in the sorority sister's backyard. They could not have imagined that toward the end of the War, when there was no coal, oil or gas, people cut down every tree they could find, indeed stole any wood they could find, even from railroad beds, etc., for fuel. Thus, finding the buried silver after the War became a difficult task.[26]

Pop realized that he needed money to go into hiding and he needed to make some real money quickly. Through his contacts in buying rugs for De Bijenkorf, he had become friendly with a Persian rug dealer, Mr. Kinnebanyan. He arranged with the dealer to take rugs on consignment and was able, very effectively, to sell them to German officers in Amsterdam, making a tidy penny on those sales. However, after a few months, when it became clear that he had to then go into hiding, he went to Mr. Kinnebanyan and said that he could no longer continue the consignment sales. Mr. Kinnebanyan understood and said to my father, "Here is a prayer rug that I want you to have and to keep as a talisman, a symbol of good luck. I know you are considered an infidel, but Allah will protect you." It must have worked. That rug together with my parents made it through the War and then spent 65 years on my parents' piano; it is now on our piano.[27]

I was never able to find Mr. Kinnebanyan.

---

[26] Sadly, that silver, a large George Jensen set received at their wedding and which they then brought to America, was ultimately stolen shortly after we moved into our second home in Port Washington. The silver had been in trays in the sideboard made by Pop in Holland. The set was never replaced.

[27] The rug, which is still in very fine shape, is a Daghestan (Caucasian) rug from 1900, approximately 5'3," made of wool and decorated with a praying niche and two hands. Pop related this story during his and Mom's interview with Steven Spielberg's Shoah Foundation. The relevant portion of the interview is included in the "Image Gallery" of the link to the Exhibition "Some Were Neighbors – Collaboration & Complicity in the Holocaust" on the website of the U.S. National Holocaust Memorial Museum.

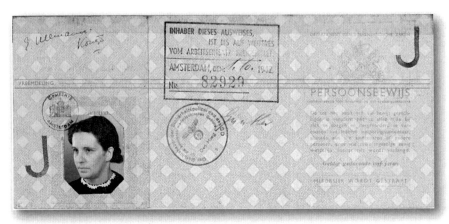

Mom's ID card, the authentic one with the "J" for "Jew."

Back of Mom's "real" ID card.

Mom's ID card, the false one without the "J" for "Jew."

Back of Mom's false ID card.

The Christian names on false ID cards were often taken from
tombstones in cemeteries.

The signature on the card was recognized immediately during a recent
visit, by Marion van Wesemael-Hoogenboom, as that of her father, Piet
Hoogenboom, Jr.

Pop's ID card, the authentic one with the "J" for "Jew."

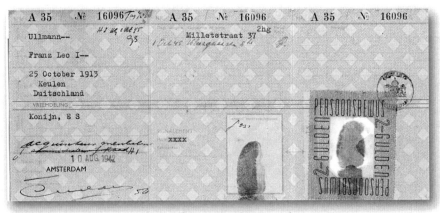

Back of Pop's "real" ID card.

Pop's ID card, the false one without the "J" for "Jew."

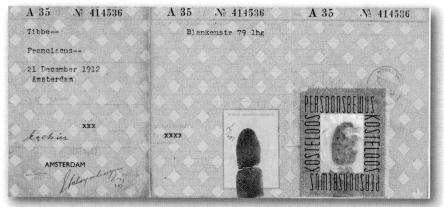

Back of Pop's false ID card.

Zentralstelle für jüdische
Auswanderung Amsterdam
  Adama v. Scheltemaplein 1
    Telefoon 97001

No.

OPROEPING!

Aan   L   No.

U moet zich voor eventueele deelname aan een, onder politietoezichtstaande, werk
verruiming in Duitschland voor persoonsonderzoek en geneeskundige keuring naar het door
gangskamp Westerbork, station Hooghalen, begeven.

Daartoe moet U op_____óm _____uur

op de verzamelplaats_____ aanwezig zijn.

Als bagage mag medegenomen worden:

- 1 koffer of rugzak
- 1 paar werklaarzen
- 2 paar sokken
- 2 onderbroeken
- 2 hemden
- 1 werkpak
- 2 wollen dekens
- 2 stel beddengoed (overtrek met laken)
- 1 eetnap
- 1 drinkbeker
- 1 lepel en
- 1 pullover
- handdoek en toiletartikelen

en eveneens marschproviand voor 3 dagen en alle aan U uitgereikte distributiekaarten met
inbegrip van de distributiestamkaart.

De mee te nemen bagage moet in gedeelten gepakt worden.

a. **Noodzakelijke reisbehoeften**
daartoe behooren: 2 dekens, 1 stel beddegoed, levensmiddelen voor 3 dagen, toiletgerei,
etensbord, eetbestek, drinkbeker,

b. **Groote bagage**
De onder b vermelde bagage moet worden gepakt in een stevige koffer of rugzak,
welke op duidelijke wijze voorzien moet zijn van **naam, voornamen,
geboortedatum en het woord „Holland".**
Gezinsbagage is niet toegestaan.
Het voorgaande moet nauwkeurig in acht genomen worden, daar de groote bagage in
de plaats van vertrek afzonderlijk ingeladen wordt.
De verschillende bewijs- en persoonspapieren en 'distributiekaarten met inbegrip van
de distributiestamkaart mogen **niet bij de bagage verpakt worden,** doch
moeten, voor onmiddellijk vertoon gereed, medegedragen worden.
De woning moet ordelijk achtergelaten en afgesloten worden, de huissleutels moeten
worden medegenomen.
Niet medegenomen mogen worden: levend huisraad

K 372

Standard form of summons/call up ostensibly for forced labor
camps in Germany.
(translation on next page)

(My translation)

Central Agency   No.
For Jewish Emigration

SUMMONS

To   [Person, Address, Date of Birth]   No.

You must appear for potential participation in a labor camp under police supervision for personal examination and medical clearance to the transit camp Westerbork, at (railroad) station Hooghalen.

For this purpose you must be present on _____ at _____ at the collection site _____

As baggage, you may take
1   **Suitcase or rucksack**
1   **Pair work boots**
2   **Pairs of socks**
2   **Pairs of underwear**
2   **Shirts**
1   **Work clothes**
2   **Woolen blankets**
2   **Sets of bedding/cover and sheet**
1   **Bowl**
1   **Drinking cup**
1   **Spoon**
1   **Pullover**
    Towel and toiletries
And also food for 3 days and all coupons (for food distributions) issued to you and the underlying distribution master card.

The luggage must be packed in sections.

a. **Travel necessities**
This includes: 2 blankets, 1 set of bedding, food for 3 days, toiletries, a plate, knife, fork, and spoon and drink cup.

b. **Large baggage**
The items listed under *b*. must be packed in a sturdy suitcase or rucksack, which must have in a clear readable manner, **(last) name, first and middle names, date of birth and the word "Holland".**
Family baggage is not permitted.
The foregoing must be narrowly followed, so that the large baggage can be loaded without a problem at the place of departure.
The various ID and personal papers and "distribution" coupons, including the distribution master card **must not be packed in the baggage.**
The residence must be left behind in an orderly state and locked, the keys must be taken with you.
Not permitted to be brought along: live pets.

K 372

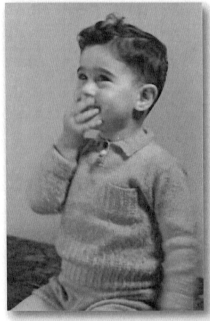

Me, Leopold (nicknamed
"Deinemanetjelief" or in short form,
just "Dein" or Deintje").

Leo starting on Chapter 1 of this book
before being placed in hiding.

Aleida Schot, Mom's sorority sister, responsible for Leo's placement.

Mom (in the middle) and her Arktos sorority sisters (1932)

An Arktos *Lustrum* (reunion) in 1942. (Mom is in the second row, 3rd from the left). Note: Jewish women were not allowed in sororities.

"Ma" and "Pa" Peyster and daughters Riet and Ellie,
my parents' "hosts" in their hiding place.

(left to right) Piet Hoogenboom Sr., who did so much to save our family,
Evertje Hoogenboom-van Maanen (spouse), Dini Hoogenboom (daughter) and
Piet Hoogenboom Jr., who made the false IDs. Photo dated 1940; courtesy of
Marion van Wesemael-Hoogenboom.

Left: Pop with the prayer rug given to him by Mr. Kinnebanyan as a "talisman" when he and Mom went into hiding.

Below: Political Investigation Department of City of Amsterdam notice of failure by Pop to register (he had gone into hiding).

POLITIEKE OPSPORINGSDIENST
District AMSTERDAM

AMSTERDAM, *3 September* 1945

VERKLARING

STATEMENT

Ondergeteekende verklaart hiermede, dat *Ullmann, Frans Leo*
The undersigned herewith declares, that

Persoonsbewijs No. *J 35 / 16096* beroep *employé Bijenkorf*
Identity Card No. profession

tot op heden nog niet bij bovengenoemden opsporingsdienst is geregistreerd,
has not been registered **up till now** at the Political Investigation Department.

Het Hoofd van den P.O.D.
i/o De Chef der afd. Inlichtingen

N⁰ 010692

Chapter 7

A Place for Me

Through the Dutch Reformed Church, I was placed with a young man, Anton Schimmel and his wife, who lived in a suburb of Amsterdam. However, at some point, Anton's marriage was breaking up (it could well have been because of me, although I'm told that Anton's wife independently had psychiatric problems).

Anton's parents, Hendrik and Jannigje Schimmel ("Oma and Opa Schimmel"), who were in their 50s, had apparently taken a liking to their new temporary grandchild, and decided to take me in, together with the dog, Ruffie, (after Anton and his wife could no longer take care of either me, or Ruffie), at their third floor apartment at van Speijkstraat 175, in a working class neighborhood in Amsterdam West. Oma and Opa shared the apartment with their daughter, Tilly. Tilly, whose real name was Mathilda (which I learned only after she passed away), was adopted by the Schimmels; she was in fact the daughter of Oma Schimmel's brother, Arnold ("Oom Nol").

Neither Anton nor his parents had any idea as to who I was or where I came from, other than knowing I was to be a hidden Jewish child. They also knew that if the Germans discovered that they were hiding a Jewish child, they would almost certainly be executed. Further, they knew that bounties were paid by the Germans for reporting or betraying a Jewish child.

At some point late in the War, Opa and Oma apparently decided that the situation was too difficult to keep me with them, especially because of the lack of food during the "Hunger Winter" of 1944-45. Children everywhere in Holland were starving to death. Accordingly, the Germans, in an apparent compassionate moment, arranged a boat to take children under 10 years of age from Amsterdam across the Zuiderzee behind the German line (the *IJssellinie*) to farming areas north of Amsterdam where they could get food. I was destined for an orphanage maintained by farmers in the area. However, after a week or so, Opa Schimmel decided that my existence there was too dangerous.

Thus, Opa, a retired policeman with a disability pension, was able to arrange a pass to permit him to pass through the German *IJssellinie* at the railroad station, to cross the river to North Amsterdam with his bike, and thus to go some 150 kilometers (approximately 95 miles) roundtrip to the orphanage from which he was able to save me and bring me back. The date was March 14, 1945.

Opa Schimmel.

Oma and Opa Schimmel.

Oma and Opa Schimmel.

Oma Schimmel and Leo.

The apartment on the third floor at van
Speijkstraat 175 where I was in hiding with
the Schimmels.

Pass for Opa Schimmel to take Leo from the orphanage back to the Schimmel's apartment.

Chapter 8

At the Schimmels

Oma Schimmel was a very religious woman. Opa Schimmel, as earlier indicated, was a (retired) policeman, who had a pension, but also owned a part interest in a bar near Centraal Station frequented by Germans (who were basically the only persons with money at the time), where a German girl, with whom Opa Schimmel was very friendly, and whom I came to know as "Tante (Aunt) Paula," tended bar.

My war sister, Tilly, was some 14 years older than I, and thus a late teenager. I reportedly teased, bothered and annoyed her mercilessly, which she somehow did not permit to diminish how much she cared for, and about, me. Among other things, I woke Tilly up every night, apparently waiting until she first fell asleep, to demand her help as I needed to go to the bathroom.

I don't know that I was ever hungry, though food was difficult to come by. I do know that at one point Opa Schimmel dropped a large pan of gravy, which may have had some slivers of meat in it, and everyone was extremely upset. One of the sayings uttered by me in yet another moment of childish insensitivity, but which has certainly become important folklore for the Schimmel family, was my saying to the Schimmels, "I wish Tilly was dead, then we'd have more food."

There was apparently one instance when I refused to eat rabbit meat. Meat was terribly scarce in the War and this was a special treat arranged by Opa. However, I refused to eat it because its eyes looked so sad. I of course did not know at the time that the Dutch word for "rabbit" (konijn) was my mother's maiden name. With Opa's connections through his bar, and with Aunt Paula, the barmaid at the bar, we were able to have food, including potatoes and even some meat once in a while. Like many Dutchmen, we at the Schimmels also suffered the indignity of having to eat flower bulbs and sugar beets, which were generally ground up and rolled to form a sort of paste, both of which tasted perfectly fine to me.

We also had the dog, Ruffie, who came with me as part of the package from Anton and his wife, to which I was quite attached, but I was not allowed to walk the dog outside the apartment. I also know that I was never without a piece of a security blanket (a "sabbellapje") throughout my stay.

I was apparently a decent looking kid with one noticeable problem; I was quite cross-eyed with a wandering left eye, which was not corrected until immediately after the War. The Schimmels dyed my hair blond so that, ostensibly, no one would know I was Jewish. They pretended that I was a grandchild.

For the first year or so, I was permitted outside of the house to play in the street, etc. Thereafter, because of the apparent dangers, I was basically never permitted to leave the apartment.

Oma Schimmel attended church often. Her abundant faith notwithstanding, she never made me take part or observe in any manner the religious faith to which she herself subscribed, because, as she later reported, her role was intended to be that of a caretaker, not a parent.

Through Aunt Paula and her German friends, Opa Schimmel often learned about impending *Razzias* (raids) by German soldiers to find hidden Jews. In the event of an impending *Razzia*, I was often shipped out of Amsterdam to stay with Anton.

Oma and Opa Schimmel also had a son, "Bas" (Bastiaan), who was married to Joyce, an English woman, and lived in an apartment in the south side of Amsterdam, the area from which I had originally come. Bas, after the War, was involved in the film industry and apparently did quite well. Personalized photos of Bas with many film stars (Rita Hayworth, Burt Lancaster, etc.) are plastered on the wall of one of his grandsons.

While the Schimmels never in fact had any idea who I was, they may have had an inkling of where I came from, as on one occasion when I was at Bas's apartment and outside with his wife, the milkman apparently recognized me and said, "Hello Sonny" in a familiar way. The only persons who knew my whereabouts (and that of my parents) were, as further described herein, the Dutch Reformed Church Minister in Haarlem and Mom's sorority sister, Aleida Schot. Aleida in fact, at least for a while, was able to deliver some food coupons to the Schimmels to help feed me.

Leo during his hiding at the Schimmels.

Anton, Tilly and Bas Schimmel.

Chapter 9

Frank, Emily and Bram in Hiding

My parents went into hiding in the attic arranged by the Peyster family (father, mother and two daughters) at Ceintuurbaan 81 on March 1, 1943. Several months or so later, they also took in with them, Mom's cousin Abraham ("Bram") Konijn, whose parents had been hauled off to concentration camps, and transported to Germany.

The three of them, or at least Mom and Pop (Bram a few months less), lived in the attic for more than 2 years and 3 months (796 days) with no heat, electricity or plumbing. There were two rooms (Pop removed the door between the rooms) and only one window. The window had to be covered with a curtain so that they could not be seen and also to comply with German requirements that all windows be darkened (generally by black paper curtains) after dusk to hinder potential bombing operations by Allied forces. It nevertheless provided a view of the Ceintuurbaan and was immediately across from the well-known Café Witteveen, an Amsterdam institution for many decades (now long gone). They would spend part of their days looking over the customers, many of whom they felt they came to know from a distance.

They slept on a couple of mattresses on the floor and could only move about when the couple in the apartment below them left for work at 8:30 in the morning and the Peysters knocked on the ceiling with a broom handle. They cooked food occasionally on a hibachi. Until the end of the War, the couple in the apartment below never knew that my parents were hidden in the attic above them!

Aleida Schot, the sorority sister who arranged my hiding, initially came to visit my parents once a month. On one occasion, when I had not yet found my final hiding place, she actually took me to briefly visit my parents. Saying goodbye again must have been heart-wrenching for my parents.

My parents undertook during their hiding to never mention my name and thus to suppress that obvious pain, even if they thought about me a lot, i.e. was I alive? If so, where? Was I happy? What did I look like?

In addition to soap and some canned food, they were able to take two suitcases filled with rice, chocolate bars and skeins of knitting wool and cotton, as well as clothes, 3 chairs, a table, bedding, and books into hiding in several trips to the hiding place from their Milletstraat apartment. The books became terribly important and they spent a great deal of time silently acting out various stories from Russian novels (which they received from Aleida Schot).

Their "hosts" were also able to get library books. They constantly played chess, as well as "skat," a card game Pop had learned from his father. On at least one occasion, when in recent years we were talking to students at schools, Mom actually said, believe it or not (and I didn't), that they had fun. They also spent a lot of time learning languages, including Russian and Sanskrit, to keep their minds from atrophying.

Pop was able to take (an illegally retained) radio that he had kept in the Milletstraat apartment, with him, which he placed in the ceiling and operated by attaching strings to the knobs. This was their lifeline to the BBC and Churchill, as well as to Queen Wilhelmina on *Radio Oranje* and periodically gave them hope.

They were able to generate a bit of light by surrounding a candle on three sides with mirrors, and they were able to look out the sole window and see across neighboring rooftops. One of the most painful memories, as recounted by Mom, was seeing a young neighboring child playing and skipping on the narrow walk between the adjacent shingle roofs and angled parapets. Suddenly, she slipped and fell to her death.

Mom could not even scream. She spent hours crying and moaning in Pop's silent embrace, "that poor little girl, that poor little girl."

One of the challenges was sanitation and keeping themselves clean. They had to use a potty which they could empty only when the couple in the apartment below left for work.

Pop told me that the only time he ever struck Mom, was when, during their hiding period, she did not want to wash (sponge bathe) herself. He was afraid that it might have been a signal of loss of hope or caring. It also may explain why, after the War, in their closets in their homes and apartment, my parents kept boxes upon boxes of bars of soap.

Pop, who, as earlier indicated, had become a capable woodworking craftsman after he was discharged from De Bijenkorf, created a false wall, using the door which had separated the two rooms in the attic, under the staircase leading to the attic with shelving on it on which there were jars of nails, hooks, etc. They hid behind that door whenever there was a *Razzia*.

Razzias occurred when the German soldiers and/or police cordoned off a block and went house to house searching for hidden Jews.

They often used dogs during such searches. My parents mentioned at least two of such searches while they were hidden and Pop has always said that if you ever hear the expression, "you could hear your heart beat," it was surely true for him while he was hiding behind that door. Fortunately, during the raids on their block, the Germans never used dogs, who would certainly have found them.

During the first year, the arrangements were tolerable and they got along very well with the Peysters. There was food and there was still some money. They were able to exchange a few letters with close relatives who were also in hiding, including Grootmoeder, Pop's parents, and Pop's brother through Ma Peyster and Mr. Hoogenboom. My parents paid Ma Peyster to travel to Utrecht to effect the letter exchanges with Mr. Hoogenboom. Some of those letters (with translation) are included in the Appendix.

The Peyster girls, on the first anniversary (March 1, 1944 at 7:45 A.M.) of my parents' entry into the hiding place, created a special poem addressed to my parents. Mom also wrote a poem to Pop on that occasion. Those poems (and translations) are included in the next chapter.

The greatest problem for my parents during that time was getting food, especially in the last year of the War during the so-called "Hunger Winter," when many thousands of Dutchmen died. In the beginning, my parents were able to pay for the Peysters to shop for food. With their false IDs, they were also able, for a while, to arrange through the Peysters to get minimal rations with food stamps. My parents were convinced, however, that the Peysters gouged them.

Yet, in 1944-45, there were no more rations.

The "Hunger Winter," which resulted in large part from a German retaliatory embargo on all shipments of food to the Northern and

Western part of Holland, including Amsterdam, is further described in a separate chapter of this book. The liberation of the balance of Holland was effectively halted for perhaps a half-year, thus contributing to the Hunger Winter, by the loss of the Allied armies in the battle for the bridge in Arnhem.[28]

Apparently, in the same manner as other starving people, their minds were almost consumed by food they didn't have. They talked about food all the time, remembering great meals and great restaurants and even arguing over recipes.

At the outset, my parents paid the Peysters rent for their hiding place. They also spent time with the Peysters during the day in their apartment, helping them make tea bags with surrogate tea which the Peysters produced on an outsource basis for a factory in Holland and for which they received some money based on their piecework.

The long poem the Peyster girls wrote to my parents makes clear that the relationship of the Peysters and my parents was excellent at the outset. My parents, Bram and the Peysters all enjoyed their daily gatherings around the table at the Peyster apartment while they glued the tea bags. However, after a time, there were no more disability payments for the Peysters and my parents also ran out of money (again, no one thought the War would last 5 years). Shortly thereafter, the relationship soured, at least with the Peyster parents.

The Peysters' two teenage daughters, Riet and Ellie, became very attached to my parents, and perhaps this created some jealousy. The Peysters, among other things, assigned to my parents tasks of cleaning their apartment daily, including cleaning the toilets and scrubbing the

---

[28] *That battle was brilliantly described in the widely-read book by Cornelius Ryan, and in the powerful movie, "A Bridge too Far" (the movie starred many famous actors, including Robert Redford, Michael Caine, Anthony Hopkins, Sean Connery, Gene Hackman, James Caan, Lawrence Olivier, Maximilian Schell and Liv Ullmann (no relation)).*

floors, in part, my parents believed, because they were envious of Mom and Pop's lifestyle before the War.

My parents, in turn, loved the Peysters' girls. They spent untold numbers of hours with the girls teaching them literature, languages, etc. The girls, in their one-year anniversary poem to my parents, among other things, expressed the hope that they would be friends long after the miserable occupation would end. In the meantime, the two girls hung around with German soldiers, enjoying cigarettes and companionship. This, of course, was immensely threatening to my parents, especially because the Germans offered bounties for the disclosure of hidden Jews, but the girls never betrayed them.

It is clear that the Peysters saved my parents' lives, yet, it has always been a mystery to me that my parents did not stay in touch with the Peysters after the War.

A few months after the War, when my parents were already living in their new home in the Velasquezstraat, Mom received a call from the two Peyster girls (my parents were surprised the girls found them) telling them that Pa (Gerard) Peyster had died. Mom and Bram (my father was on a buying trip to Paris for De Bijenkorf) went to the cemetery and no one of the Peyster family was there. The next day the girls called again and asked if my parents would join them at Ceintuurbaan 81. Mom and Bram went to the Peyster apartment and shared a meal with Ma Peyster and the girls, then left. They never returned to Ceintuurbaan 81 and never saw the Peysters again.

I tried in the last decade or so, through the Civil Registry and through the media, to find the Peyster girls, but was never able to do so.

During the occupation, and during their 796 days in hiding, my parents could not run the risk of leaving their hiding place without exposure to grave danger of getting caught, jailed, deported or even executed on the spot. This was especially the case for Pop, who as a young able-bodied man, would almost certainly have been shipped off to Germany early in the War.

Mom, however, left the attic and the house on a few occasions to try to get food, not only for the three of them in hiding, but also for the Peysters, from persons she knew who were well-to-do, including Polly van Leer, whose husband's family owned Royal Packaging Industries van Leer, one of the world's largest industrial packaging companies. The Peysters also made Mom take the girls to the doctor for hip sores. Mom was always terrified while sitting in the waiting room.

She also left twice because she had an unbelievably painful toothache, the pain of which was such that she was willing to risk whatever consequences might result by trying to find a dentist, as she simply could not live with the pain. Accordingly, at dusk one day, she left the apartment and walked a ways to De Lairessestraat, a street where a number of dentists had their practice. Without having any introduction, she knocked on the door of one of the dentists, told him that she was in desperate pain, but also told him that she could not pay him and that she could not tell him who she was or even where she came from.

The dentist nevertheless undertook to help her, but he needed to do some drill work. There was no electricity at that time, and so the drill was operated by the dentist's wife by means of a foot pump much like those on old-time sewing machines. Mom had the treatment and received some stitches and returned to the hiding place undiscovered.

She had to go back a few days later to remove the stitches. Not only did the dentist at that point remove the stitches, but he gave her a loaf of bread and some other food, which, of course, Pop, Mom and

Bram valued beyond belief, and which they were able to savor in small morsels over a period of several days.[29]

In April 1945, when things were really desperate, a bread factory nearby was baking loaves of bread and would honor certain food stamps. Mom and one of the Peyster daughters stood in a line for many hours, guarded by policemen and representatives of the Red Cross. They were finally able to get three loaves and a half pound of margarine, on which they gorged all night long until they were sick to their stomachs.

Mom and Pop (many years later) at their hiding
place, Ceintuurbaan 81 in Amsterdam.

[29] *The dentist was Dr. J.W.A. Tjebbes; he later became a professor of oral surgery at the University of Utrecht.*

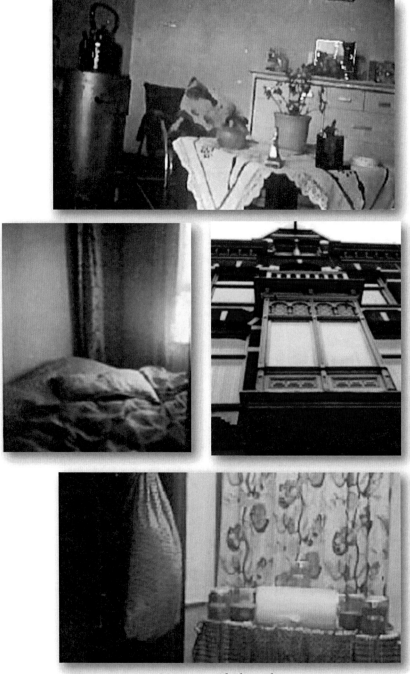

My parents' hiding place.

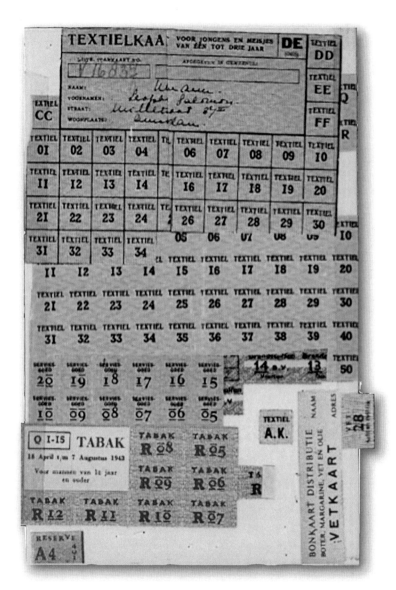

Coupons from top for: • Textiles
                        • Table service earthenware
                        • Tobacco (for men aged 18 or older) (this was
                          in fact a surrogate "shag" concoction) and
                        • (at lower right) a "fat" coupon for butter,
                          margarine, fat and oil

Wartime coupons

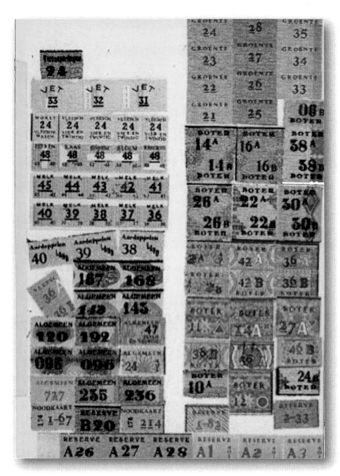

- Left, top to bottom)
- "Delicacies"
- Fat
- Sausage, meat
- Eggs, cheese, flour
- Milk
- Potatoes
- General
- Necessities
- Reserves

(Right, top to bottom)
- Vegetables
- Butter
- Reserves

Wartime coupons

(clockwise starting at top left)
- Textiles for boys/girls to age 3
- Warm food in the city of Amsterdam
- Surrogate cigarette packages
- Food (1943-44)

(far right)
Masthead of underground paper,
De Waarheid (The Truth), April 1945

Top to bottom:
• Ticket for concert at which Yehudi Menuhin, the world famous violinist,
  played to raise the spirits of the Dutch.
• Scrip used for purchases at the Therezienstadt (Terezin) and Westerbork
  concentration camps.
•U.S. cigarette packs for Dutch forces only.
•Cigarettes manufactured from "Netherlands Indies" (now Indonesia) tobacco
  and bearing the label on the package "The Netherlands shall rise again" and
  "Orange (as in the House of Orange, the Dutch Royal family) will be
  victorious."

Front and back of Distribution Base Card listing ID number of Piet
Hoogenboom and indicating items received, including bike tires,
shoes and fuel.

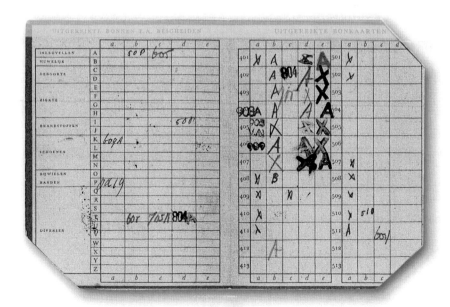

DE VLIEGENDE HOLLANDER

DAGBLAD VERSPREID DOOR DE GEALLIEERDE LUCHTMACHT   No. 66. WOENSDAG 1 NOV. 1944

Roosendaal bevrijd - Zuid-Beveland van Duitschers gezuiverd

Londen, 31 Oct.—Terwijl in het Oosten de Russen in Oost-Pruisen in harden strijd gewikkeld zijn met de Duitschers, nieuwe vorderingen zijn gemaakt in Slowakije en Hongarije en terwijl in het Westen, na Duisburg en Essen, Keulen is gebombardeerd met ongekende hevigheid, heeft in Noord-Brabant en Zeeland de campagne voor het openstellen van de haven van Antwerpen goeden voortgang gemaakt. Den Bosch, Tilburg, Breda, Bergen-op-Zoom, Roosendaal en Goes zijn bevrijd. De gevechten in Westelijk Zeeuwsch-Vlaanderen naderen hun einde. Nederlandsche troepen vechten, tezamen met de Polen van het Eerste Canadeesche Leger, ten Noord-Oosten van Breda.

Britten aan de Maas

Op Dinsdag 31 October bereikten Britsche troepen de Maas ten Noorden van Waalwijk. Daarmede hadden de reizen op het Duitsche Vijftiende Leger in Noord-Brabant alle directe onderlinge verbindingen verloren. Een klein deel bevond zich noorden de Bergsche Maas ten Westen van Den Bosch. Deze troepen gebruikten het Afwateringskanaal tusschen de beneden Heusden en de Bergsche Maas ....

Op Beveland

De correspondent van de Times gaf hebbende Britsche daghad een beschrijving van de toestang op bevrijd Zuid-Beveland....

Amphibische tanks, "Buffalos," rijden op Zuid-Beveland den wal op na de Wester-schelde te zijn overgestoken. De rupsbanden van deze varende tanks, die op het land voor de voortbeweging zorgen, stuwen de tanks ook door het water voort. Op de onderste foto ziet men de "Buffalos," vóór de landing, in rijen opgesteld terwijl de Britsche infanterie aan boord klimt.

DE STRIJD AAN HET KREEKERAK

door; GUY BYAM, oorlogscorrespondent van de BBC

Fliers dropped by the Allied Forces announcing Allied victories in the Southern part of Holland, November 1944.

Chapter 10

Writings During the Years in Hiding

Afairly unique aspect of the 796 days in hiding was that there was (limited) exchange of correspondence with other relatives who were also in hiding, but elsewhere, in separate cities, during the War, which, in the case of my parents, included Mom's mother (Grootmoeder), Pop's parents (Oma Aenni and Opa Sally), Pop's uncle (and Aenni's brother) Fritz Loeb and Pop's brother Fritz Ullmann. The occasional exchange of letters during that time was facilitated by the same Piet Hoogenboom who arranged the very hiding places of all those people, as well as their fake ID cards.

The letters describe in considerable detail the hardship of other family members while also in hiding, and the hope that they would someday "live like people" again. They all frequently prayed that they'd be together again, and that the nightmare would soon end.

The letters included in the Appendix were translated by Mom, except in those instances, as indicated, where they were translated by me in my upgraded, but still basically third grade, Dutch.

This chapter includes a couple of unique poems. One is a poem written by one and signed by both teenage daughters of the Peyster family who "hosted' my family in their attic hiding place during those

796 days. The love and admiration expressed by those girls for my parents in a handwritten poem covering eight legal-size pages, on the occasion of the first anniversary of my parents' entry into the attic hiding place, is truly remarkable.

The fact that the relationship later "turned," at least in terms of feelings by my parents toward the girls' parents, after the especially convivial first year, is equally remarkable. There are probably very few, if any, such written pieces by teenage girls on the side of the host protectors, describing the dynamics of the relationships between the hidden persons and their hosts, that have survived and been preserved after the War. This, of course, in contradistinction, for example, to the writings of a teenage Anne Frank, describing the experience of hiding from the point of view of the "hidden" teenager.

On the same occasion of the first anniversary of my parents landing in the attic hiding place, Mom wrote a poem to Pop remarking on how much trust she and Pop built for one another while truly forced to be with each other every minute of every day. The materials included here involve her original poem in Dutch, which I have attempted to translate, while Mom has created an abridged translation in English, and in rhyme!

In her translation, Mom, who never, ever, used off-color words or sayings (at least in English), in describing the air in the attic apartment referred to "farts," a word I am sure she never uttered (the original Dutch is much less graphic).

This poem, too, is, of course, a remarkable work. There cannot be many of such personal inter-spousal written expressions to have survived the War. Their marriage continued beyond the War for a total of some 64 years, and their love for each other was a burning flame that never flickered, even for a moment.

Others, who have met and come to know my parents, have marveled at their wonderful marriage. Once when my parents (and I was there) told their story at a large high school in Freeport, New York, and the floor had been opened for questions (and we, of course, expected Holocaust-related inquiries), a young man stood up at the back of the fully-populated auditorium and asked in a booming voice, "How long have you guys been married?" Mom quickly answered, "Sixty-two years!" The young man mulled it over briefly, and half-yelled, "Holy Shit!!" (which we took to be a favorable comment) and sat down.

In Remembrance of (7:45) March 1, 1944

By Rie Peyster

(Rhyming in the Dutch language – translation by me)

In honor of the 1 year stay
that you celebrate now
I want to embark on a piece of poetry.
I hope that it will please you.
I will begin with the time at
which we live now; it is brought by El and Rie.
An entire year has now passed
since our Frank and Emily ("Lot")
in this attic rear flat
were received by us; emotionally they were a wreck.
Together they came from Milletstraat 37.II
That day they can still see in their dreams,
Because such a step is not easy.
Frank's bike was loaded with packages;
Lot's arms were completely full.
Together they, tugging and pulling,
were quickly at home, in their Ceintuurbaan
hiding place pad.
They were no longer strangers.
First came introductions,
and for us "Mr." and "Mrs."
but soon enough this was no longer necessary.
And therefore the couple Ullmann decided
that "Mr." and "Mrs." were too demanding.
Thus for us it became "Lot" and "Frans."
The first days flew by.

The food stamps were arranged by Ma.
Pa came and asked every morning, "do (I) need to do some shopping?"
For a reward when he returned he received from us
a delicious buttered slice of bread
with whatever he liked, syrup, cheese or pickle.
Then the days that we had to return to your (former) *flat at night*
because there were still many items
that had been readied for us to take back.
Looking around, sweating, being careful
we walked into the Milletstraat apartment,
because if people had suspected us,
that would've been a bad beginning.
Then sneaking into the building
like thieves…
And if by chance we heard someone
we would collapse in a heap from nerves.
Then returning here (to the Ceintuurbaan hiding place),
you stayed there in fear
because suddenly some men appeared
and you thought they were the police.
If I think about the first nights (during their stay)
they did not sleep much
because they were lying there with the thought that soon
they'll come get us. Why? For What?
Also they thought a lot about their little darling
who would also now be in hiding.
How was it with Leo's new father and mother?
And thus they thought constantly about their little "Dein" (Leo's nickname)*;*
but they were soon satisfied
because they received good news.
Their little boy had received a home.

But very soon this all changed;
It could no longer continue as it was;
the couple with whom he'd been placed could no longer keep him.
Lot as a result frequently wiped a tear
for our dear little man.
Among themselves they were arguing:
at some point he'll land in Westerbork, and then???
Luckily this had not happened…,
and thus on a certain morning
our Deintje (again, Leo's nickname) *came hand-in-hand*
with Leidje [Aleida Schot, Mom's sorority sister who arranged my hiding venue(s)]
Do you recall how happy you were
with the arrival of your son?
You could not believe your eyes!
It was like love in your dreams,
but the time was soon up
and "Deineman" (Leo) *again went on his way.*
A real new home (hiding place) *had now been found*
for our little dear.
After that, everything again quieted down.
Lot and Frans again went their own way;
life did not yet bore them.
They stayed here for months.
From the beginning, Tuesday was fixed as the
cleanup day,
and everything they could find was then turned
inside out.
Also, head lice arrived.
Frans had to cut off his hair.
Lot herself grabbed scissors

and cut so neatly that the Peysters were amazed.

It was as if she herself were a hairdresser/barber

who certainly could not have done it better…

Oh; did they ever think it was upsetting

when the oven had to be turned on!

Wheezing, puffing, blowing, sweating

they prayed for fresh air,

but they got used to it,

and coming downstairs they sought some relief

not from their misery, oh no it wasn't that,

but then to have to return to that heat (in the attic)

and that future and those prospects…

Thus the days flew by,

until at a given moment

there was the biggest Razzia.

Do you not recall that?

It was on a hot Sunday morning

I had that night the flu;

you were all there that morning, concerned (about Rie)

and I was alone outside…,

but the worst was yet to come.

First I was not allowed to go to my house;

Then, when I finally arrived there,

the greatest crisis began.

Trams full of Jewish people

passed our house that day.

There were at least 24 long cars with people.

As for the Nazis, they were swine.

Then came the scum (police) *to search through your house;*

a piece of green (police) *and a civilian. Garbage!*

and they looked in every nook and cranny,

but found nothing. We fooled them.
Both our (persons in hiding)
were safely in the closet.
I was most scared
that they came to get you, the so-called "guest,"
but luckily this is not what happened,
because they noticed nothing. The Cattle!
And thus they left again with empty hands,
Down the stairs. Both very meekly.
Lot and Frans then came again in our midst.
They did not have fear for even a minute
We prayed for that,
because a Nazi and a Jew are like a dog and cat.
The weeks thereafter were relatively quiet,
until again on a given day
Pa and Ma were overcome with fright,
seeing the Blacks (Gestapo) *standing in front of their noses.*
They didn't know what to do.
Lot and Frans disappeared quickly
because the [Black Gestapo] *came upstairs,*
they heard it from their steps.
This time it was not for our friends,
But for the girls, Rie and El.
The first with her big mouth
was then in a bad spot.
An arrest was threatened
We were both pretty scared
Because we could not pay the fine
there was no choice but jail,
yet we still managed to turn the situation around so
that nothing further happened.

Otherwise we would have had to go to jail
and you would have had to get out.
This, too, didn't have to happen
because that was the biggest problem.
Still, you had to hide for another 2 hours
in the closet.
Finally (the Gestapo members) *disappeared*
and you again came out of the closet.
We did not need to bribe them;
they left, with just a couple of cigarettes
and there have been no more Black (Gestapo raids).
Quietly October arrived
and we were forced to deal with something else.
Dear cousin (Bram Konijn) *landed in our house,*
like a man from the moon.
He, too, was permitted to pitch his tent here,
because we all felt it terrible if he had to
return to Westerbork,
because they were on the lookout for him.
Therefore, Bram we thought it best to take you into our house
and happy that you would find it to your liking,
because you already feel very much at home.
Our entire life has changed
since you came in our midst;
it is quite cozy
with our Lotje, Frans and Bram...,
because you accepted correctly my extended right hand
when you came downstairs.
Full of curiosity we first viewed
our new piece of Konijn [Mom and Bram's last name],
and we asked ourselves how would he get along?

But that puzzle was soon solved,
because a couple of days later, cousin began to feel at home,
and escaped his inhibitions.
We were happy, yes very happy,
because he was not a boring guy,
and he began, just like the others,
to talk about uncles, aunts and some woman.
Eventually he began telling jokes…
and thus the days passed quickly.
The month of December arrived again.
Everyone was [wrapping presents].
and most started on poems.
St. Nicholas eve [December 5] *was very successful,*
and I'll think of it often,
all those fun stories and poems
I found "terrific.".
Next was New Year's Eve
and it was also a wonderful night.
At exactly 12 o'clock we celebrated
and right after that, the dishes of meat.
We stayed up until 2:30
and then the fun was over…
The New Year had arrived,
and we thus start with new resolve
and hope for freedom,
and that the Nazis will finally leave our country.
With these thoughts we go on living;
that's also the best thing
because we well know ourselves the Nazis
are and remain a "damnation."
Also I want to return to the gluing [of tea bags]

because we all think it fine that you in your free hours
are so helpful to Ma and Pa.
You all laugh the most when you are
Sitting at the "glue table"
Do you recall when cousin came to make us happy
with 3 potatoes hidden behind his false teeth?
Cousin is such a nut...
And thus this year has gone
in fear, concern and pleasure.
Let us thus now hope
That it will remain calm here
I myself will only be content, if
when the War will end
you will normally be known as Ullmann
and our little Bram, Konijn.
That it will then, as it is now, remain in
friendship,
because we belong to one another.
This we now understand each day
Therefore, niece and dear nephews,
promise us that, when the War is behind us,
we will remain Friends.
That is my only wish.
El Peyster • Rie Peyster

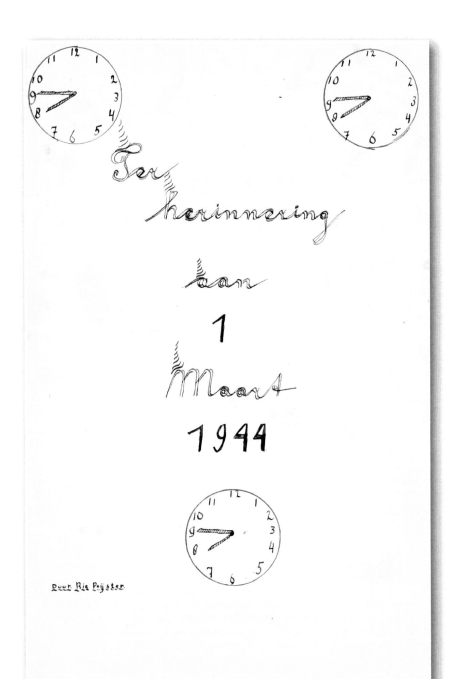

Ter ere van het 1 jarig bestaan
Dat jullie heden vieren
Wil ik een stukje dichten gaan
Ik hoop dat het jullie wal plexieren.
Ik wal beginnen bij het uur
Waarop wij heden leven
's Woids gebracht door El en Rie
Dus luister nu maar even.

Een heel jaar is nu alweer verstreken
Voordat onze Frans en lot
Op hun flatje 3 hoog achter
Door ons ontvangen werden, geestelijk
        waren ze kapot.
Samen waren zij naar hier gekomen
Vanaf de Milesstraat 37ᵉ
Die dag zullen zij nog kunnen dromen.
Want zo'n stap valt heus niet mee.
Frans zijn fiets beladen met pakken
Lot haar armen stampend vol
Kwamen zij al sleep-en sjokkend
Eindelijk in het Ceintuurbaanshol.
Zij waren hier gauw ingeburgerd
Want vreemd waren zij niet meer
Eerst nog wat bedeesd en schuchter
En voor ons Mevrouw en Mijnheer,
Maar al gauw was dit niet meer nodig
En zo besloot het echtpaar Ullmann (!)
Meneer en Mevrouw waren overbodig.
Dus voor ons werd het lot en Frans.
Zo vergleden de eerste dagen
De bonnen werden verzorgd door Ma.
Pa kwam elke morgen vragen
Moeten er nog boodschappen zijn, ja?
Voor beloning als hij terug kwam
Kreeg hij dan van onze buur
Een lekkere besmeerde boterham
Met wat hij maar lust. stroop, kaas of suur.
Kwam de dagen die wij moesten

's Avonds terug naar jullie flat
Want er waren nog vele dingen
Dat men voor ons had klaargezet.
Lourend, kijkend, pratend, oppassend,
liepen wij de Mulesstraat in.
Want als de mensen ons zouden bemerken
Was dat dan toch wel het slechtste begin!
Dan de woning in te sluipen
zoals een dief, nou dat vonden wij naar
En als je dan iemand toevallig hoorde
Kromp je van de zenuwen in elkaar.
Dan weer hierheen terug te keren
Je stond daar dan in rak en as
Want plotseling verscheen dan weer Heren
Dat je dacht dat het de politie was.
Ook die keer, ik zal het nooit vergeten
Waren wij toch haast de pisel
Toen ik uit pure benauwdheid
Over de vuilnisbak naar beneden viel.
Als ik naga, de eerste nachten
Sliepen ze niet aan een stuk door
Want ze lagen nog met die gedachten
Straks komen ze mij halen. Waarvoor?
Ook dachten ze vaak aan hun kleinen lieveling
Die nu ook onder water zou zijn.
Dog het was bij den nieuwen vader en moeder
En zo waren ze in gedachten steeds bij hun Dein.
Maar al gauw waren ze tevreden
Want ze kregen goed bericht.
Hun jongen had een vast tehuis gekregen
Dus knepen ze hun handen dicht.
Maar, heel vlug werd dit weer anders
Het kon zo echt niet langer gaan.
Ze konden hem daar niet langer hebbe
Het pinkte hierom ook een traan.
Tot ze eindelijk geen uitweg meer wisten
Voor onzen lieven kleinen man.
Onderling waren ze al aan het twisten
Straks lag hij in Wesserbork en dan???
Hoever is het gelukkig niet gekomen
Wij kwamen op een ander idee
En dus liep op zekeren morgen
Ons Heintje aan de hand van heidje mee

Weet je nog hoe bly jullie waren
Met de komst van jullie zoon
Je ogen kon je niet geloven
't Was als leefde je in een droom.
Maar de tyd was gauw verstreken
En Dineman ging dus weer op pad
Zyn echte thuis was nu gevonden
Door ons aller lieve Schad.
Na die tijd werd alles weer rustig
Lot en Frans gingen weer gewoon hun gang
Het leven zo ging hem nog niet vervelen
De zaten hier nu al weer maanden lang.
In het begin al werd de Dinsdag
Als de schoonmaak dag bepaald.
En alles wat ze dan konden vinden
Werd overhoop gehaald.
Ook kwamen er nog hoofd perikelen
Frans zyn haar dat moest er af
Lot nam zelf schaar en donderse
't had zo net, dat de Peijsters stonden paf.
't leek als was zij nog een kapster
Die bracht het er heus niet beter af
Lot vond dit altijd half een pretje.
Maar voor Frans is het gewoon een straf.
Als ik zo eens verder ga denken
Komen wij bij de zomer aan
Oh, wat vonden ze dat vervelend
Als met die hitte de kachel moest aan.
Hijgend, puffend, blazend, zwetend,
Snakten ze naar frisse lucht
Maar ze konden er nich in schikken.
En beneden komend staakten ze menige zucht.
Lijf van ellende, oh neen zo was het niet.
Maar strals terug te moeten in die warmte
En dat vooruitzicht in het verschiet.........!
Zo vlogen de dagen verder
Tot op een zekere keer
De grootste razzia werd gehouden
Of weten jullie dat niet meer?
Het was op een heten zondagmorgen

Ik vloog van de ene kant naar de ander
Tot ik eindelijk geen uitweg meer wist
En voelde mij net op die ochtend
Of ik op weg was naar mijn huis.
Maar het ergste dat moest nog komen.
Eerst mocht ik niet naar mijn huis
Toen ik daar eindelijk toch gearriveerd was
Begon pas het grootste kruis
Trams vol met jodenmensen
Kwamen die dag ons huis voorbij
Het waren wel 24 lange wagens
Het Mensen voor de ?? was het Zwijnderij.
Dan kwam het schoon je huis doorzoeken
Een stuk groen en een stuk burger. Drek.
En keken in allen gaten En hoeken.
Maar vonden niets. We hielden ze voor de gek
Onze beide onderzeeërs
hadden veilig in de kast.
Ik had het ergste in de zenuwen.
Dat hij je kwam halen de "E.G.Gast"
Maar zo is het gelukkig niet gelopen
Want ze merkten niets Het Vee.
En zo trokken ze met schone handen
De trap weer af. Beiden heel gedwee.
Lot en Frans kwamen nu weer in ons midden.
Ze hadden geen minuutje angst gehad
Daar hadden we voor niets beiden
Want een Mof en een jood is als hond en kat.
De weken daarna was het tamelijk rustig
Tot weer op een goede dag
Pa en Ma door schrik bevangen
De Zwarten voor hun neus staan zag.
Ze wisten niet wat te beginnen.
Lot en Frans verdwenen traps.
Want daar kwamen de Zwarten boven.
Ze hoorde het al aan hun stap.
Dit keer was het niet voor onze vrienden
Maar voor de spruiten Rie en El
De eerste met haar grote mondje
Had toen wel vreselijk in de knel.
Een proces verbaal werd al gemompeld
We waren toch beiden wel wat bang
Want als we het niet konden betalen

Zat er niets anders op dan het gwang.
Maar we wisten het toch zo te draaien
Dat dit niet is doorgegaan
Anders waren wij naar de hooien
En moesten jullie van onze baan.
Ook dit hoefde niet te gebeuren
Want dat was de grootste last
Toch moesten jullie je nog 2 uur vermaken
Het haasje over en de pass.
Eindelijk waren ze afgedropen
En jullie kwamen over ons je hoek vandaan
„De hadden ze niet om te kopen
Met een paar sigaretten zijn ze heen gegaan"
Dat was het eerste wat we zeiden
Tegen jullie, weet je nog wel
Ook dit is taling weer afgelopen
En geen kwartier maar in het
Zoo'tjes aan werd 't nu October
En kwamen we weer voor iets anders te staan
Deze maf is op ons huis gevallen
Als een mannetje wij de maan.
Ook hij mocht hier zijn tentje opslaan
Want wij vonden het allen beroerd
Als hij maar Westerbork terug zou moeten
Want op hem werd eveneens geloerd.
Daarom Bram vonden wij het best
Je op te nemen in ons huis,
En hopen dat het je blijft bevallen
Want je voelt je hier al aardig thuis.
Het hele leven is veranderd.
Sinds jij in ons midden kwam
Maar we hebben het erg gezellig
Het ons hoofje, Prins en Bram.
Weet je nog op Zaterdag morgen.
Toen je het je entree had gedaan
Was je eerst om te beginnen
Een poosje naar je bed gegaan.
Ik weet nog hoe het die middag regende.
En ik hoopte, ja ik bad
Dat als ik straks naar thuis zou komen
Je nog niet in de kamer zat.
Want voor een dier, zoals jij genoemd werd
Vond ik het toch lang niet pluis.

Als ik je met natte handen
Begroeten moest hier in huis.
Maar het geheel is nogal goed verlopen
Vind je ook ook niet Bram
Want je kreeg netjes mijn rechter handje
Toen je naar beneden kwam.
Vol bewondering werd eerst gekeken
Naar ons nieuw stukje Konijn
En we zaten ons al af te vragen
Hoe zou hij in de omgang zijn?
Maar het puzzel was gauw op te lossen
Want een paar dagen naderhand
Begon neef zich hieral thuis te voelen
En sprong hij wel eens uit de band.
We waren blij, ja dolgelukkig
Want het was geen saaie Piet.
En begon al net als de anderen
Over oom Jan, tante Nina en een griet.
Eindelijk begon hij met zijn moppen.
Je eerste weet ik nog heel goed.
't Was over een venstje op de kermis
Die in het donker zagen moet.
En zo verliepen snel de dagen
De Decembermaand brak alweer aan
Iedereen was aan het pakken
En de meeste ook aan het dichten gegaan.
Het St. Nicolaasfeest werd een geslaagde avond
Waar ik dikwijls nog aan denken zal
Met al die leuke cadeaux en gedichten
Vond ik uitgesproken "Koraal."
Na St. Nicolaas kwam het Kerstfeest
Waar ik niet over mee praten mag
Want die dagen was ik in Knolle
En kwam terug op mijn verjaardag
Ook die dag was fijn in orde.
Waar ik met vreugde de op tong kan zien
Al mijn cadeaux die waren geweldig
Ook die spekerlamp van jullie drieën.
Daarna kregen we het toneeltje.
Met de allerjongste spruit.
Tipsie kwam er boven water.
En lachte iedereen die avond uit.
Allen waren uit het veld geslagen.

Lotje jij had zelfs verdriet.
Je was jezelf ook af te vragen
Hoe komt die erby die jonge griet.
Jij kwam 's avonds vreselijk vrij praten
Alsof ik je zuster was
Ik trac je hartelijk uit te lachen
De spijt ervan kwam later pas.
De volgende dag was het Oude Jaar er
Het was toen ook een geweldige nacht
Om 12 uur precies werd er gerookt
En vlak daarop de schotels geslacht.
Tot half drie hebben wij het uitgehouden
Toen was 't ook met de pret gedaan
En zijn daarna allen zeven
Vlug in het "Vlooienfuik" gegaan.
Het Nieuwe Jaar is reeds ingetreden
En pakken dus weer met nieuwe moed aan
En hopen dan maar op de vrede
En de Hof eindelijk ons land uit zal gaan.
Met die gedachten leven we verder
Dat is ook maar het beste ding
Want we weten toch wel van ons zelve,
De Hof is en blijft een "Verdommeling"
Ook kom ik even op het plakken
Want wij vinden het allen fijn
Dat jullie in je vrij uren
Zo allerlei behulpzaam bij zijn
Lachen doen jullie het meest in de tijden
Dat je aan de "Plaksafel" zit
Weet je nog toen neef Jons kwam verblijden
Met drie aardappels achter zijn gebit?
Neef die is me toch een malle
O ja, komt hij ook met het verhaal dat,
Hij het Paradijs binnen kwam vallen
En met de engeltjes onder de vijgenbomen zat
Niet te vergeten de legende.
Neef gaat uit wandelen maar van dien aard
Dat hij hierbij niet veel nodig heeft
Dus gaat alleen met hoed verder in zijn blote
En zo is dit jaar verlopen
In angst, zorgen en plezier
Laten wij dus nu maar hopen
Dat het voorlopig rustig blijft hier

Ik zelf ben pas tevreden
Als de oorlog over zal zijn
Jullie twee gewoon Uffmam zullen heten
En ons Brammesje, Konijn.
Dat het dan zoals wij nu doen
Zo vriendschappelijk blijven mag
Omdat wij bij Ekander hoort
Dat merken wij nu wel met de dag.
Daarom nicht en lieve neven.
Beloof ons, dat, als de oorlog is voorbij
Wij toch Vrienden zullen blijven
Dat is de engste wens van mij.

My translation, excerpted, of Mom's poem to Pop on the one-year
anniversary of their arrival in their hiding place:

I

A whole-year has passed
for the youngest offspring of Aenni & Sal (Pop's parents)
On December 5th last year
we were all still together,
Grandmother Mum, and father-in-law (Opa Sally), *Leopold* (me), *Friet,*
[Fritz and Riet Ullmann], *and mother-in-law* (Oma Aenni).
On the table were all sorts of packages
and in the dining room Jewish things.
And little Dein [Leo] *dutifully sang his song*
for the good Sint [St. Nicholas] *and Black Pete:*
Afterward, we together put him to bed
and wished him good night.
Then we continued our conversation
for a long time about our little dear sweetheart.
This year we cannot talk about him
we have to leave him to other parents
and (Saint Nicholas) *advises you*
keep the faith because there our Deintje [Leo] *is in a good place.*
This year has truly not been very easy.
I hope that our dear son will not forget us,
because in '44, that will be the time
when we all will again be freed,
then everything will be all right.
"The year of freedom" Churchill said;
I hope so very much that it will be so;
we all again together, with our (Leo)
and Oma Mum (Pop's grandmother) *will still appear before our eyes*
as she lived with us in the Milletstraat.

II

This all as a picture is now in the past
because she died this year…
I certainly know that I will surely never forget her…
Then there were also those horrible nights,
when we lay together waiting,
with Aenni and Sally (Pop's parents), *and Riet* (Pop's sister-in-law) *also*
present,
for the Green Police.
And at night it actually happened;
we were yanked out of our sleep
by 2 men in black with dark caps.
Thank God, your parents had the idea (to send them away)*;*
and wasn't it an awful suffering
to not even be able to talk to our Fritz (Pop's brother).
But still, let it be said that
everything turned out alright for them.
Thanks to Ma and Pa (Peyster) *and the two girls*
we forget much of our sadness,
and we have
here still a very good time.
I still remember how we came here
on March 1 with your bike,
packed and loaded
with cigarettes, tea and chocolate.
Now we have here our own flat,
my dear husband!
Even if you are now without work,
we have been able to learn together…
We have whispered a lot
afraid that someone was also listening.

III

My dear [sweetheart], *so the past days*
still brought to us cozy times
Now in each other we have so much trust
we are surely building for the future
The days, they fly so hastily by
A relief for you and also for me.
on this calendar I am learning that
if you turn the page every two months,
then quickly comes the good news
of our possible rescue…

Original poem follows

I

Een lied toch dit keer weer geleden.
En een heel jaar weer is vergleden.
Wilde hij in dit bijzondere geval,
Voor de jongste telg van Anni en Sal
Nu ook eens probeeren
Dit jaar de revue te laten passeeren,
Op 5 December, vorig jaar
Waren we allen nog bij elkaar
Grootvader Leeuw, en schoonpapa,
Leopold, Piet en schoonmama.
Op de tafel allemaal pakjes lagen
En in de voorkamer Noortje's wagen.
En kleine Dien zong trouw zijn lied
Voor de goede Piet en Zwarte Piet.
Bij de kachel in de kamer ging hij staan
Met zijn blauwe hemd aan.
En als we hem dan samen in bed hadden gelegd
Hem alles goedenacht hadden gezegd,
Dan ging in de kamer nog lang ons gesprek
Over onze kleine lieve lachebek.
Dit jaar kunnen we over hem niet praten
Moesten hem aan andere ouders overlaten
En Lied haar raad jou, houd goeden moed,
Want daar zit onze Dientje goed.
De ware liefde, die leert thans.
Te kunnen afstand doen, mijn lieve Frans.

II

Dit jaar, waarachtig niet zeer zacht,
Heeft ons dat beiden lui gebracht.
Bij denken we samen, dat is heel gewoon,
Zoo vaak aan onze lieven zoon
Toch hoop ik, dat hij dit nooit zal weten,
En ons toch ook niet meer te vergeten,
Want in '44, dan komt de tijd
Dat we allen weer worden bevrijd,
Dan wordt wat krom was lui weer recht,
„Het jaar van de vrede", heeft Churchill gezegd.
Ik hoop zoo innig, dat het kan,
Wij allen weer samen, bij Oom Jan.
En Oma Mima nog voor mijn oogen staat,
Zooals ze bij ons leefde, Milletstraat,
Dit alles als beeld mij is vergleden,
Want dit jaar is ze overleden!
Met een auto van het Roode Kruis
Kwam ze aan, bij ons in huis,
En met een tosei ging ze veel later,
Toen heul alleen ook onder water.
't Is goed, dat ik zoo zeker weer,
Dat ik haar vast niet meer vergeet,
Dat ik haar beeld ook trouw bewaar,
Zij blijf voor grooter leed gespaard.'
Toen waren ook nog die ellendige nachten,
Waarin we samen lagen te wachten.

III

Met Benni en Sally, en Riet nog erg;
Op de Grüne Polizei.
En 's nachts is het werkelijk gebeurd,
Dat we wreed uit onze slaap gesheurd,
En stonden, met een donk're pet,
2 zwarte heren aan ons bed.
Goede 2ij land, zuigen je onuers gedoee,
Met onze vriend Reinders toen veilig mee.
En wat was het niet een vreselijk leed,
Het lot van die arme, lieve Frees.
Om onze Frits nog niet eens te spreken,
En liebe zag, zooveele weeken.
Maar toch, dat heb ik blij gingd,
kwam met hem alles goed terecas.
toch was het weer een groote ramp.
Zooveelen kwamen in het kamp.
Zoo waag dit jaar wel lidaar als laad.
Borg vele tranen in haar schoot.
Dana 2ij bra, Pa, en iedere Fries
vergaten we veel van ons verdries.
En leven we in leuter aan heid,
Hier toch een dolle leuse tijd.
Ik weet nog hoe we samen,
Op 1 maart hier ten kwamen,
Met onze fiets, bepast en beladen,
Met zigaretten, thee en chocolade.

IV

En Tante, Corr, Elly en Riet
Gingen ieder voor ons naar buurvrouw Schmidt.
En hebben wat er was nog meegenomen.
Zijn dik aangekleed weer bij ons aangekomen.
Wat werd voor ons zoo veel gered.
Nu hebben we hier ons eigen flat.
Mijn lieve man, een draad maakt sterk!
Al zit je nu dan zonder werk,
Dit hebben we samen kunnen leeren,
Al moet je dat je spijt nu beletteren.
Zoo hebben we hier wat afgefluisterd,
Bang dat Dien soms vaak meeluisterd.
Maar, helaas ik niet altijd zie.
Die goede volmaakte harmonie.
Trekt Dina dinsdag aan haar been,
Gaat naar haar kind in Amstelveen,
Dan kan ik met het schrobben en het schuren,
Heel veel critiek steeds te verduren.
Toch merkte ik het hier van Mia.
Dat wasschen met Amonia.
Maar is het eindelijk gereed.
En blinkend schoon ons bezige kleed,
Kom ik de trap van boven naar beneden,
Dan lieve man, ben je toch tevreden.
Dan glunder je bij al dat blinken,
En.... kun je vroolijk weer gaan stinken

_II_

na 5 minuten, 't valt echt niet mee.
Leh de hamer, echt op een .... W.C.!!
Mijn lieve Moos, zoo ging de tijd
Bracht ons toch veel gezelligheid.
In elkaar hebben we zooveel vertrouwen,
Wij zeker op de toekomst bouwen.
De dagen, die vliegen zoo haastig voort-
Een zegen voor jou en ook voor mij.
Op deze kalender ben ik dat leeren,
Als je weder 2 maanden het blaadje moet keeren.
En dan komt gauw de dolle bevrijding.
Van onze moffelijke bevrijding.
Dan zeg je: „Ziezoo". Ik ben der. "
Dit brengt je, Frans, deze scheurkalender.

March 1, 1944. One year in hiding: (Translated From Dutch)

On this day, it is right to create,

To try to commemorate.

This day, I believe, could not go by,

Without writing some verses, which I do now try.

Pa, and Ma, you know, exactly how I feel,

Your great hospitality is our safety-seal.

I hope, that soon you will bask in your glory

And able to write your happy-end-story.

And I hope, that Pa will soon be a handy waiter,

Without using a cane, walking much straighter.

But my special thought, my special thank,

Goes to you, my dear patient Frank.

We are still close together, without too much fear.

And we made it, this whole difficult year.

Though our life upstairs, was quite hard,

Our togetherness made it better, from the start.

We could share our thoughts, share our fate,

Because we can talk about it, mostly fairly late.

And to me, it is now crystal clear.

That sharing, makes things so much easier, even deeprooted fear.

We had much laughter, I really think,

Because this was a year with many farts, and stink.

Ma could buy onions galore, without too much fuss

We cooked them upstairs, called Jewish pineapple by us.

It was a year, how can I possibly forget,

That you were mad, every single Tuesday, I bet.

A whole year, I cleaned and scrubbed that day,

Polished, and worked in my special way.

A whole year, without parting, it does not seem fair.

A whole year, I am your barber and cut uneven your hair.

A whole year, I mend, and repair your suit.

A whole year, with no holes on either sock of your foot.

A whole year, our Ma visits Hoogeboom, for news of the family

Bringing them our letters, signed Frank and Emily.

A year now, without being too scared, too afraid,

For every single night, those terrible German raid.

This year has gone now, and became an historical event,

This year, in the closet, we in prayers did bent.

A year, of hard work, as Churchill eloquently said.

A year of curfew, of darkness, we went early to bed.

A whole year, now, we are mixing the glue,

To finish the envelopes, for tea or coffee to glue.

A whole year, your apronstrings look suddenly good,

We share the worries, for cooking our food.

Frans & Emily -- 11

A whole year friend Leidje, has been our monthly guest

Helping you, in your Russian Language quest.

A whole year, you are so handy, and so strong,

You help us listening, to the radio-in-the-closet-song.

A whole year, you took care of us all, and spent,

Many an hour to repair, and to mend.

I hope, no more year, after this has to come,

We lived illegal, without coupons in Amsterdam.

Quietly, whispering, and on slippers we hush,

Not even the toilet we use, can we flush.

On the floor, sleeping together we cram,

Greatful though, to share all with Bram.

This whole year, you gave me, in your sorrow,

Your optimistic, loving care for the day of tomorrow.

May the Good Lord, I pray send you His reward.

So that our own life, we soon will start.

And that Leo will come back to us, for ever more.

That I pray, dear Lord, on March 1, 1944.

Chapter 11

Amsterdam During the "Hunger Winter"

On Sunday September 3, 1944, *Radio Oranje*, the Dutch expatriate radio station operating out of London, announced that Holland was about to be liberated. That announcement was totally erroneous and based on false information. It was followed two days later by *Dolle Dinsdag* (Crazy Tuesday) when thousands of people filled the streets of Breda and a number of other Dutch cities in wild celebrations of the reported end of the War.

That jubilation, which soon ended, preceded by just days the beginning of *De Hongerwinter* (The Hunger Winter), one of the greatest tragedies in the history of the Netherlands.

On September 17, 1944 the Dutch government in exile in London ordered the Dutch Railway System to strike and shut down the entire railway system in the Netherlands, commencing on the next day, in order to prevent the Nazis from continuing to strip the country of all its rolling stock, factories, and other assets.[30]

---

[30] *In fact the Netherlands' railway strike continued until the country was liberated in May 1945.*

The reprisal by the Nazis was swift, effective and incredibly brutal. They cut off for an initial period of six weeks (the effects of which would last long beyond that) all shipments of food and fuel to the Western provinces of the Netherlands, which covered a population of some 4.5 million people including Amsterdam, The Hague and other major cities.

This embargo was made possible, regrettably, by the loss by the Allies in the Battle of Arnhem, which resulted in the Allies moving the front toward an invasion of Germany without liberating the areas of the Netherlands north of the Rhine River, thus leaving most of Holland (8 of the 11 Provinces at that time) in the hands of the Germans.

The strike by the Dutch Railway System kept potatoes from coming from the North of the country, while the German embargo kept most every kind of food and fuel from reaching Western Holland. In the meantime the winter of 1944-1945 was unusually severe, causing the canals and the inland seas to freeze, thus further preventing food and fuel transports from the South.

As there was no food to speak of, the central food kitchen in Amsterdam was able to serve only soup made out of potato peels and watered-down mashed potatoes. People were forced to eat sugar beets, flower bulbs, even dogs and cats. As there was no fuel, there was no electricity or heat. Factories and schools were forced to close. People scavenged the wood blocks from between the rails of the tramlines, and the wood floors, doors and beams of abandoned houses in the Jewish section, to provide a little bit of heat. People even took doors from occupied houses. Trees were cut down throughout the city and its nearby roads. There was no wood for caskets; they were therefore made out of cardboard. Lines of dead bodies were placed, without any caskets, in some of the churches in Amsterdam.

Garbage was left on the street and was not picked up until the end of the War.

Women on bicycles (men would be picked up and sent to German forced labor camps) made trips, referred to as *Hongertochten* (Hunger Trips), to the farms in the Eastern and Northern parts of the country looking for food and bartering textiles, jewelry and anything of value. Some Dutch farmers were able to enrich themselves meaningfully, taking advantage of desperate people's plight.

The Germans created *De Landwacht* (the Country Watch) in November 1943, consisting basically of Dutch Nazis who created control points and often confiscated anything of value, including food, from those who gave up everything to find some food in farms.

A black market was prevalent, even though the Nazis prohibited it. The Nazis created a Central Crisis Control Service, which was charged with preventing black market sales and economic sabotage. On the black market, a loaf of bread commanded a multiple of an average week's salary.

The lack of food and heat affected children disproportionately. Accordingly, as many as 50,000 children, with consent of the Germans, were sent, largely under the auspices of Protestant and Catholic churches, to farms East and North of Amsterdam for survival and sustenance. I benefitted from this effort, and, as earlier described, was shipped to the North of Amsterdam with others, but my "War Father," Opa Schimmel, with a special permit, came on his bicycle to rescue me after a week because he was fearful that I might not survive.

In late January 1945, Swedish ships under the auspices of the Swedish Red Cross brought three shiploads of flour, from which Dutch bakeries could make "Swedish" white bread. The Dutch, prior thereto, generally had bread made only out of "potato flour," when available.

Food help in larger measure for the Dutch did not come until April 29, 1945 after months of negotiations between the Germans and the Allies. At that time, over a period of eight days, U.K. and U.S. bombers under "Operation Manna" and "Operation Chowhound" in 5000 "mercy flights" dropped nearly 11,000 tons of food parcels containing corned beef, chocolate, powdered milk and other items on Western Holland. It took another 10 days before the parcels were effectively distributed to the people, but my parents didn't get any.

It is estimated that more than 22,000 Dutchmen died from hunger during the Hunger Winter.

During the last year of the War a group of photographers, professionals and amateurs, was formed to chronicle the occupation by photography. While photography was forbidden, this group, named "The Underground (hidden) Camera," under the most difficult circumstances, and without knowing one another, created thousands of photographs. They had to hide their cameras in grocery bags or under their coats, leaving a hole through which the lens could take a peek. The photographs are but small pictures of the panorama of suffering by literally millions.

The photographs included here are intended to evidence the effects of the deprivation of food and fuel during the Hunger Winter. They were exhibited just two weeks after the liberation of Amsterdam to establish memories which could not die.

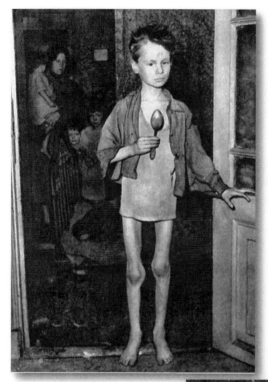

Note: Photographs on pages 152-156 were made by Emmy Andriesse, Cas Oorthuys, and/or others, and published in a book of such photographs, entitled *Amsterdam Tijdens de Hongerwinter (Amsterdam During the Hunger Winter)* published in 1947 with an introduction by Max Nord (without copyright) by Contact "in cooperation with C.V DeBezige Bij u.a."

Hunger

Children died from hunger, their bodies left on streets, wrapped in paper.

Without help or support, thousands died.

Dead bodies lined up in a church.

Women looking for food in the farm areas, sometimes traveling 100 km by bicycle.

Sifting for traces of coal.

"Demand More Food"

Scavenging in garbage piles for food or fuel.

A lucky find: enough wood
to last a week.

As a result of demolition and plunder,
the Jewish quarter came to look as if it
had been bombed.

Children looking for splinters of wood between the train rails.
In the background: VERZET! (Resist!)

Chapter 12

The End of the War

May 5, 1945 is considered as the day the War formally ended in Holland. However, for Amsterdam, this situation remained somewhat fluid until May 8 when the Canadians arrived in the heart (Dam Square) of Amsterdam. On May 4, 1945, the Germans, including Seyss-Inquart formally surrendered but initially refused to surrender "Western Netherland." The final surrender documents were signed on May 6, 1945 but were dated May 5, 1945.

On May 7, 1945, a group of armed Germans, in a last vicious act, fired shots from the balcony of De Groote Club, ("Large Club"), an exclusive men's club, on the festive crowd celebrating in Dam Square who thought the War was over, killing 19 and wounding 117 innocent and unarmed Dutchmen. I was on my way to the Dam Square with Oma when we heard the shots and turned back.

A war monument in the Square commemorates that atrocity and all Dutch persons killed in the War.

May 4th is now celebrated in Holland every year as *Dodenherdenking* ("Remembrance Day"), a national holiday and involves enormous crowds who gather at the National War Monument on Dam Square. At 8 pm on that day there is a bugle call and a two minute period of silence throughout the country.

May 5th is referred to as *Bevrijdingsdag* ("Liberation Day") and is also a national holiday. It's the day on which I always called my "War Mother" after the War to thank her for saving me.

Much of Holland was in fact liberated in late 1944 before the "Hunger Winter" and in the early months of 1945. Queen Wilhelmina even returned to Dutch soil on March 13, 1945.

The Canadian Maple Leaf Brigade freed Amsterdam and most of Holland. For the liberation of The Hague, Dutch troops, among other Allied forces, including the "Princess Irene Brigade" (named after one of Queen Wilhelmina's granddaughters) accompanied the Canadian troops. There has been a special relationship between the Dutch and the Canadians ever since those days for freeing their country and also for accommodating Princess Juliana (who became Queen in 1948) and her family during the War in Toronto, at the invitation of a cousin who at the time was Governor General of Canada.

On May 5th, every fifth year anniversary of that day in 1945, Canadian veterans of the liberation of Holland are invited to parade to the Dam Square via the same route by which they marched into the City in May 1945 (via the Churchillaan, among other roads), to great applause. Of course, there are now very few left to make the parade.

That Liberation Day is one of the few days that I truly remember, but, having regard to the above history, I'm not exactly sure whether it was in fact on May 5th, or whether it would have been a couple of days later. Did I make it to 800 days or more in hiding? And, is the title of this book wrong? My parents always maintained that it was in fact May 5, the very day we all celebrate. It would appear, based on the matters described above, that May 7th or May 8th was the more likely day when we in fact celebrated and met. Other days and other times are a bit unclear to me, because, without having reinforcement from my parents, or indeed photos, it is hard for me to know what I remember versus what I've been told that I should remember.

On that actual liberation day, there were several significant things to remember. Pop said that the way that he knew that the War was over, was that they were able to look out their window onto the Ceintuurbaan and to see German soldiers, their epaulets having been torn off their uniforms, walking with their hands on their heads and without rifles.

For me, there were a few special sights. One was the bombers flying over Amsterdam, where we could look out and see them (whereas during the War, we always had to black out our windows at night) and they were dropping food parcels on Amsterdam.

There was an incredible amount of cheering, noisemaking and hugging, etc. Also, the color orange was everywhere. Orange is the color of the House of Oranje, the Dutch monarchy. Anyone who had anything resembling the color orange wore it, waived it, hung it out the windows, and displayed it wherever possible.

It turns out that the people on the street where I had lived, from whom Oma and Opa Schimmel had so carefully hid me for a good part of the War, all knew that I was there as a hidden child, and no one betrayed us.

My parents, in the meantime, wanted to find me. Aleida Schot, the sorority sister who had arranged my placement with the Haarlem minister, together with the Haarlem minister himself, came to my parents' hiding place and had a most joyful reunion. At that point, they told my parents where I had been hidden, and my parents set out on foot to find me. This was especially difficult for my father, who had very severe edemas on his feet. His feet had ballooned to enormous proportions, basically because he had not been able to get out and walk literally for years.

They arrived at the Schimmels' apartment and Oma Schimmel, with me at her side, opened the door. I had no idea who these terribly gaunt strange-looking people were, but Oma knew immediately that these were my parents. She had expected them. To me, they were not my parents; Oma and Opa Schimmel were my parents, at least as far as I was concerned.

This must've been terribly difficult for both my parents and the Schimmels, but, fortunately, Oma Schimmel, as a compassionate, religious and wonderful woman, knew that she had to give me up. They all agreed that this should be done over a period of several days, at least, to avoid undue pain for me.

Before my parents took me back to their hiding place, I insisted on having one of those orange paper hats that were being sold that day, and I made my poor folks, who hardly had the energy to either stand or walk, stand in line for hours on a main shopping street of Amsterdam, the Ferdinand Bolstraat, until we obtained one of those hats.[31]

At the hiding place, although they had absolutely starved during the last months of the War, my parents had saved, and hidden under a floor board, a large can of baked beans for the day that they would get me back. I, in the meantime, had eaten quite well at the Schimmels, and never knowingly suffered in any respect.

When we arrived at the hiding place, they opened the can of beans with great meaning, ceremony and hope. I, however, who never lacked for food, to my continuing embarrassment to this day, said, "uughh, I hate baked beans!" They nevertheless ate them all and even wiped the plate with their fingers. Mom had also knit some clothes for me, largely

---

[31] This is one of those areas where my recollection differs from that of my parents. I remember going and standing in line on a bridge with Oma Schimmel, and I think Mom may have co-opted that story, as I don't remember standing in line with her and Pop.

from threads she culled from a discarded bedspread, but I apparently found them to be funny-looking and the legs were too narrow.

Pop's parents (Oma Aenni and Opa Sally) also came to the hiding place from Utrecht somehow, presumably through Mr. Hoogenboom (there was no public transportation at that point). They, too, learned of our whereabouts from Aleida Schot.

Mom, Pop and I then walked back to the Schimmels, a long hike on good legs, let alone on their atrophied limbs, where the Schimmels had arranged a reception (tea and cookies) with friends and neighbors. This was joyous. One of the neighbors who owned a store actually gave a bicycle to each of my parents to use (with wooden rims on the wheels, as rubber tires were impossible to come by at the end of the War). I personally was happy to be back, at least then, with Oma and Opa Schimmel.

Also on that day my parents met for the first time the couple that lived in the apartment immediately below them.

My parents and Pop's parents stayed in my parents' hiding place that night, and several additional nights, sleeping on the mattresses on the floor. Fortunately, and again probably through Piet Hoogen-boom, Pop's parents soon found a place to live in Utrecht.

Because I was seriously cross-eyed, my parents immediately arranged to have me operated on in a hospital in Amsterdam. Opa Schimmel came to see me every day in the hospital. My parents claim the operation was a complete success. They, in the meantime, had been able to find a house in Amsterdam and left the hiding place forever.

PROCLAMATIE

NEDERLAND HERWINT ZIJN VRIJHEID.

De tyrannie, die ons het hart doorwondde, is verdreven.
Onze Koningin kan het bewind weder te midden van Haar
vrije volk uitoefenen.
Vreemde smetten worden uitgewischt. Recht en wet treden
weder in de plaats van willekeur en geweld.

Door de Regeering geroepen hare vertrouwensmannen te zijn tijdens de overgangsdagen, waarin het regelmatig bestuur ontbreekt, wenden wij ons ingevolge bijzondere opdracht tot U, Nederlanders.

Gevoelens van ontroering, van innig geluk en van diepe blijdschap over de beëindiging van de bezetting, die zooveel kommer en onherstelbaar leed bracht, vervullen ons allen. Millioenen brengen God ootmoedig dank voor de bevrijding en voor de kracht, die Hij aan Vorstin en volk schonk om steeds zwaarder treffende smerten te doorstaan en het hart in tegenspoed standvastig te doen blijven.

Dankbaar zijn wij jegens het Koninklijk Huis, dat ook in den vreemde met woord en daad aan land en volk verknocht bleef. Wij achten ons gelukkig, dat indertijd wijs beleid en oHerzin, met trotseering van persoonlijke gevaren en van de mogelijkheden van verkeerde uitlegging, het zoo vruchtbaar en juist gebleken besluit deden nemen het bewind over de verschillende gebiedsdeelen van het Koninkrijk te voeren van het land der ballingschap en gastvrijheid uit.

Onze gedachten gaan naar de mannen van leger, vloot en luchtmacht, die in de rampspoedige Meidagen van 1940 en later, met die van de koopvaardij, in het belang en tot heil van het vaderland hun offer brachten, en naar allen, die nog dagelijks hun leven in de waagschaal stellen.

Met dankbaarheid en trots gedenken wij, hoe ons volk onder aanvoering van zijn leidslieden uit kerkelijke en wereldlijke kringen zich vijf jaar lang tot het uiterste verzet heeft tegen een stelsel, dat gericht was op de vernietiging van de christelijke bescheving, van eeuwenoude tradities en van de nationale eer.

In het bijzonder denken wij aan de tallooze heldhaftige ondergrondsche strijders, die zich een gevaarloos bestaan ontzegden, in verbeten kamp met stoffelijke en geestelijke wapenen de kracht van den vijand ondermijnden en door hun werk en voorbeeld onze volkskracht sterkten. Velen hunner, wier nagedachtenis in eere zal worden gehouden, lieten hun leven in gevangenissen en concentratiekampen en voor de pelotons van den niets ontzienden onderdrukker.

Wij mogen ook hen niet vergeten, die tegen hun wil als slaven naar den vreemde gevoerd, daar óf den dood hebben gevonden óf nog in handen van beulen en geweldenaars een schier ondragelijk bestaan leiden.

Al deze offers zijn niet tevergeefs gebracht. Onze nationale zelfstandigheid is herwonnen en een nieuwe toekomst ligt voor ons open. Het vaderland, dat wij in de jaren der beproeving nog meer hebben liefgekregen, biedt ons weer vrijheid en vrede, orde en rust, rechtszekerheid en een menschwaardig bestaan.

Alle krachten zullen worden ingespannen om zoo spoedig mogelijk te voorzien in de allerdringendste behoeften van de bevolking en een einde te maken aan de stoffelijke ontberingen, waaronder helaas zoovelen hebben moeten lijden.

Ondanks de groote en talrijke moeilijkheden, waarmede wij te kampen hebben, zal de arbeid tot herstel met kracht en voortvarendheid worden aangevat om zoo veel en zoo snel mogelijk de sporen te doen verdwijnen, welke het duivelsche vernietigingswerk allerwege achterliet.

Thans is het de plicht van ons volk zich de herkregen vrijheid waard te toonen. In eensgezindheid met onze bondgenooten, wier offers en wapenfeiten ons met erkentelijkheid en bewondering vervullen, zal de strijd tot een goed einde moeten worden gebracht. Op ons rust de plicht met alle kracht mede te werken aan de bevrijding van Indonesië, dat in handen is van een vijand, niet minder wreed dan de bezetter van Nederland zich toonde.

Van ieder wordt verwacht, dat hij zich stipt zal houden aan de bevelen der Regeering en aan die van het Geallieerd Opperbevel.

Met den meesten aandrang sporen wij allen aan tot een ordelijke houding en tot het nalaten van daden van eigenrichting, welke in strijd zijn met ons rechtsbesef, onze tradities en democratische opvattingen.

Wij vertrouwen, dat men zich in de begrijpelijke vreugde over de herkregen vrijheid waardig zal gedragen en zonder dwang die orde en tucht in acht zal nemen, welke passend zijn bij den ernst van den tijd, dien wij beleven.

Zooals ons volk sterk was in de verdrukking, zoo getuige het van kracht en zelfbeheersching bij de bevrijding.

De nieuwe tijd, die ons wacht, vinde een volk, dat, gestaald door het leed en gegroeid in saamhoorigheid, met opgeheven hoofd, al is het in een gebrandschat land, gereed staat voor de taak, waartoe het geroepen is.

Leve de Koningin, leve het Vaderland!

Op den dag der bevrijding,

De Vertrouwensmannen der Regeering.

(translation on next page)

(My translation)

PROCLAMATION

NETHERLANDS REGAINS ITS FREEDOM

**The tyranny that wounded us through our heart
has been driven off.
Our Queen can again carry out her leadership amid
her free subjects.
Justice and law will rule again in lieu of arbitrariness
and might.**

Through the persons called up on by the Government to be its placeholder trustees during the transition period, while the duly authorized government has not been available, we are establishing special demands for you Netherlanders.

Feelings of wonder, of great good fortune and of deep happiness as to the ending of the occupation, which brought with it so much distress and unmitigated suffering, fulfill us all. Millions bring to God humble thanks for the liberation and for the strength which He gave to the Queen and the people to withstand continually heavier wounds and to make the heart continue to beat through adversity.

We are also thankful for the Royal House, which also while abroad with word and deed remained devoted to our country and people. We consider ourselves fortunate that at the time thoughtful leadership and sacrifice while confronting personal danger and the possibility of false explanations, made the apparently fruitful and correct decision, to carry out the governance for the various parts of the Kingdom from a country of exile and hospitality.

Our thoughts go out to the men of the army, navy and air force, who in the disastrous days of May 1940 and later, with those of the merchant marine, who carried out their efforts in support of, and to the good of the fatherland, and to all who daily carried out their lives in the balance.

With thanks and pride we think how our people under guidance of its leaders from religious and worldly circles has mightily opposed rules which were directed toward destruction of Christian civilization, of centuries-old traditions and of national honor.

We especially think of the countless heroic resistance fighters who gave up a safe existence, and with physical and inner weapons undermined the power of the enemy, and who through their efforts and example strengthened our national will. Many of them, whose memories we will retain with honor, lost their lives in prisons and concentration camps and against the troops of the unscrupulous controlling power.

We must also not forget those who against their will were deported as slaves to foreign lands, there to have found death or at the hands of tyrants and oppressors to have led a nearly unbearable life.

All these efforts have not been in vain.

Our national independence has been regained and a new future lies open ahead of us. The fatherland that we, during the course of years of trial, have come to love even more dearly, again offers us freedom and peace, order and calm, the rule of law and a worthy human existence.

All efforts will be undertaken to satisfy as rapidly as possible the most urgent needs of the people and to end the material hardships, under which regrettably so many have had to suffer.

Notwithstanding the great and many hardships with which we have had to deal, the work toward recovery will be undertaken with strength and perseverance to eliminate the traces which the Devil's destructive work has left behind everywhere.

It is now the duty of our people to justify its retrieved freedom. Together with our allies, whose efforts and military deeds fill us with appreciation and wonder, the battle must be brought to a good ending. The burden rests on us to cooperate with all the powers to work toward the liberation of Indonesia, which is in the hands of an enemy, no less cruel than evidenced by the occupier of the Netherlands.

Of everyone it is expected that they will carefully obey the orders of the government and of the Overall Allied Command.

With the greatest urgency we urge all to assume an orderly demeanor and to avoid actions of self-interest which are contrary to our respect for law, our traditions and democratic views.

We trust that people in their understandable joy over the recovered freedom will conduct themselves in a worthy manner and, without being forced to do so, respect order and reason, which will be consistent with the seriousness of the times which we are experiencing.

In the same manner our people were strong under oppression, so must we evidence strength and self-control upon liberation.

The new time that awaits us finds a people, steeled by the suffering, and grown in unity, with head held high, albeit in a ravished land, standing prepared for the task to which it has been called.

Long live the Queen, long live the Fatherland
On the day of liberation
The Representatives of the Government

Last issue, dated May 10, 1945, of "The Flying Dutchman" fliers distributed by the Allied Air Command heralding the unconditional German surrender.

Chapter 13

Fritz Ullmann and Family

Fritz Ullmann, Pop's older brother, like Pop, was born a Jew in Germany. Unlike Pop, Fritz was able to obtain an advanced education (in law) in Germany before coming to Holland.

With the help of a sympathetic government official who did not feel compelled to abide by all the Nazi rules, Fritz was able to marry Riet Coebergh, a Catholic, during the War, notwithstanding the Nazi *Rassenwetten* which forbade marriage between Jews and non-Jews. In June 1942, their first son, Joost, was born.

By virtue of marriage to an Aryan, Fritz was considered a "half Jew." Accordingly, he was exempted at the outset from transport to German concentration camps. This was strangely inconsistent with the thought that such Jews were "polluting" Aryan blood. However, by decree of December 12, 1943, all Jewish partners in mixed marriages were nevertheless ordered to be deported.

Fritz did not abide by the strict German government rules, including the requirement that Jews wear the yellow Jewish star, because he believed that to abide by those rules would only ultimately lead to the destruction of the Jews. Thus, not only did he not wear the Jewish star, but he also used a bike, which, too, was prohibited.

At some point in July 1942, Fritz was riding his bike (without a Jewish star) toward the home of his parents (Oma Aenni and Opa

Sally), who in the meantime had received an order to move to Amsterdam. Fritz wanted to help them with their move. While on his bike, carrying a false ID card, also supplied by Piet Hoogenboom, Sr, and in fact made by Piet, Jr., with a Christian name often taken from tombstones in cemeteries, and without the letter "J" to identify Jews), he was stopped, just a couple of hundred meters from the home of his (and Pop's) parents (Oma Aenni and Opa Sally), by two men in street clothes. Fritz at first was not worried because he had "good papers" and he showed them those papers.

However, one of the two men after looking at his ID card yelled, "This is not you — I know you, you are Ullmann. I was a police detective and I was in your factory because of a theft claim. You are a Jew and you have to come with us to the police station." The man was indeed a detective in the Utrecht Police who was now working for the Germans. Accordingly, Fritz was taken to a nearby police station while the two men went to his home and "searched the house." While Riet stood by, they walked off with food, liquor, cigars, cigarettes and a typewriter. They could also claim a bounty for capturing a Jew.

Then began a long journey for Fritz through various police stations, jail cells, jails and "camps." He was transported from Utrecht to Amsterdam in a horse-drawn cart to the Gestapo office on the Euterpestraat in Amsterdam (further referenced in the next chapter). Fritz was then placed for a matter of weeks in a "Jewish cell" in a jail in Amstelveen together with a number of other Jews who had been picked up under generally similar circumstances.

One of his cellmates, an elegant Dutch lawyer who had a leather suitcase full of real soaps, which at that time was a great luxury, was ultimately seen by Fritz being shot dead near a barbed-wire fence because "he was contemplating flight."

After eight weeks, with very little food, basically only bread and a watery soup, he was taken to the concentration camp at Amersfoort. This turned out to be a horrifying experience for Jews who were interred there. Not only were they deprived of food, but they had to wear wooden shoes which were enormously painful after a while, causing blisters that made it nearly impossible to either stand or walk. The prisoners had to continuously "work" pulling up tree stumps under the supervision of the green-uniformed Nazi police who patrolled with dogs. They were often made to stand at attention for hours on end, and were especially severely punished if an inmate escaped. They thus lived in constant fear of whatever the next step might be. Whoever survived Amersfoort was generally well-prepared for what might later occur.

Luckily, Fritz was shipped from Amersfoort to the Dutch transit camp Westerbork, rather than directly to the killing camps in Eastern Germany. In Westerbork he was placed first in a small jail (Barrack 51) because he was considered a "lawbreaker" deserving punishment.

Aunt Riet did everything she could in the meantime to rescue him and ultimately was able to arrange a hearing with senior officers of the German SS who felt sorry for her because of the baby.

After three months, Fritz was transferred out of the jail cell to a normal barracks where he could see the freight trains leaving every Tuesday full of captured Jews, destined for an unknown ending. Thus on Tuesdays, the mood at Westerbork was extremely somber, whereas in other days, captives still had hope that they could stay in Westerbork.

At the end of the summer of 1943, without any forewarning, a decree was issued to the effect that Jewish men married to non-Jewish women were to be dismissed from the camp. This was a totally unexpected surprise. Fritz was released and could thus return to his home, where, for the first time in more than a year, he could see his son Joost. Riet in the meantime, without Joost, had been able to visit Fritz a few times at Westerbork. Although Fritz was now "free," the War was certainly not over and the search for Jews continued unabated.

After some six months of "freedom," Fritz was again called up for "work service" in a work camp in the Northern part of Holland where the Germans were building an airport. There were barracks at that site as well and it was under the administration of Germans, but there was not the sort of terror that existed in Amersfoort, for example. In fact, he and others could leave the camp and there was not very much "work" to be done, in part because there were virtually continuous air raid alarms during which he and others would go hide in nearby farms. The farmers were usually friendly and accommodating, providing milk and food to the inmates. Suddenly on June 6, 1944, all the Germans disappeared from the camp. Through the BBC, the prisoners learned that the Allied troops had landed in Normandy and would soon march through France toward Holland and on to Germany, which, in turn, had been extremely challenged by the Russian armies on the Eastern front.

Fritz decided at that point not to hang around and to take advantage of the departure of the Germans. He grabbed a bike that was parked there and rode (without the Jewish star) to the nearest train station and jumped on a train for Utrecht. To Riet's total surprise, he suddenly arrived home. It was too dangerous to stay there (there were still many collaborators), so he found a friendly family who agreed to take him "into hiding" in their attic. In September, he nevertheless returned to his home and mostly stayed inside, sometimes in a small hiding place under the floor boards when there were warnings of house-to-house *Razzias*. Even the Hunger Winter of '44-'45 hardly fazed him because Riet was able to go by bike to the northern part of the country and trade textiles, yarn, cigarettes, etc. for food. They thus survived with help from many people and with a lot of luck.

After the War, Fritz became the head of a Dutch furniture factory, UMS-Pastoe, which became a leading manufacturer of knock-down cabinets and modern furniture. The factory was founded in 1913 by Fritz Loeb, a brother of Oma Aenni. The factory still exists and the name "Pastoe" ("ready fit") is still used.

Fritz Loeb was married to the enormous Aunt Sophie. They had a daughter, Liesje, who was almost as large as Aunt Sophie. She married Hans Eiser; they had no children. They, too, survived the War through placements arranged by Mr. Hoogenboom. Liesje inherited the factory when her father died. As further discussed eleswhere, Hans and Liesje remained close to, and arranged a number of honors for, Piet Hoogenboom and his family

At some point after the War, Henk, my parents and I went to visit Aunt Sophie, whose size was remarkable to the point where their Buick had to be especially reconfigured (including widened doors) and reinforced to accommodate her. I remember my then very young little brother, Henk, sitting there staring at Aunt Sophie with his jaw open, mesmerized, as Aunt Sophie proceeded to eat a whole plate of cookies, rearranging the remaining cookies each time she ate one, into a new symmetric pattern until there were none left.

Uncle Fritz, Riet and Joost Ullmann in Utrecht
early in the War.

Great-uncle Fritz Loeb, founder of the UMS-
Pastoe furniture factory, husband of Aunt Sophie and father of Liesje Eiser-Loeb.

(l. to r.) First cousins Joost, Eric and Robert Ullmann (Joost was born
during the War; Robert and Eric were born after the War).

Chapter 14

The Plight and Separation of the Warendorfs

My parents discussed the decision to go into hiding with Mom's eldest sister, Margaret, and tried to convince her to do so as well, but Margaret, who was in great danger because her husband Hans (J.C.S. Warendorf), was active in the Resistance, hunted by the Nazis and not living at home, would not do it. She had been ill with breast cancer, and had been under intense treatment. She was terribly afraid that she would be separated from her three children and that the children, in turn, would be separated from one another..

Dutch Nazis came to their home in late October / early November 1942. The youngest daughter, Josephine, age 10 at the time, was home alone. The Nazis told her that the family had to leave. Their father, Hans Warendorf, in the meantime, came by briefly and said, "goodbye," stating that he was going to visit his mother in the Westerbork concentration camp. He by his own report attempted to convince Margaret and the family to flee with him across the Belgian border, but Margaret would not go. Shortly thereafter, Margaret and her children were picked up and taken to a school on the Euterpestraat opposite the Nazi headquarters in Amsterdam.[32] (Margaret and the children did not see their father again until after the War). She and her three children were then moved to the *Hollandsche Schouwburg* (Dutch Theater, described elsewhere herein) for a few days. On November 25,

---

[32] *The Euterpestraat was renamed after the War to honor Gerrit-Jan van der Veen, a non-Jewish resistance fighter. Van der Veen, who created the illegal underground "Central Office for Identity Cards", was one of the leaders of a group which forced their way into the offices of the Civil Registry in March 1943 and started fires to destroy that agency's records. He subsequently led a brazen attack on the main prison of Amsterdam, together with a number of other members of the Dutch Resistance. He was executed by a firing squad on June 10, 1944 in the Dutch dunes.*

1942, the four of them were sent by train from Amsterdam to Westerbork. Soon after arrival at Westerbork, Margaret was sent to the hospital; the children were placed in a nearby orphanage.

Margaret and her family, because of her husband's involvement in the Resistance, had a green "S" rubber-stamped on their identity papers. The "S" signified "*Straf*," the Dutch and German word for "punishment." This was very dangerous because persons with an "S," once arrested, were routinely and immediately sent to death camps, like Sobibor in Poland or Auschwitz-Birkenau in Germany, rather than to Bergen-Belsen, for example. Aged persons with an "S" had to remove their clothing and coats and were forced to wear pajamas.

Through a woman acquaintance married to a German officer, and also through the intermediacy of Eduard Spier, a civil law notary, who was a member of the Jewish Council (and a relative), Mom and her mother (Grootmoeder), whose husband (my grandfather, Salomon Konijn) had been, as indicated, in the diamond business, were able to bribe a German officer with diamond brooches to obtain a *Sperre*. They were thus able to eliminate the "S" and with a blue *Sperre* stamp on their ID papers, to place Margaret and the children on a "do not deport" list (the so-called *Putkammerleist*) for a period, while at Westerbork.[33] While Margaret and the children were interred at Westerbork, Grootmoeder and Mom were nevertheless able to send food and clothing to them.

Yet, ultimately, in February 1943, she and the children were deported, notwithstanding the *Sperre*, and sent to the Bergen-Belsen concentration camp in what-is-now Northeast Germany, between Hamburg and Hanover. Bergen-Belsen was generally intended by the Germans to be *Austausch-Lager* where Jews were collected with the intent ultimately

---

[33] *After the War, reparation was paid in modest sums for the diamond brooches.*

to exchange them for Germans captured by the Allies.[34]

Margaret, while at Bergen-Belsen, was able to obtain work outside the camp taking boots apart for re-use of the leather in a leather boot factory, as a result of which she was able to "earn" some rations almost daily to help sustain her kids. At the time they arrived in Bergen-Belsen, the oldest of the three children, Dorothy ("Door"), was 12, Josephine ("Fien"), was 10 and young Hans, was 8. She had Hans share her upper bunk bed in a barracks, while the two girls slept below in another bunk. The bunks were stacked three-high.

Margaret and the three kids, whom she sought so desperately to protect, all somehow survived the Bergen-Belsen concentration camp, even though they, like many others, including, as surmised, Anne Frank and her sister, Margot, had contracted typhus (if not typhoid fever), a highly contagious disease transmitted by fleas, lice or mites.[35] Margaret forced herself and the kids to keep eating turnips which, for much of the time, was the only available solid food. Two elderly aunts, sisters of Grootmoeder as well as their husbands, were also interred in Westerbork and later perished. Grandmother Warendorf, Margaret's mother-in-law, perished in Sobibor.

Josephine, in a video she made for Yad Vashem in Israel a few years ago, said that she and her siblings remember little about those days in Bergen-Belsen. As later indicated, they never really talked among themselves or even with their parents about those days, and, accordingly, not much is remembered, and much may be repressed. They apparently spent a lot of time in their bunks and standing outside for hours on end during daily roll calls. Josephine remembered

---

[34] In fact, in July 1944, 222 Jews interred at Bergen-Belsen were exchanged for 114 German Templars (a Christian monastic order of German colonists who supported Hitler) impounded by the British in internment camps in Palestine. One of the Jews released from Bergen-Belsen as part of that exchange was Liesje Polak, sister of Jaap (Jack) Polak, my predecessor and successor as Chairman of the Anne Frank Center USA.
[35] Margot and Anne succumbed in March and April 1945, respectively, just a few weeks before the camp was liberated.

little things like the woman in a bunk across from theirs who had managed to bring cosmetics to the camp in a shoe box and who spent time and effort applying those cosmetics. There was also a woman in a nearby bunk who went on and on about recipes.

Josephine definitely remembered the lavatories with a large wood plank covering a pit with a number of round holes in it over which they had to "do their business."

She also claimed that she never saw a dead person, except for one man at the camp toward the end of their confinement. Mostly, people just "disappeared."

Margaret and the three kids, in addition to surviving Bergen-Belsen, also survived one of the three "Death Trains" which left Bergen-Belsen in April 1945 with the intent to transfer 7,000 prisoners to Theresienstadt just prior to the impending liberation of the camp. Margaret and the kids apparently wound up on a train with some 2,500 prisoners, herded to the train, some five miles from the camp, together with untold numbers of ghastly sick and emaciated prisoners.

They were on that train some 13 days traveling through Germany. There was no food or water, and the train was in effect an open sewer. It is thought that as many as 50% of the persons on that train died because of starvation, disease and exhaustion. It is also believed that there were many more women on the train than men, as many fewer men survived the camp. The train stopped several times and Josephine, who by then was 13, left the train with a friend on a couple of occasions in an effort to steal food from some of the small farm houses en route. She was apparently the only one in the family at that time strong enough to do so. They did so not knowing where they were, not speaking the language and fearful that the train would start up again without them. On their first such foray, Josephine came back with only a pot of rice.

Russian soldiers on horseback ultimately stopped the train in the small German town of Tröbitz, located between Leipzig and Dresden. At that point, everyone able to do so grabbed carts and ran to private homes and farms to snatch whatever food they could find. In the case of Margaret's family, it was just the kids seeking food for their very sick Mom and themselves. Little Hans grabbed for himself an alarm clock and a small cardboard box with clay German(!) soldiers rather than the desperately needed food. He was still a little boy and he had not had any toys for years.

While in Tröbitz, they and others commandeered a house and took whatever they could scavenge, not only food, but even drapes, from which some of the women made skirts. This all took place under the watchful and supportive eyes of Russian soldiers, who also helped themselves to various spoils, including, in the case of one soldier, numerous watches which were strapped up and down his arm. One of the Russians, to be helpful, grabbed and killed a chicken and gave it to Josephine.

Incidentally, Tröbitz, which never had a Jewish resident, now has a Jewish cemetery (for captives who died on the train).

Margaret, who was terribly ill, was taken to a hospital and the kids were told by a doctor that their mom would probably die that day or the next. She did not. Margaret and the children were soon taken by American soldiers in Army trucks from Tröbitz to the city of Leipzig in what became after the War a part of Eastern Germany. They departed Leipzig by train for the city of Maastricht in southern Holland, where they were quarantined for two weeks. It was only there and then, according to Josephine, that they first learned of the gas chambers.

They soon returned to Amsterdam where they were taken by an Army truck from Centraal Station and dropped off at the corner of Stadionweg and the Beethovenstraat, a block from the house on Velasquezstraat. Their appearance in torn clothes, bald, gaunt and di-sheveled, was surely truly pitiful.

As earlier indicated, Margaret's husband, Hans, disappeared from their lives shortly before Margaret and the three children were taken from their home by the Nazis. Hans, active in the Resistance during the War, had a remarkable anti-Nazi past. At an early age he decided to devote substantial efforts to combat militant fascism in Germany and Italy. In this connection, Hans, whose family was in the publishing business, came in contact with the publishers of *Das Tage-Buch*, a liberal Jewish weekly German publication, and became a principal in the founding in Paris of *Das Neue Tage-Buch*, which effectively succeeded the German publication when it was essentially driven from Germany. *Das Neue Tage-Buch*, which had articles contributed by Churchill and Chamberlain, was published and distributed in Holland and some 50 other countries from 1933 to 1940, seeking to alert the public, which paid little attention at the time, to the political and social dangers of the rise of National Socialism.

At the outset of the German occupation of Holland, Hans became part of a small group which founded the illegal social-democratic underground paper, *Het Parool* (The Word). *Het Parool* was published sporadically during the War, beginning in 1941. It issued as many as 40,000 copies to its readers, making it the largest of several Resistance publications. It is estimated that there were as many as 1,300 "underground" printing presses turning out Resistance publications. Many of the persons involved in publication of *Het Parool* and other such publications during the War were hunted down and executed, or sent to death camps, by the Nazis. Hans was one of three Jewish members of the founding group; the other two did not survive the War. There were other Jews, beside the founders, who worked for the paper. After the War, *Het Parool* became a daily national circulation newspaper.

As previously noted, Hans fled to Paris, via Maastricht and Brussels in late October, 1942, just before Margaret and the kids were picked up and taken from their home. He managed to fly to London on May 30, 1943 after spending seven months fleeing the Nazis in France, Portugal and Spain. In England, he became a second lieutenant (although he did not actually perform any military service during the War), worked for the Dutch Ministry of Justice and served as a substitute chief prosecutor at the Dutch Maritime Court in London. After the War, he was named an (honorary) Commander of the Order of the British Empire.

Hans, who had access to British and Dutch intelligence activities, may have known where his family was, and certainly came to learn, from his contacts, that his family was still alive. When he learned, through the Red Cross, that Margaret and the kids were in Maastricht and about to be released from quarantine, he arranged to come to Amsterdam.

He was waiting at my parents' home on the Velasquezstraat with suitcases full of clothes for his wife and kids. He arrived the day before Margaret and the kids themselves arrived, on June 29, 1945. Mom told Hans he should leave, but he stayed nearby. When Margaret arrived, she, in her meager and weakened condition and appearance, asked Mom, "Do you think Hans will take me back?" The next day, Hans and Margaret indeed took each other back and together with the children experienced an emotional reunion while my parents went for a walk to leave them alone.

Margaret, Hans, two of their children, as well as, my parents, Bram and Bram's niece, Jeannette, all lived together in the house on Velasquezstraat for several days. Josephine in fact stayed with a friend as there was not enough room in the house. They obtained food (literally in buckets) from the Americans and the Red Cross.

After the reunion, and in not much more than a week, the Warendorf family, without passports, photos or other identification for Margaret and the kids, flew in a small plane from a small airport in Holland to Croydon in the U.K. and obtained a house from Hans' political contacts.

The kids were sent, on July 8, 1945, almost immediately upon arrival, to a co-ed boarding school in England, which both Josephine and young Hans attended until the summer of 1948, while Dorothy remained one more year to finish her schooling in England.

It was in December 1945, according to Josephine, during the first year in England, when a family friend came to visit their family in England, that Margaret started to talk about the War. Young Hans started to cry and Margaret stopped abruptly. She said to the children in a firm voice, "We will never again talk about the War years." She never did, nor did she ever mention her husband Hans' disappearance/apparent abandonment of his family.

Shortly thereafter, Hans and Margaret moved to Paris, where Hans had been appointed legal counsel to the newly-established UNESCO. The kids shared a couple of holidays with their parents in France, but basically stayed in England even during school holidays. The decision to send the kids off to boarding school, almost immediately after the family reunion, rather than living together at that point, a decision strongly supported by Mom at the time, has not received very favorable reviews when talking to the Warendorf children in later years. Mom later came to regret her advice, although she strongly believed it to be right for the Warendorf family at the time.

In 1947, Hans and Margaret flew to the U.S. at the urging of Margaret's (and Mom's) sister Juliemarthe, who, together with her husband and three children, were living in Port Washington, New York, to consider the possibility of emigrating to the U.S. However, Hans, with his law-background could not clearly envision a livelihood in the U.S., and the family thus determined to set their course in Europe.

After completing his tour in Paris, Hans and Margaret returned to Amsterdam, purchasing the home at Velasquezstraat 5 from my parents in November 1947, and Hans opened a law firm bearing his name, with offices at home in the first instance, specializing in business law, including matters requiring (certified) translations of documents into or from the English language. Hans became very successful, built a substantial practice and he and Margaret ultimately shared some 20 years together after the War, which all described as extremely happy times, before Margaret finally succumbed to cancer in 1968 at age 63.

Hans ultimately remarried, moved to Switzerland, but stayed in touch with everyone. He passed away in 1987 at the age of 85.

(l. to r.) Hans (H.C.S.), Dorothy and Josephine Warendorf (before Bergen-Belsen).

Mom's brother-in-law, Hans
(J.C.S.) Warendorf, Mar-
garet's husband (1944).

Anti-National Socialist publication for which J.C.S.
Warendorf was a publisher/editor prior to WWII.

Aunt Margaret and Hans (J.C.S.) Warendorf.

An issue of the illegal underground paper, *Het Parool* (The Word), of which Hans (J.C.S.) Warendorf was one of the founders. The caption, ("Vrij Onverveerd"), means "free and fearless". This particular issue contains the text of a speech made by Wilhelmina, Queen of the Netherlands, on *Radio Oranje* while in exile.

Chapter 15

Life Immediately after the War

My parents were very fortunate to be able to acquire, within weeks after the liberation of Amsterdam, a very nice home, a row house, at Velasquezstraat 5 in Amsterdam, which, when completed prior to the War, had been purchased by Mom's sister Juliemarthe and her husband, who, with their 3 children, had been able to escape Holland at the outbreak of the War to land ultimately in Port Washington, New York.

The house, which had been used by Nazi officers in the War, was made available on the condition that my parents allow the ground floor to be used on an interim basis by the U.S. Army and/or Red Cross as a soup kitchen. The house was in the "Artists Section," one of the best areas of Amsterdam South. Velasquez was a famous Spanish artist. Other streets in the area were named after Michelangelo, Rubens, Holbein, Courbet, etc. My parents previously lived in the Milletstraat in the same area, named after the French pre-impressionist. An abutting section, also upscale, was named after composers, i.e. Beethovenstraat, Bachstraat, Brahmsstraat, Chopinstraat, etc.

In any event, it was a nice quiet street, with an enclosed grassy area in the middle, not far from the Olympic Stadium and convenient to shopping. The street immediately behind us was Stadionkade, which was at the side of a canal. That canal froze over during the winter, before pollution and global warming ended it all, and I remember ice skating on the canal with open skates strapped to my shoes and pushing a wooden chair, being careful about the ice under the bridges. My best friend at the time was Wim Willems, who lived on Schubertstraat, with whom I knew I would be friends for the rest of my life. In fact, Wim passed away years ago; I had not seen him in 40 years. His parents were close friends of my parents. His father was a well-known investment banker with his own firm (Willems & Cie, which ultimately merged into a major international bank) and one of his older brothers indirectly played a very important role for me, to be discussed later.

The difficult reality for my parents after the War, living in the part of Amsterdam where most reasonably well-to-do Jewish people, and thus where many of their friends, lived, was the fact that hardly any of them survived the War.

One of the problems ultimately confronting survivors is the fact that those who survived were largely persons who could afford to pay for their hiding or had the contacts to arrange their escape. This in turn has saddled many survivors with lasting feelings of guilt with respect to the very fact of survival.

As published in *Het Parool*, the Germans listed 21,662 specific addresses where Jews lived in just Amsterdam; 61,700 persons were taken from those homes. Ultimately, some 57,800 Jews were sent to Auschwitz-Birkenau, 34,000 to Sobibor, and 4-5,000 each to Bergen-Belsen and Theresienstadt, alone. As earlier indicated, only some 5,000 of 107,000 deported from Westerbork returned after the War. The Jewish population in Amsterdam as of 1947 was down to an estimated 14,350 persons, or less than 10% of the Jewish population before the War.[36]

Accordingly, my parents spent much time thinking about who used to live in what house as they walked past the empty houses in the area. They felt that they hardly knew anyone any longer, and there were so many daily bad memories. As Jews they were members of a severely injured group in a severely injured society.

---

[36]*The Jewish population of Holland is now estimated at 35,000, or approximately 0.2%; the Muslim population is currently approximately 1 million persons.*

Ultimately, the loss of family and friends and the lack of any meaningful business or commercial life or prospects during the first years
after the War and an upsurge of anti-semitism in Holland after the War,
made the move out of Holland to start a new life elsewhere, and especially in the U.S., very compelling. It was compelling notwithstanding
the fact that Pop again had a good job at De Bijenkorf. The appeal was
also especially powerful when a number of friends and relatives had
successfully emigrated to the U.S. Thus, at the beginning of the War,
as earlier indicated, Mom's sister Juliemarthe (Jacobs) and Pop's uncle,
Harry Loeb, (and their respective families), and, after the War, Mom's
mother, Bertha Konijn-Prins (Grootmoeder), all made it to America.[37]

Dutch post-war anti-semitism was based largely on a feeling
among many Dutch persons that Jews, even returning Jews from concentration camps, should not be accorded more favorable treatment
than ordinary Dutchmen. Resistance fighters, by contrast, were always
accorded special status and privileges as heroes.

Perhaps the most compelling reason for leaving Holland, as
stated by Pop on numerous occasions, was an abundant and overriding fear that the Russians might ultimately take over all of Europe,
as Russia had already taken over, or at that time never left, many
countries in Eastern Europe, just a few hundred kilometers from
Holland, including Poland, Czechoslovakia, Eastern Germany, Hun-
gary, Yugoslavia, Rumania, Bulgaria and Albania. He and Mom could

---

[37] *In addition to persons earlier mentioned, others who made it to America included, without limitation,
Grootmoeder's sister-in-law, Sientje Konijn, who lived on Riverside Drive in New York City, Wim Konijn
(who, as earlier mentioned, did not return in 1939 from his traineeship in the U.S.), together with a
brother and sister who both moved to California, and Philip and Cornelia ("Corry") Prins. Corry was the
daughter of Grootmoeder's brother-in-law and Philip was the son of one of Grootmoeder's brothers. Their
son, John, born in April 1940 still lives in Rockville Center, N.Y. The story of Philip and Corry Prins is interesting in that in 1940 they were living in Paris where Philip was in the diamond business. They had
come in contact with Aristides de Sousa Mendes, the Portuguese consul in Bordeaux, France (whom they
had come to know when he was consul in Antwerp, Belgium) who ultimately, without authority to do so,
issued large numbers of visas; some reports estimate the number as high as 30,000; others say it was just
hundreds. In any event, Sientje Konijn, as well as Philip Prins' family all made it to the U.S. through
Sousa Mendes, who was honored posthumously by Yad Vashem.*

not contemplate, countenance or endure the thought of suffering the type of oppression they had just survived, potentially yet again, at the hands of foreign invaders.

For many months after the War, my parents spent a great deal of time at local offices of the Red Cross and the Dutch Civil Registry trying to learn what might have happened to their many friends and relatives, going almost daily to those centers for any information they might obtain. At first, this was focused almost entirely on finding Mom's sister, Margaret, and her three children, who had been deported to Germany and wound up in Bergen-Belsen. Miraculously, Margaret and her three children survived Bergen-Belsen, as described in another chapter.

One challenging problem for my parents was to get rid of my *sabellapje* (security blanket) which I still carried with me at the time. They put it on top of an armoire where I couldn't reach it, and I screamed for days.

I went to school briefly to a nearby Montessori School. Opa Schimmel came to our house and walked me to school almost every day. He truly loved me and missed me. It was at that school where we learned penmanship by writing in quadrille paper pads. At the moment when I ultimately left Holland, I had only learned to write from the bottom to the top of each square rather than corner to corner, and I have maintained this (childish) script for the rest of my life.

Also, shortly after the War, while in our new home on the Velasquezstraat, Pop was able to buy a very small 4-cylinder British car, a Standard. It was barely larger than a Fiat 500 and it was shiny bluish-gray with chrome here and there. I was immensely proud of that car and helped wash it frequently.

It was during the couple of years that we lived in the Velasquez-straat that I embarked on my passion for collecting. At that time, like many Dutch kids, I started collecting cigar bands. Cigar bands were sold separately from cigars and often in extended series covering historical events, famous rulers, movie stars, automobiles, etc. I started by pasting them in notebooks. There were actually history books, as in the "History of Flight", or a four-volume "History of America", with specific spaces in which to place the relevant cigar band. The bands, in turn, were often beautifully printed/embossed with gold colors, etc.

Many Dutch cigar companies produced such series and they were sold in toy stores, including one nearby in the Beethovenstraat as well as in open air markets, where dealers traded in stamps, cigar bands and coins. One such market was on the Spui near the Queen's palace every Wednesday.[38]

I also collected stamps and had a nice collection of Dutch stamps, including the colonies ("East and West Indies," now Indonesia, Surinam, Curacao, Aruba, St. Maarten and Bonaire), with many "overprints" created during the War. However, my cousin Hans Warendorf had a better collection and he was helped by his father, so I eventually quit when I came to the U.S.

Incidentally, my cousin, young Hans (H.C.S. Warendorf), joined his father, J.C.S. (Hans) Warendorf, the husband of Mom's sister Margaret, in the practice of law in a firm later named Warendorf & Warendorf, which ultimately merged into a large law firm, Trenité van Doorne, and the Warendorf name disappeared, at least for a while.

When young Hans retired from the merged firm, a few partners in that firm, who had worked with Hans, decided to break off and create their own firm, and asked Hans if they could use his name for a new firm, rather than their own, (these are concepts totally incom-

---

[38] *In recent years I did in fact pick up a bit on my cigar band collection (thank you e-Bay) and now have some 20,000 bands, including such special items as Monica Lewinsky bands, as well as beautifully printed cigar box labels. The problem is, that unlike stamps, there are no catalogs for cigar bands. I thus really have no idea if they're any good, or how many tens of thousands I am missing.*

prehensible to me - note the famous New York law firms, *Ullman Van Ginkel* and *Ullman, Miller & Wrubel*, from which the Ullman name has disappeared, with no chance of a return.) Hans agreed and, accordingly, there is now the law firm in Amsterdam of "Warendorf," of which Hans has been "of counsel" until his recent retirement as a lawyer after 50 years at the (Dutch) bar. I cannot imagine a greater measure of respect for a person's achievements, integrity and reputation.

Abraham (Bram) Konijn, who was hidden with my parents, lost most of his family. However, a niece and nephew, Jeannette and Peter Kalker, children of one of Bram's sisters, survived, also in hiding with families who saved them; Jeannette with seven different families and Peter with one. My parents undertook to have Jeannette (whom we called "Nettie") move in with us and she stayed with us for some 15 months, effectively as my post-war sister.

Bram, his wife Hanny, Jeanette and Peter emigrated to the U.S. in September 1954. Their story is further chronicled in Chapter 16.

My parents, through Mr. Hoogenboom, also located Mom's mother (Grootmoeder), who had been placed by Hoogenboom in a Catholic residence in Utrecht and who, despite her Jewish upbringing and background, had apparently converted seamlessly to Catholicism, much to my parents' amazement. Mom went to meet Grootmoeder in Utrecht, within a day or two after the War's end, hitching a ride on a beer barge on the Amstel River to Utrecht, as there was no public transportation, and then getting a ride on the back of Mr. Hoogenboom's bike through the city streets of Utrecht. Grootmoeder's conversion was ultimately deprogrammed, but it was, at least for a while, both amusing and a source of serious concern.

Pop's parents (Oma Aenni and Opa Sally) survived in Utrecht, even though they had been thrown in jail at the end of the War, but, fortunately, too late to be transported to a concentration camp. They spent a substantial part of their war days with false IDs in the apartment of a German woman who had a Jewish lover. Many German soldiers visited this apartment and socialized with Oma and Opa, who were introduced by their German friend and landlord as her parents. They went to jail only through a surprising fluke, after they had moved to another boarding house, during a search by the Germans, looking, as usual, for hidden Jews.

The Germans had obtained a copy of a "potato list" on which were names and addresses of Jews in hiding who were to be given potatoes by underground supporters to help them survive. As the Germans were about to leave their apartment, having reviewed their (illegal) birth certificates, one of the soldiers asked Opa Sally for his wedding band, which he removed, only to reveal that the initials inside the band did not match his illegal certificate, nor that of his spouse.

My brother, "Henk," was born, according to my wife's calculations, virtually nine months to the day after the War ended. So we think we have a pretty good idea how my parents celebrated the end of the War. "Henk," whose full birth name was Hendrik Jan Ullmann, was named after my War Parents, Oma and Opa Schimmel, respectively, Hendrik and Jannigje (a Frisian name from the Dutch Province of Friesland) Schimmel. Opa (Hendrik) Schimmel died in 1951. Sadly, neither my parents nor I went to Holland for the funeral.

My parents had given to Opa Schimmel in thanks for his efforts in saving me, a valuable gold pocket watch that had belonged to Mom's father, on the lid of which they had inscribed, in Dutch, "in thanks for saving Leo." That watch was kept and never returned by Aunt Paula to Oma Schimmel, though Oma asked for it. Mom gave to Oma Schimmel a ring that Mom had worn throughout the War.

In all the years I visited with Oma after the War, she never mentioned "Aunt Paula," and we'll never really know the nature of that relationship. I do know that in her last years, Oma often said that she could not wait to rejoin Opa in heaven.

Pop, as a German-born Dutch resident, had a busy time immediately after the War, and during the next following two-year period, having to prove that he was a trustworthy person and neither a Nazi sympathizer nor a collaborator. His employer, civil law notaries[39] and police departments all had to certify as to such trustworthiness. This was critical in again arranging employment at De Bijenkorf and also to establish eligibility for compensation for lost wages during the years following termination of his employment.

Pop's citizenship in the meantime remained in question. As his application for Dutch citizenship, for which he first applied in April 1940, less than a month before the Germans attacked Holland, was never acted on, he was therefore from that time forward basically neither a Dutch nor a German citizen (his German citizenship had been terminated by a German decree issued on November 25, 1941 terminating citizenship of all German Jews living outside Germany).

Pop again applied for Dutch citizenship in 1946. This apparently required a letter/written submission to the Dutch Ministry of Justice. In his case, the application was made by a lawyer and the lawyer's letter referenced support by a number of leading citizens, including the CEO of De Bijenkorf, the head of an investment banking firm, a leading civil law notary and others.

---

[39] A civil law notary is quite different in background and status from a notary public in the U.S. A civil law notary in the Netherlands is appointed by the Crown and there are only a limited number of notaries, generally assigned to separate geographic districts. Qualification as a civil law notary requires completion of (civil) law studies as required for most any lawyer, as well as additional graduate study of notarial law. Thus, in effect the civil law notary is a super lawyer of highly elevated status. Fees are established by law and a notarial deed, prepared by the Notary (who will typically have assistant notaries working for many years in his office) is required for corporate organization documents, wills, real estate transfers and other such deeded transactions. A document prepared and certified by a civil law notary, unlike a U.S.-style notary public, is presumptive and conclusive evidence (and the only required proof) of a transaction.

Not only was he stateless, but the status of his (and Mom's) two Dutch-born sons, little Henk and me, at ages 1 and 7, clearly upstanding and innocent citizens of the world, was, as reported by the lawyer who submitted the application for Pop's citizenship, "unclear." While Pop's new application for Dutch citizenship was submitted early in 1946, it was never acted upon, despite a number of inquiries by the lawyer, before our family arranged to emigrate to the U.S. in late 1947.

We nevertheless were able to obtain exit permits and immigration visas to the U.S. from the U.S. Consulate based in large part on sponsorship (at that time critical to potential immigrant visa status) by Joost and Juliemarthe Jacobs, Mom's sister and brother-in-law, who had landed in Port Washington, New York after escaping from Holland in 1940.

Shortly after the War ended, in my case, and several years after that, in the case of my brother, when he, too, was about 7 years old, my parents engaged a then well-known Dutch sculptor, Louise Beyerman, to create a wooden (life-size) bust of each of us. Those wooden busts were proudly displayed in our home and my parents' apartment for their entire lives.

My parents always loved these wooden busts and insisted that they looked exactly like us and that the genius of Ms. Beyerman was that she could foresee our facial features, evolution as we matured. My brother and I hated those busts and remain absolutely sure they don't look like us at all.

Upon Pop's passing, Henk and I had to deal with these two busts in attempting to divide the modest "estate." This was a problem: I insisted he should have both; he insisted I should have both. We ultimately each kept our own and I suppose we'll keep them until our respective ends of life, when I suspect they'll then become firewood.

Leo with Ruffie on the back patio at
Velasquezstraat 5.

Three sisters, (l. to r.) Margaret (the oldest), Mom (the
youngest) and Juliemarthe (with Leo).

Bram and Hanny Konijn. Bram and Hanny formally adopted his niece Jeannette, her younger brother Peter and a cousin, Julie.

Jeannette and Leo at Velasquezstraat 5 in Amsterdam. (I don't recognize the animal). The photo was taken on December 19, 1945, the wedding date of Bram and Hanny Konijn.

Leo and Jeannette.

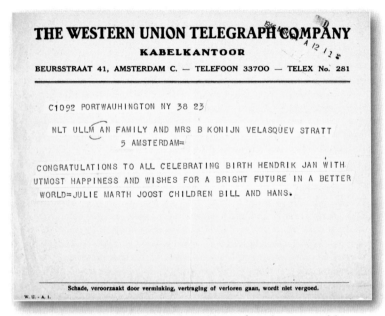

Congrats on Henk's birth and hope for a better world.

Telegram from Mom's sister Margaret.

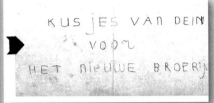

"Kiss from Dein (Leo's nickname, as
in "Deinemanetjelief")
for the new little brother."

Mom and Henk.

The house at Velasquezstraat 5 in Amsterdam.
Note the furniture, bookshelf, wing chairs, coffee table (made by Pop), baby
grand etc. duplicated in all my parents' homes.

Leo's report card in 2nd grade (after the War) at an Amsterdam music school.

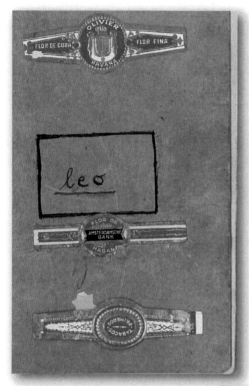

Leo started collecting cigar bands while still a young boy in Holland (and hasn't stopped); the collection now numbers an estimated 20,000 bands.

Cigar bands inserted on one page of a 4-volume book on the "History of the U.S."

Dutch cigar box labels.

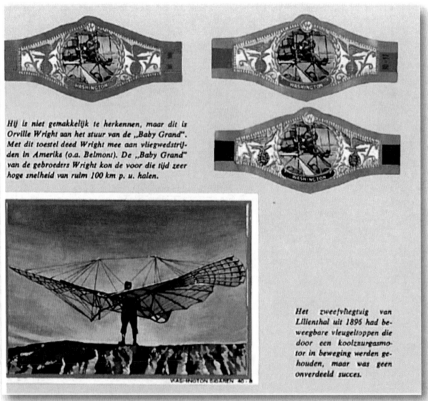

Hij is niet gemakkelijk te herkennen, maar dit is Orville Wright aan het stuur van de ,,Baby Grand". Met dit toestel deed Wright mee aan vliegwedstrijden in Ameriks (o.a. Belmont). De ,,Baby Grand" van de gebroeders Wright kon de voor die tijd zeer hoge snelheid van ruim 100 km p. u. halen.

Het zweefvliegtuig van Lilienthal uit 1895 had beweegbare vleugeltoppen die door een koolzuurgasmotor in beweging werden gehouden, maar was geen onverdeeld succes.

Dutch cigar bands inserted in a book on the "History of Flight." At the top is Orville Wright at the controls of the "Baby Grand" with which the Wright Brothers competed in flight competitions. At the bottom is a glider with movable wings which, as reported, was not a great success.

2 April 1946

Betreft:
Verzoek tot
naturalisatie
F.L. Ullmann.

Aan Zijne Excellentie
den Minister van Justitie.

Excellentie,

Ten verzoeke van den Heer Frans Leo Ullmann, wonende te Amsterdam,
Velasquezstraat 5, die , wegens de opheffing van het kantoor van
Mr. I. Kisch te Amsterdam, thans te dezer zake te mijnen kantore
domicilie kiest, heb ik de eer het navolgende onder Uwer Excellentie's aandacht te brengen.

Op 17 April 1940 is een verzoekschrift ingediend voor het verkrij-
gen van het Nederlanderschap door naturalisatie door Frans Leo
Ullmann te Amsterdam. Door den oorlog kon dit verzoekschrift niet
worden behandeld.

Nu dit weer mogelijk is, wil verzoeker nog de noodige gegevens
verstrekken, welke voor een beoordeeling thans van belang zijn.
Ik laat deze gegevens hier volgen:

      1. Verzoeker heeft in November 1941 door de algemeene dena-
tionalisatieverordening de Duitsche nationaliteit verloren en is
thans statenloos.
      2. Uit zijn huwelijk, op 10 November 1936, met de Nederland-
sche, Emily Konijn, is, behalve het reeds in het verzoekschrift
vermelde kind, op 25 Maart 1946 te Amsterdam een tweede kind geboren, genaamd Hendrik Jan.
      3. Eind Februari 1943 bis verzoeker met zijn gezin ondergedoken,
teneinde aan deportatie te ontkomen.
      4. Verzoeker is in het bezit van een door den Politieken
Opsporingsdienst te Amsterdam afgegevenboekje van politieken
betrouwbaarheid no. 010002 (fotocopie gaat hierbij).
      5. Omtrent zijn politiekex opvatting, zijn houding tijdens
de besetting en in het algemeen zijn persoon geven een beeld de
bijgevoegde verklaringen van
A. Goudsmit, directeur der N.V. Magazijn " De Bijenkorf ", Amster-
dam,
P. Hoogenboom, hoofdwachtmeester der politieke Utrecht,
Mr. M. H. de Jong, luitenant ter zee 1e klasse, K.M.R., Amsterdam,
A.J. Leeuwenburgh, directeur der n.v. Hollandsche Belegging en
Beheer Maatschappij , Amsterdam,
Mr. W. J. van Lier, destijds secretaris der gemeente Amsterdam,
Mej. A. C. Schot, beëedigd translatrice bij de arrondissements-
rechtbank te Amsterdam,
E. Spier, notaris te Amsterdam,
W. Willems, commissionnair in effecten te Amsterdam.

Ik moge nog in herinnering brengen, dat verzoeker, die sedert 1932
hier te lande woonachtig is, een Nederlandsche moeder had en ook
overigens door vele familiebanden met Nederland was verbonden

welke banden hij

Application by Dutch counsel for Netherlands citizenship for Pop,
citing, among other things, Pop's political trustworthiness and his
conduct during the occupation, attested to, by, among others,
Alfred Goudsmit (the CEO of De Bijenkorf), Notary Eduard Spier
(brother of Jo Spier and a member of the Amsterdam Jewish
Council), Wim Willems (investment banker and father of Kees
Willems), Aleida Schot (Mom's sorority sister who arranged my
hiding) and Piet Hoogenboom (the Utrecht policeman who helped
us all). All of them are mentioned elsewhere in this book.

DR. MR. D. SIMONS   's-GRAVENHAGE,   2 April 1946
Lid Ned. Inst. v. Accountants   Kantoor Hooistraat 7
advocaat en accountant   TEL.XXX33X   114063.
                                     GIRO NO. 224003

Onderwerp:
Naturalisatie.

Bijlage: 1.   Aan den Weledelgeboren Heer
                              F. L. Ullmann
                          Velasquezstraat 5
                          Amsterdam - Zuid.

Geachte Heer Ullmann,

Hierbij zend ik U een afschrift van mijn brief
aan den Minister van Justitie, welken ik heden
  bij den behandelenden ambtenaar heb ingediend. Ik
heb daarbij aangedrongen op een spoedige be-
handeling.

De kwestie van de nationaliteit Uwer kinderen
heb ik nagegaan. Mijn conclusie leidt helaas
tot twijfel. Daarom heb ik dit punt in den
brief niet aangeroerd.

Mocht U over eenige maanden nog niets gemerkt
hebben, wilt U mij dit dan berichten. Dan zal
ik weer eens porren.

                    Hoogachtend,

                    D. Simons.

Letter from emigration counsel advising Pop that "the question of the
nationality of your children, leads alas to the conclusion that it's unclear."

Het Nederlandsche Beheersinstituut

NEUHUYSKADE 94
'S.GRAVENHAGE
TELEFOON 774855-56-57-58

WFA256   'S-GRAVENHAGE, 18 Augustus, 194 6

Afschrift

Het Nederlandsche Beheersinstituut, bedoeld in het Besluit
Vijandelijk Vermogen;

Gezien het verzoekschrift van Franz eo Ullmann,
Emilie Ullmann-Konijn, en Leopold Salomon Ullmann,
wonende te Amsterdam, Velasquezstraat 5,

waarin wordt verzocht afgifte van een verklaring als bedoeld in
art.34 lid 1 sub f, van genoemd Besluit;

Overwegende, dat de gronden, waarop het verzoek rust, het ge-
vraagde rechtvaardigen;

Gezien het terzake uitgebrachte advies van het bureau van het
Nederlandsche Beheersinstituut te Amsterdam.

Gezien de desbetreffende wettelijke voorschriften

verklaart dat F.L.Ullmann, E.Ullmann-Konijn en L.S.Ullmann,
voornoemd

niet langer vijandelijke onderdane(n) is (zijn) in den
zin van het Besluit Vijandelijk Vermogen met de aanteekening,
dat deze beschikking niet vrijwaart voor eenige andere eventueele overheidsmaatregel te hunnen/haren/hunnen opzichte te
nemen.

Aldus gedaan en gewezen te 's-Gravenhage 18 Augustus,1946.

                              De Directie van het
                              NEDERLANDSCHE BEHEERSINSTITUUT:

T.47.688/Bgh/BM   J.A.Deknatel.   K.W.J.Michielsen.

FH.

Declaration to the effect that Pop is no longer considered an enemy.

N.V. Magazijn de Bijenkorf

Directie.

Amsterdam C, 24 Augustus 1945.

Telefoon 38080

VERKLARING

De ondergeteekende, Alfred Goudsmit, Directeur der N.V. Magazijn "De Bijenkorf", Amsterdam, verklaart hiermede den Heer Frans Leo Ullmann, thans woonachtig Velasquezstraat 5 te dezer stede, van kindsaf te kennen. Sedert 1 Maart 1932 is de Heer Ullmann bij de N.V. Magazijn "De Bijenkorf" als employé werkzaam.

Verder kan hij met zekerheid verklaren, dat genoemde heer in politieken zin volkomen betrouwbaar kan worden geacht, zich met politiek nooit heeft beziggehouden en wat zijn gezindheid betreft, als anti-nazi kan worden gekenschetst.

Gedurende zijn werkzaamheden bij de Bijenkorf heeft hij er naar beste weten naar gestreefd de Nederlandsche belangen te dienen.

Alfred

Declaration by CEO of De Bijenkorf to the effect that Pop always strived to serve the best interests of the Netherlands.

A declaration by the City of Amsterdam that Pop, residing at Velasquezstraat 5, is trustworthy, anti-national-socialist (anti-Nazi) and is a good citizen.

Politie te Amsterdam
Recherchedienst   Amsterdam, 2 Oct.   1945.

XXX
                                         Verzoeke bij beantwoording datum, letter en
Vr. No. 627./1945.   nummer van dit schrijven aan te halen.

Axxkxxx

Oxdexxoxpx
Bjxbxgxxx
Axxxxxxxxpx

            Franz Leo ULIMANN, geboren 25 October,
            1913 te Keulen, van beroep inkooper, wo-
            nende Velasquezstraat No 5 huis, te Am-
            sterdam, werd 19 Februari 1935 bij den
            Vreemdelingendienst alhier ingeschreven,
            komende van Utrecht.
            Hij is, voor zoover mij bekend, politiek
            betrouwbaar.

                    DE HOOFDCOMMISSARIS VAN POLITIE,
                          namnes dezen,
                    De Hoofdinspecteur van Politie,
                    Chef Bureau Vreemdelingendienst,

                            H.R.Stoett.

                            (H.R.Stoett.)

Certificate of Amsterdam Police to the effect that Pop is "politically trustworthy."

A cover note from the military director in the Province of North Holland to a Dutch Notary referring to an enclosed certificate as to Pop's "trustworthiness."

[handwritten letterhead]

Amsterdam C.   2 September 1946

VERKLARING

Wij verklaren hiermede, dat de heer Frans Leo Ullmann, wonende Velaequezstraat 5 te dezer stede, van 1 Maart 1932 af bij onze vennootschap werkzaam is. De heer Ullmann heeft tal van afdeelingen in onze zaken doorloopen, is eerst verkooper, daarna assistent-inkooper en vervolgens afdeelingschef van de huishoudafdeeling geweest, en bekleedt thans de functie van centraal-inkooper voor de afdeeling huishoudelijke artikelen in onze drie zaken.

Doordat de heer Ullmann gedurende al deze jaren een zeer grondige opleiding in ons bedrijf heeft genoten, heeft hij zich tot een voor onze firma zeer waardevolle werkkracht ontwikkeld.

Waar onze firma gedurende de oorlogsjaren een zeer belangrijk aantal van haar oude ingewerkte employé's heeft verloren, is de aanwezigheid van menschen, die ons bedrijf door en door hebben leeren kennen, van nog grooter belang geworden dan voorheen.

Wij kunnen met zekerheid verklaren, dat genoemde heer in politiek opzicht volkomen betrouwbaar kan worden geacht, zich met politiek nooit heeft beziggehouden en, wat zijn gezindheid betreft, als anti-nazi kan worden gekenschetst.

De heer Ullmann is te Keulen geboren, heeft echter een Nederlandsche moeder en is met een Nederlandsche gehuwd.

Alle faciliteiten, die den heer Ullmann kunnen worden toegestaan, worden door ons ten zeerste op prijs gesteld.

N.V. MAATSCH. "DE BIJENKORF"

Goudsmit
Directeur-Generaal

AG/vD

Certificate of Pop's employer as to his "trustworthiness."
(translation on next page)

(My translation)

Sepetember 1946

Certificate

We hereby certify that Mr. Frans Leo Ullmann, residing at Velasquezstraat 5 of this city, has been employed by our company since March 1, 1932. Mr. Ullmann has been involved in a number of departments in our business, he was first a salesperson, thereafter assistant purchasing agent and thereafter head of the department of household articles in our three stores.

As Mr. Ullmann during all these years has benefited from a very thorough training in our business, he has developed into a very valuable employee for our company.

Whereas our company during the War years lost an important part of its previously-trained employees, the involvement of persons who have thoroughly learned our business has become even more important than was previously the case.

We can certify with certainty that the above-named person with respect to political views can be viewed as completely trustworthy, never having been involved with politics and, with respect to his personal views, can be characterized as anti-Nazi.

Mr. Ullmann was born in Cologne, however has a Netherlands mother and is married to a Netherlands citizen.

All courtesies which can be extended to Mr. Ullmann will be very much appreciated.

"   N.V. Department Store
                              De Bijenkorf"
                              A. Goudsmit
                              Director-General

ZATERDAG 6 AUGUSTUS 1955

T.R.OUW voor de VROUW.

„Ik houd altijd 't meest van m'n laatste werk"

Louise Beyerman:

Oudste beeldhouwster in ons land

(Van een onzer verslaggevers)

VAAK zweeg ze alleen maar en glimlachte dan. Ze heeft trouwens weinig verteld. En dan waren het bijna steeds van die kleine belevenissen, die zo weinig gewicht leggen in de schaal van de moderne publiciteit. Dat ze op bezoek was geweest bij Gustave Cohen,

Louise Beyerman werkt nog altijd. Nu is ze bezig aan het portret van een Amerikaans jongetje. Het staat hier geboetseerd in klei en wordt straks gehakt in mahoniehout.

Foto hieronder: Een jonge moeder met haar kind. Ziedaar een verhaal, dat Louise Beyerman met haar handen vertelde.

An article on Ms. Beyerman as the oldest sculptress in Holland. The caption reads "I always like my last work most." She's shown with brother Henk's (handsome) bust.

Mom and Pop at their apartment in front of the beautiful wooden busts of Henk and Leo made by Louise Beyerman.

Chapter 16

Jeannette Kalker, Bram Konijn and Family

As mentioned in the prior chapter, Jeannette Kalker came to live with our family after the War. Her story is also especially remarkable. The following is but a short overview of her experience, also as a hidden child; this story, as you will note, involves other very close relatives and a significant portion of our extended family whose lives were very much intertwined with ours, and many of whom also somehow survived (while, sadly, others did not).

Jeannette is the daughter of Max Kalker and Martha Frederika Konijn. Martha was a sister (one of five siblings) of Abraham (Bram) Konijn, who, of course, as earlier chronicled, became the third person in the hiding place with my parents. Bram's mother, Julie Konijn-Prins, was the sister of my maternal grandmother (Grootmoeder; Bertha Konijn-Prins), while Bram's father, Soesman Konijn, was the brother of my maternal grandfather, Salomon Konijn. Thus, Bram and his siblings were in fact double cousins of my Mom. Soesman and Salomon, as reported in an earlier chapter, were partners in the diamond business which defined (and sustained) the family.[40]

---

[40] One of Bram's two brothers, Wim ("Bill") Konijn, incidentally, founded and owned the Nassau Stores in Manhasset, New York and was my father's boss, and later his partner, in the U.S. 5 & 10¢ store chain. (see Chapter 24)

Soesman and Julie lived in the De Lairessestraat,[41] a principal street in Amsterdam, in a large luxury apartment.[42] They were later forced by the Germans to move to the *Afrikaanerbuurt* (African neighborhood), a very poor area of the city. When my parents made the decision and arrangements to go into hiding, they tried desperately to convince their beloved "Uncle Soes" and Aunt Julie to also go into hiding, but they wouldn't go; they thought they'd be safe. But they weren't; they were betrayed and ultimately sent first to Westerbork and subsequently to Bergen-Belsen, where they perished.

It was after his parents were taken away that Bram came to land in my parents' hiding place (he was apparently located by Ma Peyster, my parents' host, who undertook to find Bram after his parents were taken to Westerbork, at his last-known address, which Mom had remembered). Bram, who, like my father, had been a bicycle courier for the Jewish Council and was thus safe at least for a while, arrived at the Ceintuurbaan apartment having just "lost" his parents, scared and, as related by the Peyster girls, soaked in a desperate sweat.

Jeannette's mother and father arranged hiding places for their children, Jeannette and Peter, through an underground Resistance group in Deventer, in the Eastern part of Holland, near the German border.

Jeannette, born in 1939, was a bit beyond 2 ½ years old when she was placed initially with a family in the small town of Neede, also in the Eastern part of Holland, in the late fall of 1942. Her brother, whose

[41] Note that this is the street where Mom found the dentist who helped her during a time in need while in hiding. It's also the street where Hans Warendorf Senior and Junior located their law firm over a period of many years.
[42] A photo of the entrance to that apartment (at De Lairessestraat 39) was included in an article in "Amstelodamum" (no. 101-2; 2014) on the "interior architect" Ad Grimmon, who designed its interior and who, incidentally, was a principal furniture designer for the Utrechtse Machinale Stoel-en Meubelfabriek (UMS) founded by my great-uncle (Oma Aenni's brother), Fritz Loeb.

name at birth was Abraham Benjamin Kalker (he was named after Bram), was born in June 1942. He was thus only a few months old when he was placed at that same time with a family named Blanksma in Deventer. The Blanksma family gave him the Christian name "Peter" and he was able to stay with that family, who were very poor, but who nevertheless also kept a small handful of other Jewish children, for the entire War and indeed for another 6 months after the War. The name "Peter" stuck and he still uses that name.

Jeannette was not quite as lucky. She wound up in seven or eight different homes, including one of a minister and his family, moving in large part because of the danger both to her and the host family. For example, others would point to Jeannette, when she was playing in a sandbox at a playground, and say "there's the little Jewish girl." Theo and Marie Janssen, the last couple who hid Jeannette, took Jeannette and, on occasion, other adults, under their wing. During the last months of the War and until the War ended, the Janssens went successfully into hiding on a farm, taking Jeannette with them. The Janssens, incidentally, have been honored for their efforts and bravery at Yad Vashem.

In the meantime, Jeannette's and Peter's parents, Max and Martha Kalker, once they had placed the children, tried to escape via France to Switzerland, as Max's brother and wife had been able to do (reportedly sneaking past Swiss border guards in a rain storm while the guards were taking shelter). However, Max and Martha were caught and sent back to Lyon, France, and then to Drancy in a northeastern suburb of Paris, a transit camp much like Westerbork, from which they were ultimately deported to Auschwitz-Birkenau, where they were killed.

At the end of the War, Bram sought to find Jeannette and Peter, and had some difficulty doing so. Bram especially had difficulty with the Janssen family who apparently wanted to keep Jeannette, and, accordingly, the relationship, and communications between Bram and Theo Janssen, became strained and contentious. The relationship was complicated, as presumably were many others where families wanted to keep the children for whom they had cared during the War, by the introduction in the Dutch Parliament at some point shortly after the end of the War, of draft legislation, thankfully never enacted, that would have permitted persons who sheltered hidden children during the War, to adopt such children if they had not been (re-)claimed within three months after the War's end.

Bram reconnected with his pre-war sweetheart, Hanny Weijl, at the War's end. Hanny who was raised in Middelburg, Holland, came to Amsterdam to attend *Huishoudschool*, a school for home economics, and met Bram in Amsterdam. They married in December 1945, at which time they took Peter to live with them in Amsterdam.

Jeannette, after having been discovered on the Red Cross rolls, came to live with my family in the Velasquesstraat initially in June 1945 together with Bram on the third floor of the home (I was on the second floor where we apparently had a big bathroom but had to take cold-water baths). Bram moved later that year when he and Hanny married, to a home on a street near De Lairessestraat in Amsterdam, and Jeannette moved in with them in September of 1946.

Mom was pregnant during much of the time Jeannette was with us, giving birth to my brother Henk in late March of 1946. Mom and Pop thought that Jeannette as a playmate would be very good for me (and for her). Yet, Jeannette believes that her relationship with Mom, probably starting during those months, was never terrific, perhaps as a matter of Mom protecting her turf; Jeannette's relationship with

Pop, however, was always very good, even to his last days some 60 years later. I, in turn, aware of my personality as now developed, was almost surely difficult for Jeannette in terms of protecting my turf and competitiveness. As Jeannette and I have such a shared history. I regret that we did not stay close, but I have long admired her from afar.

Bram, Hanny, Jeannette, Peter, Julie (born in 1946) and Louie (born in 1948) lived together in Holland until 1954. After an exploratory stay by Bram, the entire family emigrated to the U.S. in September of that year, settling in San Mateo, California. A private U.S. Congressional bill, introduced by New York's Senator Herbert Lehman, had been required to permit Jeannette and Peter to enter the U.S. "as if" they were Bram and Hanny's children. Bram and Hanny served as their "guardians" until they were able to adopt them, once they were admitted to the U.S. When they were thus officially adopted, Jeannette kept the name Kalker while young Abraham, known as Peter, the name given to him while in hiding, all his years, formally changed his name to Peter (A.B.) Kalker Konijn.

Bram apparently had a good practice in Holland as a CPA and financial advisor, but, nevertheless contemplated a move to New York. However, the barriers to qualification as a CPA in that state were daunting. Bram's brother Henk and sister Margaret had wound up in California and eventually beckoned Bram, Hanny and the kids to San Mateo where Bram first practiced accounting (California apparently had uncomplicated reciprocity rules) and ultimately joined a company which provided janitorial supplies and services to big companies like H-P. He carved out a good life for his family.

Jeannette, married to a prominent psychiatrist, is now a grandmother and lives in Menlo Park, California. She is also a highly prized translator of a number of Dutch books into the English language. Peter ultimately returned to Holland. Julie and Louie live in California.

Bram passed away in October 1969; Hanny in July 1986.

Chapter 17

Oma and Opa Schimmel and Family after the War

After the War, I visited Oma Schimmel often (Opa, as earlier indicated, passed away less than six years after the War, on March 10, 1951) and I made it a point to either visit her or call her on the Fifth of May every year when the whole country of Holland celebrates the anniversary of the end of the War.

I asked her on at least one occasion why she would take the incredible risk of harboring a Jewish child with nothing in return when it was certain death if she were discovered, and she replied, "Because it's the right thing to do." She apparently never wavered.

Oma Schimmel died in an old-age home in Holland, to which she committed herself (against family wishes), almost 30 years after the War. Her brother was in the same home. I visited her almost every time I was in Holland and I used to travel to Holland on business many times a year.

During a visit, when Oma Schimmel was on her death bed, within the last couple of days of her life, I asked her if there was anything she wanted, anything at all. She said she wanted a pocketbook. I then drove back to Amsterdam as fast as I could and went to the Beethovenstraat, the elegant street with, at the time, many haute couture stores. I bought the most beautiful, expensive Gucci (or equivalent) pocketbook I could find. This was completely out of character for Oma, who never seemed to care for worldly goods, but perhaps she wanted once to have something of the sort. I raced back with the pocketbook, she held it and stroked it many times, but she never had the chance to use it. She was buried in a cemetery at the outskirts of Amsterdam on the road to Haarlem. Her family held a funeral dinner at a nearby restaurant. I met Anton, her oldest son, there for the first and only time since the War ended. He, too, died soon thereafter.

Oma and Opa Schimmel's second son, Bastiaan (Bas), and I remained good friends and we saw each other often. Bas remarried after the War to Willy Olijslager (who is now 85 and whom I still see often), and they in turn had three sons.

During the War in 1943, Bas was conscripted, as were most able-bodied Dutch young men, to work in factories in Germany to support the German War effort. He was shipped to the Zeiss Optical Factory in Jena, located some 45 miles southwest of Leipzig in the eastern part of Germany. When the War ended, he was installed temporarily by the Americans as Mayor of that city, because he spoke both English and German well.

Bas was an attractive man, took good care of his appearance, lived on the Churchillaan, one of the best addresses in Amsterdam, and apparently retired from the film business (Universal), which he joined after the War, with a nice pension. He was also a wonderful raconteur.

Some 12 years prior to this writing, he contracted cancer and was in great pain. He determined to end his life in a programmed assisted suicide, as permitted in Holland, subject to consent of an independent, certified M.D. The family all came together and they apparently enjoyed a wonderful last day together on September 12, 2002, during which, believe it or not, Bas insisted on taking all his pills only a few hours before the hour he was to be put to sleep forever. To this day, his widow, Willy, whose English is perfect (she attended high schools in England and the U.S. during the War), and whom I still see whenever in Holland, and who is still going strong, living in the same apartment on the Churchillaan in Amsterdam, in which Bas lived during and before the War, continues to speak enthusiastically about the beauty of his chosen final day.

We have subsequently had several get-togethers with Bas and Willy's son, Peter, his wife Kicky and their family. A few years ago, we had all of them, plus Willy, at our home for Christmas and a Christmas family dinner.

The only thing that they ever asked of me was to help one of Bas and Willy's grandsons apply for admission to Phillips Academy, Andover, my old prep school, to which I have given a fair amount of money. I wrote letters, explaining the history, etc. I thought it was a good story. Moreover, at 6'6" or so (all Dutch kids are tall), he might help the school's basketball or volleyball teams. Nevertheless, they turned us down.

Tilly, sadly, passed away in a hospital near Utrecht after a heart attack in the evening of May 31, 2012, just as I was completing the first version of these very chapters. She had been all there mentally, although physically at the end she was almost immobile. She smoked all the time; her rental home in the village of Wilnis was always full of cigarette butts. Visits with her, when I brought family members (Kay and I visited her last in March 2012), were a bit difficult as she basically spoke no English other than a few words from T.V. shows. She ultimately apparently overcame the difficulties I caused her, as I visited her often when I came to Holland and I always brought her flowers. In fact she told her son, Martin, (who stayed with us in Port

Washington in 1980), and her daughter Pauline, how much she valued our visits. She had absolutely the same characteristics as Oma, of complete modesty, coupled with memorable and insightful sayings with plain common analogies. For example, when I last asked her if she was lonely, she said, "the walls don't talk."

Met veel verdriet, maar met warme herinneringen, hebben wij afscheid genomen van mijn lieve Bas, onze dierbare toegewijde vader en schoonvader en allerliefste Opa

Bastiaan Johannes Schimmel

* Amsterdam, 3 januari 1919   † Amsterdam, 12 september 2002

Amsterdam: Willy Schimmel - Olyslager

Amsterdam: Robert Jan Schimmel
Marja Korteman
Maarten, Eric

Eelderwolde: Hein Schimmel
Alice Meijer
David, Lolotte

Bussum: Peter Schimmel
Kicky Hamer
Michiel, Jonathan

Churchilllaan 210
1078 EV Amsterdam

De crematieplechtigheid zal in kleine kring plaatsvinden.

Announcement of the passing of Bas Schimmel, my "War Brother," on September 12, 2002. "With great sorrow, but with warm memories, we have taken leave of my dear Bas, our beloved father, father-in-law and dearest grandfather".

Tel uw zegeningen, tel ze één voor één,
tel ze alle en vergeet er geen.
Tel ze alle, noem ze één voor één,
en ge ziet Gods liefde dan door alles heen.

Net voor haar 86e verjaardag is na een goed, liefdevol leven van ons heengegaan
onze moeder en oma

Mathilda Johanna Visser - Manschot
Tilly

* 8 juni 1926   † 31 mei 2012

weduwe van Simon Visser

Pauline

Martin en Carla
Wouter
Laura

Scheepswerf 6
Wilnis

Correspondentieadres:

Martin Visser
Wipmolen 35
3642 AD Mijdrecht

De crematieplechtigheid zal plaatsvinden op woensdag 6 juni om 15.30 uur in
Uitvaartcentrum en Crematorium Bouwens, Noorddammerweg 40, Uithoorn.

Voorafgaand hieraan kunt u van 15.00 - 15.15 uur afscheid nemen van ma.

Na de plechtigheid is er gelegenheid tot condoleren.

The announcement of the passing of Tilly, my "War Sister," on May 31, 2012
just before her 86th birthday.

Tot onze diepe droefheid is na een kortstondige ziekte, in volle vrede, op 88 jarige leeftijd overleden, onze allerliefste, zorgzame moeder, schoonmoeder en oma

JANNIGJE MANSCHOT,
weduwe van H. M. Schimmel.

Hoogeveen:
    M. A. Schimmel
    P. Schimmel - Dekinga
Amsterdam:
    B. J. Schimmel
    W. Schimmel - Olyslager
Uithoorn:
    M. J. Visser - Manschot
    S. Visser

    en kleinkinderen

IJsselstein, 1 november 1980,
Bejaardencentrum ,,Ewoud",
Jan van der Heijdenweg 2.

Correspondentie-adres:
Elsschotlaan 42,
1422 CL   Uithoorn.

Geen bezoek aan huis.

De overledene is opgebaard in de aula van het bejaardencentrum ,,Ewoud", alwaar gelegenheid tot het tekenen van het condoleance register dinsdag 4 november van 19.30 tot 20.30 uur.

Een rouwdienst zal gehouden worden woensdag 5 november a.s. om 11.00 uur in de kerkzaal van bejaardencentrum ,,Ewoud".

De teraardebestelling zal plaats hebben woensdag 5 november op de algemene begraafplaats ,,Vredenhof", Haarlemmerweg te Amsterdam, om 14.00 uur.

Vertrek van het bejaardencentrum ,,Ewoud" om 13.00 uur.

Na de teraardebestelling is er gelegenheid tot condoleren in de ontvangkamer op de begraafplaats.

The announcement of Oma Schimmel's passing on November 1, 1980 at age 88 at the old age home, "Ewoud" in IJsselstein (near Utrecht), Holland.

A certificate making Leo a member of the Schimmel (which in Dutch means both "white/gray horse," as well as "mould") Clan upon their visit at Christmas 2007.

Mom with Oma Schimmel (after the War).

Chapter 18

Anne Frank —
Connections and Comparisons

M any persons, after hearing our story make the perhaps-under-standable comment that our story of hiding in Amsterdam is "just like" Anne Frank. Yes, we were all in hiding, but there are, at least in my mind, a number of important differences. First, Anne and her family came to Amsterdam as fugitives from Germany and Austria. They and others like them, unlike Mom's family or indeed Pop's mother's family, were not fully integrated into Dutch society, as were many generations of Jews dating back to the 15th century in Holland. There was thus in place for Dutch Jews, an established support system resulting from such long-term commitments. By contrast, the new immigrants did not speak Dutch, had heavy German accents and often congregated in ghetto-like circumstances with other recent immigrants from Germany and Austria. Anne and her family settled in Merwedeplein, an area of Amsterdam where there were many other such immigrants.[43]

The old-time, well-assimilated Dutch Jews, did not generally welcome the new immigrants and in fact in many cases looked down on them as seriously dilutive to the elevated standing of Dutch Jews in

---

[43] *The apartment where the Franks lived, at Merwedeplein 37-2, has been restored to its appearance in the 30s, by funding in large part from the Anne Frank House Museum. It has been owned by Woning-corporatie Ymere, a social housing cooperative, since 2004 and is leased to the Dutch Fund for the Arts, which welcomes visitors with paid admission to the apartment.*

Dutch society. Correspondingly, many German Jews looked down at the Dutch Jews, because German Jews had achieved so much in the arts and literature as part of German culture.

The business, Opekta, of Anne Frank's father, Otto Frank, in the heart of Amsterdam's commercial area, four blocks from the Queen's palace, was a busy one involving a number of employees, including, again, German and Austrian immigrants. Miep Gies, the young assistant who found and preserved the pages of Anne's diary when, in 1944, Anne and the others in hiding in the "back house" were betrayed and arrested, herself was Austrian, although she came to Holland as a young child many years before the War. There were not only many employees, but many service providers and contractors who came to the factory.

Once the "back house" became a hiding place, it took a lot of food and other provisions to keep the occupants in the hiding place alive. Thus, many of such delivery persons, contractors, and suppliers, could have surmised, if not known of, the situation.

Further, there were burglaries at the Opekta factory and the burglars may well have made discoveries.

Finally, the eight occupants of the hiding place could not have been totally quiet.

Couple all this with the fact of complicity of many Dutchmen with the Nazis and the bounties paid by the Nazis to persons who discovered or betrayed hidden Jews. As a result, it is fair to assume that the Frank family and the others in the "back house" hiding place were effectively doomed.

By contrast, my parents' hiding place was known only to the family who hid them and to just a couple of people in the Resistance, including the minister in Haarlem, Mom's sorority sister (Aleida Schot) and Piet Hoogenboom. As earlier indicated, even the couple immediately below them did not know they were there for the entire 27 month period they were in fact living above them.

There have been some interesting personal contacts/connections that I have had with the Anne Frank story. Almost from the beginning, I was one of a small handful of directors of the Anne Frank Center USA, which was first organized by the Anne Frank House Museum in Amsterdam, as an affiliate. The U.S. organization was thus at the outset intended to be only an appendage, or even just a "feeder" organization, for the Dutch official Anne Frank House Museum.

The U.S. organization, the Anne Frank Center USA, during the six years or so I was its Chairman, achieved, and had frequent battles to retain, independence from the Anne Frank House Museum in Amsterdam. The Anne Frank Center USA created its own traveling exhibits, largely using panels it had to purchase from the Dutch official Anne Frank House Museum, and, importantly, created its own study guides for the Diary, trained docents and galvanized community involvements at the various venues around the country where we placed exhibits on the life and death of Anne Frank.

It was while I was Chairman of the Anne Frank Center USA that Cornelis ("Cor") Suijk, the former Chief Financial Officer of the official Dutch Anne Frank House Museum (who had been fired by the principals of the Dutch Anne Frank House Museum) came to me with a secret. Cor had 5 pages from the original diary in Anne's own handwriting that he said were given to him by Otto Frank, to keep, and they were not supposed to see the light of day. Cor had become close to Otto Frank over a period of more than 15 years, as he had been the liaison between the Anne Frank House Museum in Holland and the Anne Frank Fonds (Foundation) in Switzerland, a separate entity established by Otto Frank. Otto Frank transferred all copyrights to the Anne Frank Diary to that Swiss Foundation when he moved to Basel, Switzerland in 1953/1954. The Fonds was run, after Otto's death, by Anne's cousin Buddy (pronounced "Boody") Elias, with whom I had many pleasant dealings and whom I visited in Basel. Buddy, incidentally, who at this writing is 89 years old, started his career as a skater with the Ice Capades. There were many fairly contentious turf wars involving the Dutch official Anne Frank House Museum and the Swiss Fonds (as well as our Anne Frank Center USA) involving copyrights, etc. The Dutch Anne Frank House Museum was particularly angry, for example, that Buddy let the Japanese use the Anne Frank name for cartoons and T-shirt designs.

Cor spent a lot of time in the U.S., and we named him "International Director" of The Anne Frank Center U.S.A. with responsibility for helping to establish new venues for the exhibits. Cor's interest in those pages was apparently not purely academic or truly charitable. He really wanted to sell them and use the proceeds, which, of course, could be quite substantial, if sold at auction, for example, to fund his own Holocaust Education Foundation.

The subject matter of those pages was in fact incredibly important to the Anne Frank story, and I was thrilled beyond description, but also a bit nervous, to be among the first couple of people ever to view and read them. Those pages contained Anne's own thoughts and admissions on sexuality and her views/feelings toward her own parents, which were especially negative toward her mother. Otto, according to Cor, did not want the world to see those pages or to learn of Anne's thoughts on these points as it might diminish the world's regard for Anne (and the value of the Diary). Otto died in 1980 and Cor kept those pages.

Cor in 1998 asked me to help deal with these matters (I was Dutch by origin, a lawyer, close to, but completely independent of, the principals of the official Dutch Anne Frank House Museum, and Cor trusted me.) The problem that quickly arose when I approached the Dutch Anne Frank House Museum with the information on the pages was that the principals of the Dutch Anne Frank House Museum were absolutely convinced, or at least took the unalterable position, that Cor had stolen the pages from Otto and they would never consider paying a "ransom" for these pages. On a personal basis, Hans Westra, the impressive (now retired) head of the Anne Frank House Museum in Amsterdam, really disliked Cor.

After getting an indication of value from the Morgan Library and others, a deal was ultimately struck (and I returned the pages to Cor) with NIOD, the Netherlands War Documentation Institute, pursuant to which the Dutch government's Ministry of Culture agreed in 2000 to "contribute" $300,000 to Cor Suijk's U.S. Center for Holocaust Education foundation in exchange for those pages (to the consternation and anger of the folks at the Anne Frank House Museum in Amsterdam), which, accordingly, were transferred in 2001.

The payment arrangements were concluded on the eve of a potential public auction of those papers when it was feared that some (American) billionaire might pay exorbitant amounts therefor and the pages would perhaps be held in a country far from the Diary itself.

The Netherlands War Documentation Institute, subsequent to Otto Frank's death, but before these pages were published, issued in 1989 a "Critical Edition" of the Diary of Anne Frank documenting all the changes and edits that had been made and authenticating the handwriting etc. of the Diary. A "Revised Critical Edition," including these special five pages, was published by the Institute in 2003. The five pages, after they were acquired by the Netherlands War Docu-

mentation Institute, have since been placed in the archives of the
Anne Frank House Museum in Amsterdam.

Extracts from those 5 pages were published in the Amsterdam
daily paper "Het Parool" in August 1998. No one knows who "leaked"
these pages. Presumably it was Cor. The article indicated that the
proceeds of a sale would go to our Anne Frank Center USA in New
York for which he was then working. This did not happen, as the payment went to Cor's own foundation. "Het Parool," incidentally, as earlier indicated, started life as the illegal flier published by the
Resistance during the War, and was co-founded by Hans (J.C.S.)
Warendorf, the husband of Mom's sister Margaret.

Ultimately, as reported in the media, the Anne Frank Fonds pre-
vailed in court in the Netherlands (the decision was not appealed to
the highest court) on control of the royalty rights and exploitation
thereof. The Fonds, under direction of its re-constituted Board, has
taken a number of steps effectively avoiding much of the continuing
role of the Museum in Holland with respect to at least the copyrighted
materials. Thus, as reported, the Fonds has transferred substantial
rights and archives obtained from the Dutch Anne Frank House Museum pursuant to the victory in court, to the Jewish Museum in Frank-
furt for the creation of an Anne Frank Family Center, but has also
championed a new play, "Anne", which opened in a new theater, built
ostensibly for this production, in Amsterdam in May 2014 and which
is apparently intended to more effectively humanize Anne as apposed
to making/keeping her a pure "icon". The new play, thus, brings in
elements of Anne's feelings toward her mother and of her own sexual
awakening which reflect the very thoughts in those five pages.

The fact of the opening in Amsterdam in light of the nasty dispute
between the parties can be clearly justified as appropriate, because it

is where the events took place, but it can also fairly be viewed as a bit of what-we-would-call in basketball, "in your face."[44]

In a continuing show of further actual or potential commercial exploitation of the powerful Anne Frank "brand", the Fonds, as reported, has already announced, inter alia, proposals for animated cartoons, films and other presentations.

The Diary itself, has remained in Amsterdam at the Anne Frank House Museum, and will presumably always remain there, as contemplated under Otto Frank's will.

Miep Gies, who found and preserved the Diary came to the U.S. a couple of times while I was head of the Anne Frank Center USA in New York (we appeared together on several T.V. programs) and she and her husband, Jan, stayed with my parents in their modest apartment in Port Washington. They, as well as Buddy Elias, Eva Schloss and others involved in the Anne Frank story, have had dinner in our home. Miep and Mom got along famously; they were both cut from the same modest cloth. I also had the pleasure and honor of accompanying Miep to the Justice Department in Washington, D.C. to meet Janet Reno, then our U.S. Attorney General, a marvelous woman, who bounded out of her enormous office to meet Miep. Ms. Reno spent a good 45 minutes with Miep, telling her that she had read the Diary several times and how much that meant to her. A photo signed by

---

[44] *Kay and I saw the play in Amsterdam on May 24, 2014. It had received a blistering front page negative review in one of the major Dutch newspapers, and some harsh comments on T.V. from Ted Musaph, a long-time director of both the Anne Frank House Museum and the Jewish Historical Museum in Amsterdam. Kay and I, and apparently the entire audience, from whom you could hear a pin drop and who gave it a standing ovation, thought it was an outstanding production, with especially effective staging, including moving panels of videos of Germans marching into Amsterdam, a young boy with his hands up guarded by a German soldier, Allied bombing runs, and the Allied invasion of Normandy, to enhance the context of the story. The complaints included disapproval of the concept of Anne dancing and falling in love with a publisher (sitting at a bridge table in front of the stage during the performance), an imagined scenario many years after the War, and the fact that the production was in the nature of a mere "evening out" with a "borrel box" (alcoholic drink and snack box) available during intermission, thus ostensibly detracting from the import of the story.*

Janet Reno with Miep, myself and several others, has hung for years in the Justice Department at the Human Rights and Special Prosecution Section of the Criminal Division of the Department, which has been responsible for prosecuting Nazi war criminals. Miep was "knighted" (named to the Order of Oranje-Nassau) by Queen Beatrix nearly two decades ago.[45] She passed away in January 2010 at age 100.

---

[45] *At that very same ceremony, Carina Benninga, daughter of Ben Benninga and my cousin Josephine Benninga-Warendorf, whose own family story of survival is chronicled in Chapter 14 of this book, was also "knighted" in recognition of her exploits as the captain (1989-1992) of the Dutch women's national field hockey team which won the gold medal at the Los Angeles Olympics and bronze at the Seoul Olympics (both of which we witnessed with a bunch of relatives). Among many other individual and team honors, Carina carried the Dutch flag at the opening ceremonies (the first Dutch woman to do so) at the Barcelona Olympics. Carina was also the assistant coach of the U.S. National Women's Field Hockey Team from 1993 to 1995 and the (interim) head coach of the U.S. team in 1998. Her brother, Marc Benninga, was on the Dutch Olympic men's field hockey team in Seoul and, as a physician, was the team doctor for the Dutch team at the Beijing Olympics.*

Leo in 1998 with Miep Gies, who retrieved the Anne Frank Diary when Anne was arrested in August 1944, and kept it safe for Anne's father, Otto, when he returned from Auschwitz-Birkenau in 1945.

An embroidery made by Mom for me for my work with the Anne Frank Center USA. The church is the Westerkerk, with the Wester Toren (tower of the Western Church in Amsterdam), located a few meters from the Anne Frank House Museum, whose bells tolled Anne's hours.

Anne Frank's statue at Merwedeplein in Amsterdam (where Anne lived before she went into hiding and where very few visit); in the background is Holland's first "skyscraper," unique in its day; another statue of Anne, seen by millions, is located next to the Anne Frank House Museum in the heart of Amsterdam.

Chapter 19

Resistance by the Dutch and Dutch Jews

A greater percentage of Jews, nearly 80%, living in Holland, were killed at the hands of the Nazis in World War II, than Jews in any other country of Western Europe. This despite meaningful and substantial, and sometimes overlooked, effective resistance by Dutchmen, including Dutch Jews, to the Nazi occupation.

My family's and my own survival in the War, as reported herein, was clearly the product of such resistance.

I fear that the horrible destruction of the Dutch Jewish population was in fact in large measure the result of acts of brutal retribution by the Nazis to acts of brave resistance by the Dutch. It was unbounded acts of hatred by the Nazis for such very acts of resistance that set the stage for the death of many tens of thousands of Jews.

Above all, the incredibly fierce and violent reactions by the Nazis to any acts of resistance, created an overwhelming, overbearing and omni-present factor of utter and abject fear of jail, deportation or death.

Barriers to Resistance

There are a number of factors which greatly challenged the ability of Dutch citizens to carry out resistance:

- *The fact that Holland had been neutral in WWI and Hitler "guaranteed" that neutrality just before invading Holland; Holland was therefore not in a position to present an effective military defense initially nor to conduct substantial para-military armed partisan resistance;*

- *The geography of the country – the essential lack of forests, hills and other hiding places from which resistance took place in other countries, and the corresponding largely fully-built landscapes;*

- *The extremely efficient Dutch civil service system which tracked the existence of any one living in the country; there are, for example, maps (reproduced herein) created by the German occupiers identifying the specific location of Jews in Amsterdam;*

- *The limited number of Jews (less than 2%) of the population of the country and, accordingly the lack of ethnic strength and support in numbers;*

- *The lack of a strong Jewish community, led by important rabbis, for example (this in turn reinforces the earlier-described assimilation of Jews into Dutch society);*

- *The role of the Jewish Council, established by the Germans to "control" the Jews, which became an instrumentality of accommodation with the Nazi occupiers;*

- *Hitler's desire to annex Holland as soon as possible as a Jewish-free part of an Aryan German empire.*

The Strikes

As first referenced and described in Chapter 5 of this book, the first meaningful acts of such active resistance, leading to violent retribution, took place in January and early February 1941, when roving groups of Nazis attacked Jews in the Jewish quarters of Amsterdam.

On one such occasion, a group, estimated at 40 Nazis, came into the area near the Portuguese synagogue to attack Jewish youth. As many as 125 Jewish youth were waiting and proceeded to beat up the Nazis. On another occasion the Nazis beat up a bunch of Jews at a favorite ice cream stand.

When one Nazi died as a result of those fights, the reaction of the Nazis was immediate and harsh. There were many arrests and subsequent trials with resulting long prison terms and hard labor. One person, a co-owner of the ice-cream stand, was sentenced to death and executed. Fully 425 young Jewish men were arrested and deported to the Mauthausen concentration camp, where all but one perished shortly thereafter.

In response to these arrests, executions and deportations, there was a major strike, as previously detailed in Chapter 5, known as the February Strike, or the Dockworkers' Strike, on February 25th and 26th, 1941, by literally tens of thousands of municipal employees, dockworkers and many others in Amsterdam, and subsequently in other cities, bringing transit and other services to a halt in support of the Jews.

That major strike, which was preceded by a couple of small strikes organized by the Communist Party, represents the only such national strike in any German-occupied territory. It was an enormous act of Dutch (not just Jewish) national resistance and resulted in brutal reactions and retribution: 450 men, deemed leaders of the strike, were executed by the Nazis. It was made abundantly clear to the Dutch that such active resistance was futile and would almost certainly result in deportation or execution.

As mentioned in Chapter 5, there were other strikes in 1943 and 1944, although not necessarily limited to support of the Jews, including the April-May 1943 "Milk Strikes," when farmers refused to deliver milk to the factories and allowed private citizens to pick up as much milk at the farms as they wanted. However, as indicated, at that point a preponderance of Jews had been deported.

Also note the Railroad Strike of September 1944, referenced and described in Chapter 11 of this book, which, again, in terms of retribution, led to the death-ridden "Hunger Winter" in Holland (See Chapter 11).

Other Measures of Resistance

It was clear that the reign of terror by the Nazis after the February Strike in 1941 could thereafter be resisted only and primarily by more passive actions and occasional acts of bravery involving few people. Yet such measures of resistance were extensive and cannot be underestimated. They involved as many as 22,000 Dutch men and women in non-violent resistance and 3,000 at the early stages in para-military pursuits. Those acts of resistance were virtually limitless; they included, for example:

- *Hiding Jewish children and families (as in my and my parents' case). It is estimated that as many as 25,000 Dutch Jews went into hiding and that between 12,000 and 16,000 survived. Of those in hiding, approximately 4,500 were children, of whom an estimated 3,500 resurfaced after the War. Of those surviving children, 2,000 were not reunited with their parents (many staying with their Christian War Parents).*
- *Providing fake ID cards, false ration cards and other forged documents.*
- *Raiding ration offices to steal coupons.*
- *Paying monetary stipends to people willing to accept Jews in hiding.*
- *Providing passage to England (several hundred made it during the first couple of days after 5/10/40).*
- *Assisting escape through Belgium and other borders (an estimated 9,000 persons escaped across the Belgian, British, Swiss and Portuguese borders with help).*
- *Killing Nazi collaborators.*
- *Killing Nazi officers and policemen.*
- *Defying orders to wear the Jewish star.*
- *Gentiles wearing the Jewish star in support of the Jews.*
- *Publication of underground anti-Nazi papers and fliers (see the references to "Het Parool" and J.C.S. Warendorf). Note that 23 persons working for "Trouw" ("Faith"), another underground Resistance paper, were captured by the Nazis and were offered release if they stopped publishing; their leader refused and all were executed.*

- *Keeping radios and listening to Churchill on the BBC or the Queen on Radio Oranje.*

- *Making small radios.*

- *Catholic and Protestant churches refusing support of certain measures against Jews.*

- *Catholic clergy arranged "Our Lady of the Safe Hiding Place."*

- *Catholic church circular prohibiting Catholics from joining the Nazi party.*

- *Churches asking members to help people in hiding.*

- *Churches asking members to quit unions once the unions were taken over by the Nazis; only 5% stayed in the unions.*

- *Burning public records identifying Jews; burning buildings housing such documents (see the footnote on Gerrit-Jan van der Veen).*

- *Thefts of millions from the Netherlands National Bank.*

- *Student and faculty protests at the Universities against discharge of Jewish professors (Universities at Delft and Leiden were subsequently shut down by the Nazis).*

- *Providing food and other necessities.*

- *Providing medical help.*

- *Males taking female identity to avoid capture.*

- *Hiding healthy Jews as "sick" patients in hospitals for days until they could escape.*

- *Doctors falsely certifying that Jewish men had been sterilized.*

- *Notaries and police certifying essential services/employment.*

- *Helping Jews escape Westerbork and other Dutch concentration camps like Amersfoort.*

- *Helping Jewish children escape from the "crèche" (day care center) near the Hollandsche Schouwburg ("Dutch Theater") (as many as 1,100 children may have been rescued largely by student organizations).*

- *Helping Jews escape the Dutch Theater.*

- *Creating and using fake arm plates to obtain duty as part of the air raid defense (ostensibly to enforce blackouts, but providing mobility at night).*

- *Honoring the Royal Couple on birthdays, wearing white carnations as symbol of Resistance.*

- A Utrecht (primarily student) organization, Naamloze Vennootschap (Anonymous Company; this is also the Dutch term for a corporation), saved an estimated 600 children (and was honored by Yad Vashem).

- Attacking prisons (see also the footnote on van der Veen).

- Sabotage of rail lines, including those used for deportations.

- Failure to complete forms accurately.

- Hiding assets and ownership.

- Failing to turn in all metal items when, late in the War Germans demanded all items of any metal to continue the war efforts.

- Bribing Nazi officers, police, etc. to avoid punishment.

- Bribery to facilitate escape (to Belgium, France or Spain, for example) at a cost, when effective, estimated at $35,000 to $400,000 in current U.S. dollars.

- Destroying telephone lines.

- Destroying naval repair facilities.

- Espionage for Allied troops – information on German troop movements and concentrations.

- Collecting weapons.

- Failure to report for service.

- Surviving concentration camps.

- The whole Village of Nieuwlande organized and cooperated to hide at least one Jew in each home (and was also honored by Yad Vashem).

- The Kindertransport, which on May 14, 1940 managed to send 74 Jewish children to England.

- Additional national strikes, including railroad strikes, in 1943 and 1944.

- A Dutch Group, the "L.O." (Landelijke Organisatie voor hulp aan Onderduikers en de Landelijke Knokploegen) (National Organization for Help to Persons in Hiding and National Armed Squads) was formed and joined by thousands.

- In late 1944, as many as 60,000 persons signed up for military resistance and as many as 1/3 actually participated in attacks.

- The Dutch Government in exile in 1944 guaranteed loans to fund the Resistance to the tune of 47 million guilders (worth approximately US $192 million today).

Again, I wish to stress the role of fear as the overarching limiting factor and deterrent to acts of resistance. Ultimately, 20,000 persons were arrested for resistance and nearly 2,000 were executed. Yet, note how much resistance by Dutch Jews and other Dutchmen to the brutal Nazi occupation actually took place, saving thousands of Jews, including, of course, my family and me.[46]

Dealing with Refugees

The enormous problem of refugees, primarily Jewish, from Germany and elsewhere in Europe, which in turn constitutes an essential aspect of resistance to German annihilation of Jews, is far beyond the scope of this book.

We have noted that many tens of thousands of German refugees, including in essence my father and his family, managed to land in Holland or arrange passage beyond Holland to Great Britain, the U.S., Canada and elsewhere during the 30's, until the Dutch border with Germany was essentially sealed to all but a trickle of immigrants. Note that only 140 German Jewish refugees entered Holland in 1939. Literally hundreds of thousands of Jews (an estimated 400,000 in Germany) seeking havens outside Germany were effectively doomed. While Germany appears to have supported mass emigration and liberally issued exit visas during the late 30's and early 40's, few, if any, countries including Holland, Great Britain and the U.S., responded with open borders to a potential influx of immigrant Jews.

As earlier indicated, Holland actually sent immigrant refugees

---

[46] *There has been a Museum of the Resistance (Verzetmuseum) which first opened in a former synagogue in 1985. Since 1999 the Museum has been housed in a landmarked building, the Plancius building, at the periphery of the former "Jewish Quarter in Amsterdam" where it displays many exhibits relevant to the acts of resistance described above.*

back to Germany, including a number even sent to concentration camps.

The foregoing notwithstanding, there were extraordinary efforts by Dutch persons to help Jewish refugees escape Nazi Germany. Some of those efforts took place before, and even after, Nazi occupation of Holland, through various organizations both Dutch (i.e. the Amsterdam Refugee Committee) and foreign, created to help Jews. They included, for example, arranging a number of boatloads of Jews to slip out of Holland, for Palestine and elsewhere. They also included, paradoxically, the creation of residential camps, such as Westerbork, and model working farms and factories, populated by German Jewish refugees (until the residents were ultimately hauled off to German and Polish concentration and killing camps by the Nazis).

The aforementioned Amsterdam Refugee Committee facilitated the emigration of an estimated 18,500 Jews from Holland to the U.S., U.K., Australia, Bolivia and elsewhere from early 1933 to the end of 1940.

The extraordinary efforts to support Jewish refugees are described in remarkable detail, backed by voluminous scholarly research, in the book, *The Ambiguity of Virtue: Gertrude van Tijn and the Fate of the Jews*, by Bernard Wasserstein (Harvard University Press; 2014).[47]

---

[47] *An earlier version was published in Dutch by Nieuw Amsterdam (2013) as "Gertrude van Tijn en het lot van de Nederlandse Joden".*

Netherlands National Monument, located on Dam Square in Amsterdam, dedicated on National Remembrance Day (May 4) 1956 in memory of victims of WWII.

Monument of Jewish Resistance in Amsterdam, located on the Amstel River near the Jewish Historical Museum of Amsterdam, which reads (translation): "In Commemoration of the Resistance of Fallen Jewish Citizens".

There is an annual gathering at this monument on November 9, the date on which *Kristallnacht* ("Night of Broken Glass") took place in Germany in 1938.

Statue on Apollolaan in Amsterdam a few
hundred feet from the Hilton Hotel,
with a plaque reading (translation):

*"As reprisal for an action
by the Resistance,
the German occupier took
29 prisoners from the jail
on the Weteringsschans to this spot
and in the early morning of October 24, 1944
executed them before a firing squad"*

Author's Note:

As indicated in earlier chapters of this book, the most important connection of our extended family with the Resistance has been with Piet Hoogenboom, Sr. and his family, who arranged the hiding places, fake IDs, food and food stamps, correspondence, etc. to and for our family during the War. Piet Hoogenboom Sr.'s granddaughter believes that the Hoogenboom family in fact helped arrange hiding places for many persons other than just our extended family and that, accordingly, he was probably part of an organized Resistance group, but we have not been able as yet to establish such connection. Piet's efforts were recognized, among other things, in certain Certificates and Awards arranged by Hans Eiser and Liesje Eiser-Loeb to commemorate Piet's deeds. Liesje, as earlier indicated, was the daughter of Sophie and Fritz Loeb, brother of my grandmother Annemarie Ullmann-Loeb (Oma Aenni) and founder of the UMS-Pastoe furniture factory, of which she inherited sole ownership after her father's death. Hans and Liesje had no children. Copies of certain representative Certificates/Awards are inserted here with my translation, where applicable

Piet Hoogenboom's Police ID card.

(My translation)

40 YEARS IN FREEDOM
to
Piet Hoogenboom Sr. in memoriam
from
Liesje and Hans Eiser
In grateful commemoration of the help in the darkest days.

Forty years in freedom is a moment to remember. Remember in order not to forget. For many, to achieve such freedom was linked to persons who evidenced great courage and will. The Jewish National Fund has issued this "Certificate of Thanks" to Netherlands citizens who by virtue of their fearlessness and selflessness made such freedom possible for others. On the one hand as a tangible memento on the occasion of this remembrance of the liberation, on the other with the funds that are awarded with these certificates, to serve a goal that offers a better future to Israel. The total amount raised with the thousand numbered certificates, which is estimated at 250,000 guilders, shall be used in Israel as additional funds for enhancement of raw land, for forestation, irrigation, and residential development (within the former borders), thus to help ensure the continued existence of the country and people of Israel. The Jewish National Fund in the Netherlands is extraordinarily grateful to the issuer and recipient of this certificate for that which was done for the Jewish people in the past and to date.

(My translation)

In Israel in the Joop Westerweel
Woods, a tree will be planted
in the name of
Mr. & Mrs. P. Hoogenboom Sr.
By Liesje and Hans Eiser
on the occasion of 25 years of liberation

Chapter 20

Leaving Holland and Coming to America

Pop, who had lost his job at De Bijenkorf when De Bijenkorf was forced to terminate the employment of all Jewish employees, received, at some point after the War, compensation for lost wages from the time of his termination to the end of the War. With those payments, Mom's inheritance and the proceeds of the sale of the house on Velasquezstraat to Aunt Margaret and Uncle Hans Warendorf, Mom and Pop had the means, though Dutch currency was immensely devalued against foreign strong currencies like the U.S. dollar, to make the move to start a new life in America.

Mom's mother, Bertha Konijn-Prins (Grootmoeder), had come from wealth. She left Holland and moved to New York City shortly after the War through arrangements made by her daughter (and Mom's sister), Juliemarthe. Juliemarthe, the middle sister (Margaret was the oldest; Mom, the youngest), and her family, had landed in Port Washington (Long Island), New York shortly after the War started.

Grootmoeder, through Hans (J.C.S.) Warendorf, and through International Corporation Service, and/or other entities controlled by him, was able to transfer substantial funds to the U.S. and to arrange

U.S. dollar accounts prior to commencement of the War. Those funds were administered by a transplanted Dutchman, Harold Beenhaur, and traded through transplanted Dutchman Maurits Edersheim at Burnham & Co. (later Drexel, Burnham & Co.) in New York City.

Grootmoeder, who thus moved to New York City by herself at age 66, shortly after the War ended, (with, incidentally, very little command of English), moved into the residential hotel, The Adams, on the corner of Fifth Avenue and 86th Street. The Adams, together with its neighbor, The Croydon, were among the most elegant residential hotels in the City at the time. Grootmoeder's good friend, Annie Cohen, whose family founded Maison de Bonneterie, an elegant Amsterdam ladies' clothing store, lived in The Croydon. Another good friend was Tonie Soep, whose family was also in the diamond business. The Soeps also emigrated to the U.S. after the War and lived in Hampshire House on Central Park South.[48]

Both Grootmoeder and Mom were able to continue to shop for meat (especially fresh-made quality beef cervelat and steak tartar), poultry, and fish with a transplanted famous Dutch butcher, Baergo, at 88th Street and York Avenue in New York City.[49]

One of my favorite stories involving Grootmoeder is that she was used to truly royal treatment in her Amsterdam surroundings (before the War), and considered herself, at all times, to be of the elegant upper class. Thus, when she would leave The Adams and the doorman

---

[48] Mrs. Soep's daughter, Ina Polak, together with her husband, Jaap (Jack) Polak, wrote the book and starred in the movie, "Steal a Pencil For Me," about their exchange of love letters while at the concentration camp, Bergen-Belsen. Ina passed away on May 14, 2014 at age 91; Jack, passed away on January 9, 2015 at age 102. I visited both of them just weeks before they died. Jack, who was both my predecessor and successor as Chairman of the Anne Frank Center USA, and I on my last visit even shared some "very old" Jenever (Dutch gin) which I brought back from Holland for him.

[49] Baergo was founded by relatives of the Baer and Gottschall families, German immigrants, who had a butcher shop by the same name in Amsterdam prior to the start of WWII. Lore Baer, daughter of the butcher shop owners, was herself a hidden child (in a farm in northern Holland), during WWII before immigrating to the U.S. with her parents; her story of survival is the subject of an illustrated children's book "Hiding from the Nazis" by David Adler.

would say to her "Have a nice day", she would immediately retort "That's none of your business." After all, who was he, but a lowly doorman, to wish her a nice day!

Grootmoeder had arranged to purchase a house for our family at 36 Carlton Avenue, on the corner of Second Avenue, in Port Washington, the same town where Juliemarthe and her family had purchased a home.

On December 8, 1947, we arrived in the U.S., landing in Hoboken, New Jersey after a 9-day voyage on the Westerdam, a cargo-passenger ship with approximately 140 passengers.[50] Because we had regular passage, rather than steerage, for example, we did not wind up in Ellis Island. My parents, for immigration purposes, decided that we should drop the last "n" of our name so that we would become immediately well-assimilated. Even though we never landed there, I nevertheless tell people we lost that "n" on Ellis Island; it somehow sounds more authentic. Several years ago, we bought bricks at Ellis Island with the names of Bertha, Mom, Pop, Henk and myself to commemorate our coming to America.

I remember distinctly going outside on the deck together with everyone else onboard the ship in the fog and rain on the date of our arrival when we first saw the Statue of Liberty rising out of the mist.

Like the day the War ended, it's a moment I'll always remember. I looked at Mom, and the tears were streaming down her cheeks. It was then that Mom uttered a phrase which dominated her thought throughout her life, and repeated by her verbally on many occasions, "We made it; we beat Hitler"; we survived and our lives will go on, with children, families and a future in America.

---

[50] This ship was sunk several times while it was being built, both by the Nazis and, when the Nazis took over, by the Dutch Resistance; it was commissioned after WWII as one of the smaller converted cargo ships of the Holland-America Line.

(My translation)

EXTRACT

From the CIVIL REGISTRY of the City of AMSTERDAM evidences that: *Ullmann,*
Franz Leo born 25 October 1913 in Cologne, Germany, and spouse, Konijn, Emily born 9 May 1913 in Amsterdam, and two children, Leopold Salomon, born 14 July 1939 in Amsterdam and Hendrik Jan born 23 March 1946 in Amsterdam, have given notice on 10 October 1947 of departure on 29 November 1947 for Washington, currently residing at the address: Velasquezstraat 5.

18 October 1947
The Mayor
The Secretary

Extract from Civil Registry confirming departure for "Washington" [sic]
on 11/29/47.

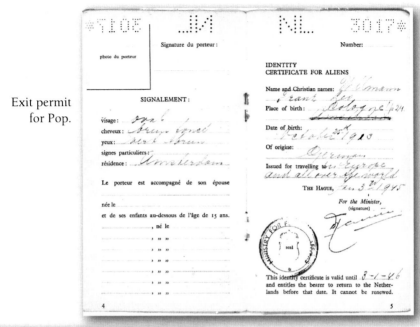

Exit permit for Pop.

Exit permit to move to "Port Washington" 11/29/47.

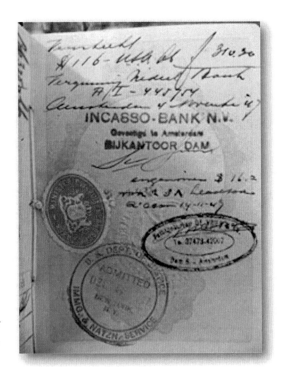

U.S. Immigration Stamp for
Pop – 12/8/47.

Henk and Leo on the Holland-America Line's "Westerdam"
on the way to America.

PART II:

Our First Years in America:
1947-1957

Chapter 21

My First Days in Port Washington

Upon landing in Hoboken that first day, we were met by Groot-moeder and Juliemarthe and her husband, Joost, who took us, our furniture and the sweet little Standard automobile that traveled with us in the cargo hold on the Westerdam, back to Port Washington to our new home on Carlton Avenue. It looked enormous – three stories, a side porch, a corner lot and a separate (one car) garage.

Aunt Juliemarthe insisted that I attend the private grade school, The Manhasset Bay School, virtually immediately across the street from our home on Carlton Avenue. My mother, in those first couple of days, had no idea that there were public schools and that the public grade school, The Main Street School, was just two blocks away. Our neighbors on Second Avenue, the Ganchers, alerted us to the existence of public schools and the potential cost-saving benefits thereof.

Immediately across the street on Second Avenue were the Hickeys. They had a bunch of sons roughly my and Henk's age and we played together a lot, but my parents always thought that they were unkempt. The Hickeys had a 6 or 8 foot stone wall which dropped off from their yard to the sidewalk below and the boys would throw mud pies on, or at, unsuspecting pedestrians below.

Further down the street on Second Avenue were the Browers, who owned a moving company. These were rough guys and I learned my first English from them, including a lot of bad words. I came home one day early in our American life, after playing with the Browers, asking Mom if we were having "shit pie" for dinner, and being spanked without knowing exactly why, as I didn't know what these words meant.

After a few days at the Manhasset Bay School, Mom enrolled me at the public Main Street School, where the principal was a larger-than-life woman, Charlotte Merriman. Ms. Merriman, herself, was an institution in Port Washington.[51]

Mom asked Ms. Merriman what would happen to me at school, as I didn't speak any English. Ms. Merriman's reply, an indication of her no-nonsense approach to education, was, "during the first couple of weeks the other kids will beat him up, but thereafter, everything will be fine." I guess that's what happened. This, of course, was long before the schools had programs such as, "Teaching English as a Second Language" ("TESL" or just "ESL"). Accordingly, I spent time after school on many days in her office when Ms. Merriman would ask me to identify in English the words for "belt," "pants," "shirts," whatever.

The historic Main Street School building is a big Beaux-Arts/Georgian-style 3-story building dating back to 1909. It dominates the view of the Port Washington landscape as seen from Manhasset Bay. Incidentally, that building's use as a school was ended in 1985 at a very contentious School Board meeting, after months of strife within the Community, with the deciding vote by my spouse, who was then Vice President of the Board of Education. The building, now listed as

---

[51] *A grade school, later demolished and now a park, bears her name. She also authored a history of the Port Washington peninsula, going back to the American Indian days, entitled "Tales of Sint Sink."*

a federal and state landmark, became a successful community center and a residence for elderly persons.

Ms. Merriman and the 3rd grade teacher, Ms. Wylie, I guess primarily to help my English, placed me in a school play as "Prince Charming." I remember that I had a what-I-thought-was a silk cape with gold embroidery and a crown of some sort, of which I was very proud.

Mom thought that to meet friends and to become assimilated quickly, she should become active in the Main Street School PTA, and she did. She quickly became Secretary of the Board, the job almost nobody wants. Her reports, lacking standard governance concepts and legal English, were highly prized. One day she had to introduce the grade school orchestra (I was there with my cello) after a perfunctory meeting of the PTA Board. After reading the minutes, Mom, who never in fact understood off-color words or double entendres in English, announced to the audience that they could now "enjoy the grade school orchestra concert and coffee will be served during the intercourse." This, of course, for the assembled parents, was the highlight of the evening.

We were amazed by the snow and the cold that first winter of '47-'48 in America. We rarely had snow in Holland and the temperature never reached far below freezing. That winter in Port Washington we had seven or eight feet of snow at a time. Manhasset Bay, just down the street from us, froze-over completely. Cars actually drove on the ice and a gas pump was set up somewhere in the middle. There was also ice boat racing.

Our house on Carlton Avenue was apparently infested by termites. The wooden columns and window frames had been gutted, with only the white paint somehow defining the shape of the columns; you could stick your fingers right through the paint. Regrettably, my parents had never heard of termites, let alone termite inspections, because termites apparently never migrated to Europe. The termites surely surprised Pop. We then had to spend quite a bit of money, which was very dear, on refinishing the woodwork in the living and dining rooms.

My parents furnished the house with a couch, winged grey living room chairs and oriental rugs all brought over from Amsterdam, and built-in bookshelves, outlined by wood strips made by Pop, plus the dining table and credenza exactly as it was in our house on Velasquestraat and before that in their apartment on Milletstraat and just as it would be later in a new house and ultimately in their apartment in Port.

We rented-out the third floor attic apartment to Mr. and Mrs. Soriano, both of whom were gym teachers in private schools. We liked them very much; they apparently paid their rent, although it became really hot up there in the summers, but they were almost never around.

Perhaps my parents' closest friends in the area, who also came to America from Holland, were Jo and Tineke Spier, who arrived in this country in 1951 and purchased a home on Circle Drive in nearby Plandome (Long Island), New York. Jo Spier, who was remotely related to Mom, separated by several degrees of consanguinity, had been one of the most famous political cartoonists and illustrators in Holland. He had published many books and was in effect comparable to a combination of David Low and Norman Rockwell, with both political commentary and pen and ink representational drawings. During the war, Jo and his family were sent first to Westerbork and then to the concentration camp, Therezienstadt (also known as "Terezin"), located some 45 miles from Prague, in what is now the Czech Republic. While a prisoner of Westerbork, Jo decorated the children's rooms with drawings with whimsical figures. While at Terezin, which was largely and purposefully filled with Jews from the cultural world in Holland and elsewhere, including artists, actors, musicians, writers and poets, as well as some government officials, and which, as such, was not primarily a killing camp (even though many people died of disease in that camp), Jo made several drawings depicting attractive scenes of life at the camp, with cafes, couples strolling on the streets, musicians playing in the gazebos on town parks, etc. Those pictures were commissioned by the camp directors and subsequently used to deceive Danish and International Red Cross visitors to the camp into thinking that the concentration camps were attractive Jewish safe havens[52]. As a result of those drawings, which clearly kept Jo and his family alive, he was pilloried by the Dutch media after the War and came to the U.S., to be near my parents, in perceived disgrace. He achieved modest success in this country as an illustrator, most notably with "The Spice Cookbook" published in 1964.

Their son, Peter Spier, absolutely had his father's artistic skills and became one of the most highly-prized illustrators of children's stories in the U.S. with more than 30 books to his credit.[53]

I, during my early years, was fascinated by Richard Halliburton's "Book of Marvels," which concentrated on seven structures that had long disappeared (the Lighthouse at Alexandria, the Hanging Gardens of Nebuchadnezzar, the Colossus of Rhodes, etc.). I convinced Jo that we should do our own Book of (Modern) Marvels, and he made beautiful drawings of the Eiffel Tower, the walled city of Carcassonne, the Sphinx and others. Regrettably, Jo died long before we ever completed a chapter.

My Aunt Grace is an important ingredient in my Americanization. Aunt Grace was a real fun woman. She was born in Brooklyn and

---

[52] *The visit was at the urging of the Danish Red Cross in support of the well-being of its citizens incarcerated in the camp. No such support came from the Dutch side. Note, incidentally, that in the last months of the War, 1200 prisoners were liberated from Terezin for payment by a U.S. rabbinate to Himmler of $5 per head.*

[53] *Peter Spier's color illustration of Port Washington's lower Main Street has been an initial access feature of the Port Washington's Public Library's website.*

somehow landed in a boarding school in Switzerland where she was in the same class as Pop's mother, Aenni Loeb (Oma Aenni). Grace was introduced to her future husband, Aenni's brother Otto, as a result of that boarding school relationship. She and Otto married in Europe and moved to the U.S. before the War. Otto opened a toy store in Albany, which, regrettably, was not successful, and he and Grace struggled financially. He died not long after the war, and Aunt Grace continued to live in Albany.

Aunt Grace took it upon herself to teach me about baseball as the great American pastime and she would come down often and take me to see the Brooklyn Dodgers at Ebbets Field. 1948 was my first full baseball season in America and this was Jackie Robinson's second season. At that point, the Dodgers also brought in a number of other talented black players including Dan Bankhead, Don Newcombe, Roy Campanella and others. They already had great players like Duke Snider, Gil Hodges, Carl Furillo, Preacher Roe, Carl Erskine, etc.

It was a wonderful ball club. Correspondingly, Ebbets Field was a wonderful ballpark, barely the size of a band box. The outfield walls were covered with advertisements; one that was particularly famous and which was the subject of a widely circulated New Yorker cartoon, was the advertisement for Abe Stark's Haberdashery, which would give a men's suit to any ballplayer who hit the sign on the fly ("Hit Sign, Win Suit"). The cartoon showed Mr. Stark in his suit, a hat and a baseball glove standing behind the right fielder in front of the sign making sure that nobody would hit it. Few people did.[54]

I became a rabid fan immediately and listened almost every night (the ball parks were not lit) to the abbreviated re-caps of the day's

---

[54] Carl Furillo, the Dodger right fielder, in an interview after he retired, said that he could not remember anyone hitting the sign, but he, himself, hit it twice.

Dodger games broadcast at 7:00 PM by Marty Glickman.[55]

One day Aunt Grace and I were walking up the ramp at Ebbets Field where perhaps 20 or 30 feet away, Pee Wee Reese, the Dodger shortstop who famously stood up for Jackie Robinson when Robinson broke the color barrier in baseball, was being interviewed by a reporter. Aunt Grace said to me, "Leo, who is that?" "That's Pee Wee Reese, Aunt Grace," I said (Pee Wee wore #1 and was therefore relatively easy to identify). Aunt Grace then yelled, "Pee Wee!" "Pee Wee! – It's Auntie Grace from Albany with my nephew, Leo," pointing down to me. Pee Wee turned around, smiled graciously, waved and said, "Hi Auntie Grace, nice to see you."

Aunt Grace and I would then head to the bleacher seats (which cost a quarter). In the bleachers, which were filled with local black citizens cheering on the new Brooklyn players, Aunt Grace would sit next to some woman and start a conversation. If that person responded appropriately and was reasonably garrulous, we would stay, and otherwise we would simply move around until we found a suitable conversation partner for Aunt Grace during the ballgame.

Manhasset Bay frozen over in the winter of 1947-'48.

---

[55] Marty Glickman, himself a member (for broadcasting) of the National Jewish Sports Hall of Fame (located in a small section of a Jewish Center in Commack, NY), was a former U.S. track star, who at the age of 18 had made the 1936 U.S. Olympic team as a member of the 4x100-meter relay team. He had the second fastest sprint times in the U.S. at the time (after Jesse Owens). However, the day before the event at the Berlin Olympics that year (after he had made the trip), he was denied a chance to compete because he was Jewish.

Henk and Leo (posed).   Leo with Henk as Hopalong Cassidy.

Henk and Leo at Carlton Avenue (Henk has subsequently grown to be as tall and at least as wide as Leo).

Our home on Carlton Avenue (1947-54; it's still there).

The Main Street School.

Uncle Otto Loeb and Aunt Grace Loeb

Aunt Grace, Oma Aenni and Opa Sally Ullmann on our Carlton Avenue porch.

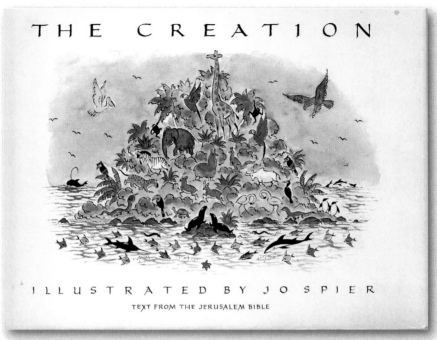

(above) Jo Spier's illustrations for a children's book after he came to the U.S.

(below) A book, illustrated by Peter Spier, about a fort on St. Simon's Island, Georgia, where Kay's family has owned a "cottage" for more than 6 decades.

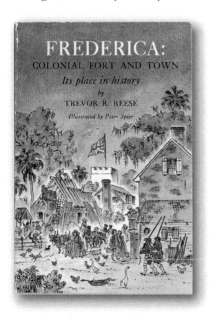

Jo and Tineke Spier

Chapter 22

Our First Few Years in Port Washington

I remember playing with a ton of kids during our first years in Port Washington. Parents were not so afraid to let their kids roam in those days. A few blocks from our home, there were woods, a stream and a pond (now part of Stannards Brook Park), with a "haunted" house. That's where I would meet many friends, all of whom lived nearby, and we'd play "Ringalevio" or "Kick the Can" for hours. In the winter when the pond would freeze over, we'd play a version of ice hockey without skates. I remember those days as very happy times. I also now realize for the first time that none of those kids were Jewish. I, for that matter, in those days, never knew I was Jewish.

I was always burdened by having to carry a cello around. I started the cello in 4th grade and became fairly good at it. One day, a (not-so-great) friend, decided to throw one of those glass insulators that hold telephone wires in place on a telephone pole, at my cello and splintered a good chunk of my borrowed school instrument. He and another friend came home with me and swore to Mom that I didn't do it.

One of my friends, Tommy, lived nearby on Port's own Madison Avenue. Mom had become a Cub Scout den leader and many of those nearby kids joined our pack. But she would not let Tommy in because

266

she felt that he was unwashed and always had dirt under his nails. We all regretted that decision. I, of course, have been careful ever since to monitor my nails.

I was apparently hyperactive in those days, and Mom did not quite know how to handle me. She consulted Ms. Merriman, the tough Main Street grade school principal, and they concocted a scheme whereby every day after school I was to run around the block while Mom held a stop watch. I thought I was potentially one of the world's great runners and might even break a four-minute mile. I had no idea it was just to wear me out and calm me down.

At the end of the 4th grade, my first full school year in America, I received a bad attitude grade from Ms. Gardner, so I wrote to her what I thought was an anonymous note in my own handwriting with the type of stupid nastiness you might have expected at that age, like "you're so fat, you need a girdle..." She retired shortly thereafter.

Probably as early as 4th grade, but perhaps shortly thereafter, I learned a good lesson from Mom. I had my hair cut at the barbershop across from the local Beacon movie theater. One day, I shaved a nickel off the 10¢ tip I was to give to the barber, because I was accumulating nickels to be able to buy a red and white polka-dotted rayon cap at a kiosk on Times Square where they'd also embroider your name on the visor. Mom was absolutely furious when I confessed. She made clear that the barber worked hard for a living, had performed his duties well, and deserved to be rewarded, and that I had been both dishonest and had cheated him out of a reward to which he was entitled.

I had to go back to the barber, pay him double the nickel out of my own money and apologize profusely. I later acquired the beautiful cap anyway. I still go to the same barber shop, now run by a Russian lady, to whom I always give a nice tip, although she gives me a terrible haircut.

I guess to replace "Ruffie," my dog while in hiding with the Schimmels, and thereafter while living in Amsterdam, my parents adopted a schnauzer at the Bide-a-Wee dog home. It contracted distemper shortly thereafter and started biting people. Hence no more dogs.

The only real task at home that I remember was to cut the lawn and weed the flower beds. Cutting the lawn was a mother of a task because we lived on the top of the hill on Second Avenue. There were no motorized mowers in those days and, while downhill was easy, uphill was no fun at all. It was almost as bad as having to practice my instruments.

When outside the house in those early years, I, of course, wanted to become immediately assimilated and didn't want the whole world to know that I belonged to foreign parents. Again, as a kid without much sense, I would generally walk 20-30 feet in front or behind them, seeking to pretend that I was not theirs.

Mom and her Cub Scout den.

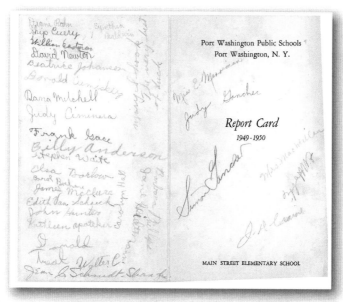

My fifth grade report card bears signatures by my principal (Ms. Merriman), my teacher (Edith Van Schaick), our neighbor (Simon Gancher and his daughter Judy); and a bunch of kids from my class, most of whom remained friends throughout our local school days—not too bad and, anyway, as you will note, I was promoted to Grade 6.

CERTIFICATE OF AWARD

THE MAIN STREET ELEMENTARY SCHOOL

Awards this certificate with sincere thanks and appreciation

Leo Ullman

for outstanding effort in the school's behalf. The good service and the faithfulness shown
in the carrying out of your tasks show the essential qualities for true citizenship

Carrie P. Weber   *Warren A. Spence*   *June 19, 1951*

Principal   President   Date

Notice the signature of Carrie P. Weber, whose name now graces Port
Washington's middle school.

PRESENT THIS STUB AT DOOR

String Festival & Convention

Carnegie Hall Participation Registration

57th St. & 7th Ave., New York, N. Y.

SUNDAY, MARCH 30, 1952 at 5:30 P. M.

Leo Y Ullman

NAME OF STUDENT

Peter Mesrobian

NAME OF TEACHER OR SUPERVISOR

VISIT OUR EXHIBITS AT BARBIZON PLAZA HOTEL

Leo as an 8th grade cellist.
Q: "How do you get to Carnegie Hall?" A: "Practice, practice, practice."

L I F E   S C O U T
RECORD OF PROGRESS

I. SCOUT SPIRIT

☐ Satisfy your Scout or Explorer leaders that you do your best, in your everyday life, to live up to the Scout Oath or Promise; Scout Law; Scout Motto; Scout Slogan.

II. SCOUT PARTICIPATION

1. While a Star Scout for a period of at least three months, show to the satisfaction of your leaders that you:

☐ a. Accept and carry out responsibilities in meetings, outdoor activities and service projects of your Unit.

☐ b. Do your best to help in your home, school, church and community.

☐ c. Take care of things that belong to you and respect the property of others.

☐ d. Have completed a conservation project approved in advance by your Unit leader.

☑ 2. Have earned the FIRST AID Merit Badge.

Date earned 2/3/63

3. Have earned TWO Merit Badges from the CITIZENSHIP group.

Badge earned: Date earned

☑ Citizenship in Nation   3/3/53
☑ World Brotherhood   2/3/63

III. SCOUTCRAFT AND LIFE INTERESTS

1. Have earned the following Merit Badges: ONE from CAMPCRAFT group;

Badge earned: Date earned

☑ Cooking   3/3/63

ONE from OUTDOOR SPORTS or AQUATICS group;

☑ Lifesaving   10/52

ONE from NATURE or CONSERVATION group;

☐

ONE from PERSONAL DEVELOPMENT group;

☑ Reading   12/52

ONE from any of the following groups: ANIMAL HUSBANDRY, PLANT CULTIVATION, COMMUNICATION, TRANSPORTATION, BUILDING.

☑ Home Repairs   4/7/53

2. Have earned any TWO other Merit Badges.

☑ Swimming   10/52
☑ Safety   2/3/63

UNIT LEADER'S APPROVAL

_____ has been a Star Scout since _____ 19___ He has qualified in all requirements for Life Scout rank, and I hereby approve his application.

Date _____ _____

Signature

YOUNG MEN'S   CHRISTIAN ASSOCIATION

SENIOR LIFE SAVER

Name _Leo Tillman_   Date _June 1954_

HAS SUCCESSFULLY COMPLETED THE
NATIONAL Y.M.C.A. SENIOR LIFE SAVER TESTS
AND IS ENTITLED TO THIS REGISTRATION CARD

Thomas Great
Aquatic Director, Instructor or Leader Examiner

Camp Kittatinny.
Field Agent or Aquatic Commissioner

T.K. Cureton Jr.
Chairman National Aquatic Committee

Proud Grandparents Oma Aenni and Opa Sally (Pop's parents) on the porch at Carlton Avenue.

A chore which was not fun, especially on the hill in back.

Chapter 23

Mom's Early Days in America

Mom was an extremely modest woman, who studiously avoided the trappings of her well-heeled upbringing and who never evidenced any pretentiousness. She never spent money on herself and if you would ever compliment her on a dress, for example, she would immediately tell you that she bought it at Loehmann's (she loved Loehmann's for dresses at a fraction of their original price) for $5.00.[56] This reflected a turn away from her elite and wealthy beginnings before the War and to some extent, a counterpoint to her sister Juliemarthe's lifestyle of personal care and glamour, fancy clothes, tennis and the like.

The one luxury that was of great importance to Mom was her baby grand piano. It was always front and center in our home and always front and center in her life. She loved to play, and she played very well. She gave piano lessons to several girls in my class and she herself took lessons from Leonid Hambro, a concert pianist who was best known as the straight-man foil of the comedian-pianist, Victor Borge.

Mom decided at the outset when we came to the U.S. that she would become truly involved in the community in which we lived.

---

[56] Loehmann's, founded in 1920, finally liquidated, after three bankruptcies, the last of its 39 stores in January 2014.

She committed much of every day from the moment we landed to an enormous number of community activities, some of which are further highlighted below. She, above all, embraced our new life and steeped herself in it to a remarkable degree.

Mom in general was a good and creative cook. She, for example, made the most fantastic chocolate mousse and apple tart, all without specific measures. If you'd ask her for the recipe, she would describe generally how she made it, but she'd always leave out one ingredient, intentionally or unintentionally, and it made the chore of copying her signature items very difficult. Herring salad was one of her signature dishes, easy to make, and we ate tons of it. She loved the pressure cooker for some reason and we had a lot of stew, soup and boiled beef kind of stuff which was basically inherited Dutch cooking. Dutch cuisine, other than Indonesian (Holland's former East India colony) dishes, and beside local fish and eel (smoked or fresh), consists basically of farmer food, such as *hutspot* (potatoes, carrots and onions, generally mashed together, and often covered with a slice or two of boiled beef).

We had it frequently. Boiled tongue was one of Pop's favorites. It was usually ugly-looking and salty, but with a lot of good mustard it was okay. We had some strange foods which now would be largely taboo, like marrow bones, where we took out the marrow and spread it on sliced bread; also cod liver (not just the oil, but the liver), which, too, we spread on bread and sprinkled liberally with salt.

We inherited some great Dutch breakfast traditions, such as Holland Rusk (like zwieback toast) with butter and piles of real chocolate sprinkles.

Also in the Dutch tradition, we ate tons of cheese. My parents lived to be 87 and 96, respectively, surviving on bread and cheese as critical parts of their daily sustenance.

Other hybrid cuisine items, apparently brought over from Holland, as we settled-in in America, included sliced tomatoes with sugar on bread. One, about which I can still laugh, yet gag at the thought, was sandwiches with peanut butter and prosciutto, which she wrapped for us when we went to Robert Moses beach on weekends. This was/is a horrible combination, which in fact has nothing to do with Dutch cuisine.

Talking about food, I was always impressed by Mom's mother (Grootmoeder), who, while in the U.S., continued to enjoy her Dutch delicacy, fish eyes. As for me, no thanks.

Certainly Mom's greatest time and psychic non-family commitment was to Henry Viscardi's Abilities School in Albertson, founded in 1962, where she spent 30 years as a volunteer every Friday. She always believed that she should spend one day a week helping others, a commitment she inherited from Grootmoeder. Mom's charitable social work, of course, was how she was able to arrange the hiding place with the Peysters in the War.

Many of her students at the Viscardi School, which specializes in educating and empowering children with severe physical disabilities, were thalidomide babies without limbs, or with hands growing out of their chest, etc. Some of these kids could only perform tasks by blowing into a gadget on a computer. Hardly any could walk. It was a remarkable commitment and it fulfilled Mom. She once agonized and cried for days about yelling at one of these poor kids without hands or developed arms, when his penmanship was poor. In fact, he probably needed the discipline, and she eventually got over it.

Perhaps the second most important commitment by Mom, and where she said she found her greatest joy and peace, was with the local Music Study Club, where she had a bunch of close friends who were also fine musicians. They would meet at a different home each month and there would be prepared programs with research papers and performances.

Mom also started the 50-50 thrift store in the public schools with another Dutch friend, selling (used) clothing and other items, and splitting the proceeds between the schools and the donor.

Another commitment of both my parents, but Mom was the clear driving force, was the local Play Troupe. They acted in innumerable plays. Mom was a born actress with all sorts of facial expressions and suitable movements. Pop was basically a stiff on stage, which may have been passed down to at least this son as an actor.

Mom apparently learned to cross-stitch at an early age and it was a very important form of relaxation for her, although unlike knitting, for example, it requires intense concentration. Cross-stitching is done on woven linen or other cloth, and in intricate patterns. Schoolgirls in Mom's day made sampler patterns by cross-stitching. You can buy patterns, some from famous designers, or you can create your own, which Mom did. The intense concentration involves counting the holes, which are the size of a pinhead, before inserting the needle and thread. Mom made cross-stitch clock cloths (6" wide and, say, 4' long) or 16" x 20" or so designs for special occasions – significant birthdays, events (college graduation, weddings) for my brother and me, and later for our kids, but also for people like our cousins, Juliemarthe's kids, Margaret's kids, etc. They're beautiful and colorful, depicting people in various regional Dutch costumes, famous bridges, various types of windmills, and personalized messages; they became highly-treasured true souvenirs.

Mom also loved to write. She took a creative writing course, and as a result of that course, was able to write about her past, a fairly cathartic exercise, and create a bunch of stories which Pop later made into a book at Kinko's.

Both parents were very active in organizing and running the Community Concert series in Port Washington, which brought leading classical musicians to our town for concerts. One of their most memorable moments was a winter concert, when Richard Goode, then a marvelous young concert pianist who had summered at the Marlboro (VT) Music Festival, was the scheduled headliner. Unfortunately, because there was a snowstorm, the rented grand piano for the concert could not be delivered. Nevertheless, Mr. Goode, a really good sport, performed on a plain-old upright piano and delivered a sterling concert. Mr. Goode is now co-director of the Marlboro Music Festival and, when approached by Mom and Pop at Marlboro many years later, said that he remembered it fondly.

Mom and Pop both read a lot and never watched television. They belonged to a Great Books discussion group. Pop especially thrived in those sessions; Mom was content to let others, especially him, talk.

The Port Washington Public Library was also special to Mom and she became the head of the Library's Music Advisory Council. The Chair of the Library's Board, at that time, Dick Wittemore, was a good friend and Mom was asked, on the occasion of a Gala in Dick's honor, to introduce him, which, she did, ending with the now-famous, albeit innocent, creed, "what this town needs is more Dicks!"

I hope to convey a sense that my Mom had an extraordinarily large circle of friends from these many and varied interests and activities. She also devoted a great deal of time, thought and care to family outside our nuclear family. When her sister, Margaret, died, she became almost a surrogate mother to their three children, the older two of whom had been very much affected by the War. She did the same for her sister Juliemarthe's children, especially Bertien Jacobs, who was a kindred soul. Others with whom she became and stayed very close were Leontine and Monique Van Lent, the children of Juliemarthe's brother-in-law, Leo, and his Dutch wife, Ilse. Leo and Ilse first lived in Manhasset (Long Island), New York, but soon moved to Ithaca, New York. While there were other motivating factors, they, too, like my parents and their friends, the Spiers, were confronted with the fear that they would spend their lives under the dominating thumb of Aunt Juliemarthe. Leo changed his name from Jacobs to Van Lent and became Presbyterian and/or Episcopalian. Leontine, who was especially beautiful and a year older than I, incidentally, was my "trophy" date at my prep school junior prom.

Mom always embroidered intricate pieces to mark special occasions; this one for the birth of her grandson Frank Clifford Ullman, named after his two grandfathers.

Herring Salad

2 large jars of herring in wine sauce,
  drain, and cut the whole onions and
  the pieces of herring in small
  pieces
2 cans of diced red beets, drained
3 apples, cut in small pieces
3 hard boiled eggs, chopped
6 large Kosher-style pickles, chopped
3 cold boiled potatoes, diced

Mix this very well with mayonnaise,
and chill in refrigerator for three hours
before serving. Decorate with pickles.

Emily Ullman.

Mom's signature (literally) dish.

A recent version of the herring salad made by Mom's granddaughter Laura
Ullman Schwartz (who says it's easy) served in Mom's Lalique bowl.

Mom

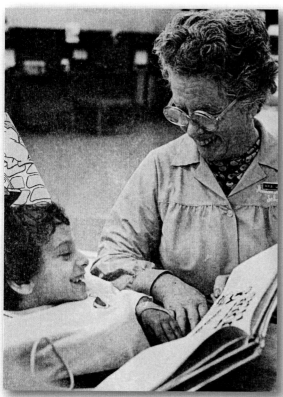

Mom with a student at "Abilities," the Viscardi School, in Williston, New York, where she volunteered every Friday for decades.

One of the students at the Abilities School.

Port's 1989 Mother(s) of the Year

Adult Category:
1st Place **Emily Ullman**
submitted by sons Leo and Henry

To The Editor:

The undersigned, Henry and Leo Ullman, hereby respectfully submit that our mother, Emily Ullman, should be Port's 1989 Mother of the Year.

Emily, her husband, Frank and their two sons came to Port Washington from Holland in 1947. She had survived, because of the war, perhaps the hardest thing imaginable--to go into hiding and to leave a 2½ year old child with others for a period which turned out to be three years of war, fear and terror. When she settled in Port, Emily immediately did all things a mother could do to make her children welcome in a new country and a new community. She valiantly entered every conceivable PTA activity, dragged her children to dancing school and music lessons, became a cub scout den mother, watched her kids in P.A.L. games, etc. She even acted with her children (and grandchildren) in many children's plays.

In the meantime, she worked in her husband's five and ten store while continuing to expand her voluntary activities in the community. She was active for many years in the play troupe, in various music study groups and parent-teacher organizations, she helped run a thrift shop, she helped establish Community Concerts etc.

During the past 20 years or so, she has served as a principal volunteer, and indeed as director of volunteers at the Human Resources School in East Williston. She has also served for years as a member of the Port Library's Music Advisory Council, and now serves as the treasurer of the Senior Citizens's Center.

Not only has she brought up her own children, she effectively serves as surrogate mother to five cousins who have lost their parents and moreover as a surrogate parent to an enormous number of disabled children at the Human Resources School.

Our mother is now 76 years old and still going strong. She has been supportive not only of our every effort over these past 40 plus years, but also those of her six grandchildren in Port Washington. We have all learned about, and benefitted greatly from the values and citizenship she has contributed to this community.

We sincerely hope that you will see clear, as we believe appropriate, to select Emily Ullman for Mother of the year.

Leo S. Ullman
Henry J. Ullman

Port Washington, N.Y.

Thursday, May 11, 1989

Established 1903

35¢

Port Washington New

A Vow Of A Lifetime:

Port Washington's Golden Couples!

A Very Special Couple

Article featuring my parents' 50th, recounting the Holocaust years and again a photo with those annoying busts.

Cranenburg 8.

Lieve tante Lot

Het was vandaag heel erg moeilijk om afscheid van je te nemen.

Je bent niet zomaar een tante; je hebt allen die een beetje extra liefde nodig hebben in je armen gesloten. De kinderen van je zusters, familie die ouderloos uit de oorlog kwamen, die hun ouders te vroeg moesten missen of door omstandigheden moederliefde te kort waren gekomen. Voor intellaren ben je een moeder geworden. Zo heb je jezelf van ons allen onmisbaar en onmisbaar gemaakt.

In het NRC heb deze maand een advertentie gedaan die precies onder woorden brengt, wat ik met mijn tired touches, je niet zeggen kan.

" God saw you grow so weary,
And will do what he thinks best
He will put his arms around you
And take you home to rest".

De kracht die grootmoeder aan jou gaf en die je mij voorjaar in mijn handen stopte, zal ik als een fakkel dragen.

Ik hou ontzettend veel van jou.

X x Am

DIT IS DE LAATSTE BRIEF DIE LOT HEEFT
GELEZEN, OP 10/23, EN DIE HAAR ERG ONTROERD HEEFT.
THANK YOU, DOOR!

Letter from my cousin Dorothy Cohen-Warendorf to Mom and notation
by Pop.
(translation on next page)

(My translation)

Dear Aunt Lot:

It was today extremely difficult to take leave of you. You are not just an aunt; you have embraced everyone who needed a bit of extra love. The children of your sister's family, who returned from the War without parents, who were forced to lose their parents too early or who through circumstances were deprived of motherly love. For countless persons you became a mother. You thus made yourself irreplaceable and indispensable for all of us.

In the NRC (*New Rotterdam Newspaper*) there was an advertisement this month which expressed exactly in words, that which I with my excess emotions, cannot say to you:

"God saw you grow so weary
And will do what he thinks best
He will put his arms around you
And take you home to rest"

The brooch which Grootmoeder gave to you and which you placed in my hands last year, I will wear as a torch.

I love you very much.

XX Door (Dorothy Cohen-Warendorf)

[Note from Pop:]

This is the last letter that [Mom] read, on 10/23 [2000 – 2 days before she died] and which moved her greatly.

Chapter 24

Pop in America

As a disclaimer in advance of telling the story, please be advised that Henk and I loved and greatly admired that strong-headed father of ours, despite certain foibles which might appear in the following text. Henk wears Pop's pinky ring on his pinky finger, and I have his wedding band on my key ring. We were both there, and I held his hand, when he took his last breath.

Regrettably, Pop's first business venture in the U.S. turned out to be a complete disaster. He had come in contact with a Mr. Jack Vandenbergh, who had come from a textile family in Deventer, the Netherlands, the very area where the Prins (Mom's) family traces its roots and had a textile factory. Mr. Vandenbergh (the name sometimes appears as "Van den Bergh") had established Knightsbridge Mills, Inc., a textile factory, in Lawrence, Massachusetts, in September 1947, to manufacture fine novelty knit fabrics. The fabrics included some that were "nubby in texture, soft and springy to the touch" for dresses under the "American Exclusives" label. Mom invested U.S. $14,000 plus another 26,700 Dutch florins (approximately $260,000 today)[57]

---

[57] *Dutch florins were fixed by the Allied liberating forces at 2.052 to the U.S. dollar. Average annual inflation from 1947 to date was approximately 3.66%.*

of her inheritance, in the factory venture in October 1947 before we even arrived in America, to purchase 480 shares of a total of 2,000 shares issued and outstanding in the Knightsbridge Mills venture.

Pop, in turn, for such investment, was granted a fee of $420 a year (approximately $4,500 today) as "advisor of the corporation" and was named a director of the Company. The factory quickly failed and ultimately Mom received $43.60 for the shares, representing the amount of the transfer taxes. Creditors received approximately 10¢ on the dollar; shareholders received nothing..

With the failure of the factory effectively as early as 1948, Pop was taken into the existing business established by his brother-in-law, Joost Jacobs, together with Mom's cousin, Bill Konijn, and a third partner, Vincent Garofallo. They had a relatively thriving 5 & 10¢ business called "Nassau Stores 5 & 10," with stores at that time in Port Washington (that was Joost Jacobs' store), Manhasset (that was Uncle Bill's store) and Hicksville, where Mr. Gary, as we called him, had the Rogers 5 and 10¢ store. Pop first worked at Uncle Bill's store, and shortly thereafter, the partners opened a new store to be run by Pop on Hempstead Turnpike in Franklin Square. The manager there was Mr. Horn, an experienced 5 and 10¢ store manager, who had fairly little patience or regard for my then-inexperienced father as his new boss. Shortly after joining the 5 and 10¢ business, Pop, with Mr. Horn as passenger, was driving in the winter in our beautiful little Standard which had crossed the ocean with us, and got into a terrible accident near St. Francis Hospital on Port Washington Boulevard, where Mr. Horn was injured and promptly commenced a lawsuit against Pop. This did not help their relationship. It also did not help our pretty little Standard. No such vehicle had ever come to the U.S. as far as we know. It was quickly replaced by a 1936 Chevrolet convertible with a rumble seat and a hand crank to help turn over the engine to start the car, when necessary, which was almost all the time. My brother and I sat in the unprotected rumble seat with no seatbelts, of course, and we enjoyed that car. Joost Jacobs in the meantime had a Dodge coupe of about the same vintage, and you'd think as owners of a growing business, they might have done a little better.

Uncle ("Oom") Joost Jacobs, Juliemarthe's husband, had perhaps the most successful of the Nassau Stores, located in Port Washington, on the north side of Main Street. There was in fact another 5 and 10¢ store at that time, Woolworth's, but Oom Joost put it out of business. Oom Joost also at one point brought back from Italy a huge and beautiful espresso machine with copper, brass and chrome all over. He placed it at the checkout counter, which, in those days, was in the middle of the store (people were trusted not to run out from the front of the store with the merchandise). He offered espresso coffee free to anyone shopping at the store. Nobody drank the stuff; it was bitter, and, therefore, tasted "un-American." Soon after its introduction the espresso machine was relegated to the basement where it eventually rusted and rotted away. We could've been Starbuck's if our timing had been a little better. In fact, if Uncle Bill, Oom Joost and Pop had gotten along, we could've been Wal-Mart because there were soon more Nassau Stores than Sam Walton had 5 and 10¢ stores in the late '60s.

I think there was always a feeling of resentment, especially by Uncle Bill, that Pop came into the business without any capital and that they essentially gave him a piece of the business. Correspondingly, Oom Joost and Uncle Bill always lived well, while Pop worked very hard for a relatively modest lifestyle. Once the "Blue Laws," restricting work at night and weekends, disappeared, he worked six days or more and at least one night a week.

They opened a new jointly-owned store on Lakeville Road in New Hyde Park for which Pop also had primary responsibility and later Pop opened a store in Bellmore. They also opened a separate Nassau Stores near Mr. Gary's Rogers store in Hicksville and, subsequently, stores in Merrick, Farmingdale and Seaford.

When they opened the Bellmore store, Pop was confronted by some (union) goons who threatened to slash the employees' tires and break the windows if he didn't agree to certain payments, etc. He then called Mr. Gary (and I assume Mr. Gary remained their partner for just such assignments, as he was not a "hands on" owner) who "took care of it" and we never heard from those people again.

I spent a part of my vacations in Uncle Bill's store in Manhasset, New York, working in the pet department, where I cleaned the fish tanks, re-stocking them with goldfish, guppies and some more exotic fish, took care of the turtles, cleaned the canary and parakeet cages and re-stocked all of the fish foods, songbird seed, etc. My favorite job actually was in Mr. Gary's store, where he permitted me to make window displays which I loved doing and which were so artistic that Mr. Gary was very proud of me. Specifically, the Nassau Stores were quite famous for their notions departments, i.e., thread, yarn, rick-rack, ribbons, patterns, sewing and darning needles, etc. I made a window display entitled, "A Stitch in Time..." and loaded the window with every conceivable kind of thread, yarn, button displays, etc. I especially loved helping to order buttons, from Mr. Schwanda, who specialized in mother-of-pearl buttons and who gave me at some point a beautiful mother-of-pearl conch shell.

The partners split up eventually. Mr. Gary retired; Uncle Bill and Oom Joost kept their own stores. Pop was permitted to buy the Bellmore store. It was part of the deal that Pop would not use the "Nassau

Stores 5 & 10" name. Pop apparently circumvented that agreement by using the name "Nassau Stores Bellmore." The purposeful retention of a closely-related name angered Uncle Bill and he cut off all further communications. This is a sad ending because Mom loved Cousin Bill, and I did too. Out of respect for Pop, I never again met Uncle Bill, though Uncle Bill and I never had a quibble. Early on, long before that ending, I wanted to show Uncle Bill my then most recent collection (as reported, I was always a collector) which consisted of pictures of female movie stars. He said that was not a good thing to do and I stopped. Who knows where that would have led?

Pop, in his Bellmore store, was greatly respected; he was a good merchandiser, kept meticulous notes, and could calculate accurately in his head. Pop had a small cadre of incredibly loyal and wonderful salesgirls, some of whom stayed with him for more than 40 years. He was like a father to them, helping them buy a home, dealing with family problems, and together with Mom, even teaching them how to drive. The salesgirls and their spouses joined my parents on many occasions for meals and evenings out to the theater. The store lost money during the last few years, kept open in large part to give the girls and my brother a living.

The 5 & 10¢ business, which for the Nassau Stores depended on non-food necessities and especially notions and cheap toys and housewares, was largely eclipsed in the small Nassau County communities by the larger drugstores and by the big-box Kmart and Wal-Mart stores, which in turn were successors to various 5 & 10¢ stores like McCrory's, McLellan's, S.S. Kresge, Woolworth's, H.L. Green and Ben Franklin stores. Today, of course, the 5 & 10's have returned in the form of "dollar stores" like Dollar Tree, Dollar General and Family Dollar stores.

Mom worked in the store as a bookkeeper several days per week, once they could no longer afford to employ an outsider. They shared offices in the basement with the excess inventory and supplies. My brother came to work for Pop and the Nassau Stores for 18 years after a 4-5 year tour in a carpet business in Longmeadow, Massachusetts and a few years at J.C. Penney.

Pop was strong-willed, as was Henk, and periodically they would almost come to blows. That's when Mom said that Pop had to get out of the store, as either she or Henk might kill him if he didn't.

Because of his enormous love of books, and encyclopedic knowledge, he was able to land a part-time job at the Manhasset Public Library. While he carried chairs and shelved books, he was, of course, an incredible resource and fount of information on most any subject. There, at the library, he had a wonderful second career, surrounded by books and adoring older ladies, for 23 years, becoming the oldest paid library employee in the country, and recognized as such with a photo in *American Libraries* magazine.

Pop was an immensely smart man, learned beyond belief in many subjects although he had never received a formal education beyond high school. He was a voracious reader, consuming untold quantities of books in Dutch, German, English and French. He especially loved French novels. He could steep himself in tomes on politics, finance, music, art, mythology, religion, theater, science, medicine, architecture, history, numismatics, or whatever you might mention that would pique his curiosity.

And if he became interested in something, he would pursue it until he had a deep understanding. Thus, for example, he travelled to Cambridge and took a course at Harvard on time measurements and standards. He would never be content with just a cursory overview, nor just enough to survive at a cocktail or dinner party, which is more my style.

One of the saddest moments in Pop's life was the passing of his brother Fritz as a result of a freak accident. Uncle Fritz, after he retired from the Pastoe furniture company founded by his uncle, Fritz Loeb, and from the Dutch furniture trade associations, remained active in the Rotary and often presented papers at local Rotary meetings in Utrecht. It was on one such lunch occasion that, after the meeting, he stepped into his car, his neighbor and best friend was in the passenger seat, and the car shot into reverse, crashed through a fence and plummeted into a canal in the heart of Utrecht, where his neighbor drowned immediately and Uncle Fritz spent several ultimately hopeless and anguished days in a coma before we lost him.

Pop was interested in clocks from his early days, and we always had special old clocks in our house. He built a large table clock from a kit with his good friend, Frank Trama, whose wife, Mimi, was one of the original salesgirls in the Bellmore store. Pop learned clock repairs from Frank and took a couple of courses on clock repairs. With his special set of tools, he became a highly-valued service provider to untold numbers of friends. He could have made a good living doing this, but he wouldn't dream of charging anyone for his services. My clocks miss him a lot. It's as if they "stopped short, never to run again when the old man died."[58]

---

[58] *From the 1875 song by Henry Clay Work, "My Grandfather's Clock."*

The Standard, our first car, bought in Holland and
subsequently totaled in the U.S.

Our '36 Chevy Convertible   Our Alfa Romeo
(with a rumble seat)

Our Rover (then referred to as "the poor man's Rolls Royce").

Our Willys-Overland Jeepster

Our Sunbeam Alpine.

Our (1956) Ford Fairlane Convertible with red and white leather seats.

The mother-of-pearl conch shell from the Schwanda salesman.

The Nassau Stores specialized in notions, including, for example, ribbon sold by the foot.

The Bellmore Store.

Jo Spier drawing to announce an expansion.

Library aide at 94
Manhasset (N.Y.) Public Library has Frank Ullman, 94, working as a library aide. He has been with the library for almost 24 years, and MPL believes he is the oldest active library employee in the country. He was born in the Netherlands and, after surviving the Nazi occupation, emigrated to the United States following the Second World War.

"American Libraries Magazine," December 2007.

The remarkably complex clock made by Pop with Frank Trama.

Pop in his 90's.

Rear view of my parents by Jo Spier for their 25th wedding anniversary.

Drawing by Kathy Ullman, Henk's prize-winning artist wife, for my parents'
50th wedding anniversary.

Brittany Taylor's Interview

I interviewed Frank Ullman. He is my great grandfather. Opa has lived in Port Washington for 59 years. Port Washihgton has changed in that there are more houses, there were no shopping centers, and there only was one grocery store where Eckerd's is on Port Washington Blvd. Main Street has stayed practically the same. Alpers, the Post Office and the movie theatre were all here. Opa likes living on the bay and that you can sleep on the train because it's the end of the line, Most of all Opa loves having a son, three grandkids, and five great grandkids who live here with him.

Brittany Taylor, oldest daughter of Valerie and Scott Taylor, was born in 1999 and arranged this interview while at the John Philip Sousa Elementary School in Port Washington.

Pop with great-granddaughter Brittany Taylor.

Chapter 25

Religion

My parents married in a Dutch synagogue, now part of the Jewish Historical Museum of Amsterdam, and both sets of grandparents were Jewish. As described, my parents had a very difficult time in WWII, solely because they were Jewish, and many friends and relatives were killed at the hands of the Nazis. Yet my parents, and in turn, my brother and I, and all our respective offspring did not pursue our Jewish heritage or a Jewish religious congregation when we settled in the U.S. We basically let our Judaism lapse. One of the explanations for not pursuing Judaism, or indeed any religion, given to me once by a survivor, was that it was very hard to believe in a righteous God after what happened to them during the Holocaust. It is estimated that some 25% of the Jews remaining in Holland after WWII "lost their religion." Many said that "God had left them" or, conversely, "I left God in Auschwitz-Birkenau." In the case of my parents, and also, I should add, Jo Spier and his family, and indeed others in my parents' extended family, I think it was their intent to start anew in the U.S. in an effort to become assimilated and also perhaps to explore new avenues of religious pursuits.

My Aunt Juliemarthe was quite anxious to have my parents join her synagogue. Juliemarthe had been a founding member of the Community Synagogue, a reform Jewish congregation in Port Washington which was permitted to purchase, after contentious lawsuits, "The

Chimneys," the former Fleischmann (margerine) estate in Sands Point, a part of Port Washington, subject to closing down the swimming pool, squash courts, and bowling alley in the building. The Chimneys had previously been the residence of the Commander of the Naval Special Devices Center where the Navy tested various underwater devices. Juliemarthe was not only a founder, but the first president of the synagogue's Hadassah women's group. While not intending to hurt her feelings, I think my parents, especially Pop, did not wish to have Juliemarthe, no matter how well intended, direct their lives.

My parents then and thus sought alternative comfort in some form of religion. While Pop never talked about his relationship with God, if any, Mom always affirmed her religiosity and definitely said she believed in God. At our early ages, Henk and I followed my parents, and their route became very easy for us. They found compassion and comfort early on (by 1950) with a very small Unitarian congregation in Port Washington.

Within the Port Washington congregation, which was established in 1945 with a handful of families, they especially admired the minister, Gerald Weary and his wife Alma.

Jerry Weary was a true intellectual who delivered insightful, thoughtful and thought-provoking sermons on a wide range of social issues. He and Alma and their two children lived in a relatively large private home, where the services were held, on Murray Avenue in Port Washington. Sunday school was held in the basement and, as far as I can recall, Sunday school consisted only of artwork and clay figures which we crafted with the help of Dan and Aida Whedon. He was a printmaker; she was a prodigious artist who produced many whimsical pictures of Port Washington which are prized possessions on the walls of many homes in Port Washington, including those of all of our family.

According to my brother and at least one of the Hartog daughters, my parents were also very much influenced in their embrace of Unitarianism by their very close Dutch friends living in Scarsdale, Jo and Ada Hartog, who immigrated to the US in 1948 and who right at the outset became staunch Unitarians. We visited them often. My brother spent hours rolling down the double hills in their backyard with the Hartog girls, Anna and Fay. Fay (Fay Hartog-Levin) later served as US Ambassador to the Netherlands from 2009 to 2011.

Unitarianism or not, my brother and I were not allowed to have a regular Christmas tree, presumably as a nod to my parents' Jewishness. Reluctantly, I was granted permission to have a small 12" (fake) tree ("Hanukkah bush") in my room.

We did, however, celebrate Christmas with presents. As Pop had a 5 & 10¢ store, we had access to unlimited quantities of styrofoam, ribbons, pipe cleaners, glitter, and Christmas decorations of all sorts including Santa Clauses and reindeer of all sizes, angels, crèches, etc. With such items, Henk and I made elaborate gifts. We also had access to boxes of all shapes and sizes, so that we could create a series of boxes inside one another like a Russian matryoshka doll set, until you reached the smallest one with the present.

The presents themselves, we found, as did our children after us, in the very Nassau Stores owned by our parents. We would comb the aisles and all the counters until we found just the right present in their own store, which, predictably, they usually returned to the relevant bin after Christmas, hopefully for successful resale.

In the Dutch tradition of creating poems for most any occasion, we also made poems with our presents, often hinting clearly what the present might be. This could also give rise to severe disappointments. Henk once received a very large box from Pop, with indications that he could sit in the present inside the box, it floats, his friends could also sit in it, etc. Henk thought he was getting a boat - it turned out to be a Rubbermaid garbage pail.

In Holland we celebrated the precursor to Santa Claus, *Sinterklaas*, a shortened form of *Sint Nikolaas* (St. Nicholas), who comes from Spain on December 5th every year with a golden staff and a white horse. He is believed to ride on rooftops and to drop presents down chimneys where they land in (wooden) shoes. *Sinterklaas* is accompanied in these endeavors by a Moorish black helper, *Swarte Piet* (Black Pete). While now being questioned as to political correctness, many Dutch folks dressed up as *Swarte Piet* in blackface, including store employees and bank tellers, for example, on December 5. Henk thoroughly believed in *Sinterklaas* and *Swarte Piet* until the neighboring worldly Bobby and Billy Hickey made nasty fun of Henk's beliefs, which he ultimately gave up reluctantly; the abuse and humiliation at the hands of the Hickeys bothers Henk to this day.

Gerald Weary, himself and his small flock of Unitarians, were as poor as a church mouse. The congregation consisted at that point in the late forties, early fifties of only perhaps a dozen families.

Unitarianism, moreover, was not a clearly defined religion. The reference to unity was in the sense of monotheism, worship of a single God. Unlike traditional Protestant denominations, Unitarianism rejects the concept of Christ and the Holy Spirit as part of God as three persons-holy trinity. Jesus is viewed as a great person and prophet, but nothing more.

The Unitarianism of Murray Avenue in Port Washington was probably much more liberal than that of Boston, for example, where the movement was headquartered, which was reportedly much closer to Protestantism and New England-style Puritanism. I know we sang a lot, never about the Holy Trinity, of course, but mostly about the beauty of the earth and of the skies, which "all around us lies." The Unitarian congregation eventually merged with the Universalists (to form the "U-U") and became even more liberal, which in fact may not have suited Mom very well, although Pop always thrived in the Congregation's discussion groups, usually taking the conservative (straight *Wall Street Journal* editorial pages) line.

At the funeral service for Pop at the U-U, Henk and I chose, among other things, the Thanksgiving hymn, "We Gather Together," based on the Dutch hymn, *"Wilt Heden nu Treden,"* because we all loved it, and it was one of the few hymns we identified with our exposure to the Unitarian Church. Much to our consternation, and I think my parents would have been equally dismayed, the hymn, presumably after merger of the Unitarian and Universalist Congregations, had been revised to take out the references to "God." Thus, the phrases "to ask the Lord's blessings, he hastens and chastens his will to make known…" have all been taken out after the words "We gather together…" of this most wonderful and famous hymn, and replaced with some kind of agnostic pablum.

In the early 50's, Caroline Veatch, widow of a geologist for a major company, who lived one block from the Weary's, and had befriended/ felt sorry for, Jerry Weary, and who was not herself a member of the Congregation, offered to Jerry, a small royalty interest in an oil and gas concession, which her husband had acquired for himself, in Germany. It threw off at the time only $100 or so per annum and she was glad to give it to Jerry if he wanted it.

Jerry then arranged to have Jim Nickerson, a partner at the law firm Dewey Ballantine Bushby Palmer & Wood, assign the royalty interest to the Church. That interest, now having given rise to the

Veatch program, which was founded in 1959, generates tens of millions of dollars a year for the Church, and provides grants for all sorts of social, civic and charitable pursuits. It has a large staff, a board of directors, etc. It still provides funding reportedly for an overwhelming portion of the costs of the entire UU movement. It also provided an endowed chair at the Harvard Divinity School, funding for the Freedom National Bank, etc. Most significantly it permitted the Congregation to buy the Payson estate on Shelter Rock Road in Plandome/Manhasset and to build an enormous church, incorporating a beautiful mansion on that gorgeous estate. Mom was a trustee of the Congregation for a brief period which may not have extended beyond a year. I think she was disgusted and upset about the gap between religious thought and principles on the one hand, and the money being thrown around by the Trustees, especially in contrast to how they treated Gerald Weary.

Jerry Weary was forced out in 1958. Jerry's problem was apparently that he was too intellectual and that he didn't minister enough to his congregants, including visits to the ill and needy. He and Alma and their two kids retired in Maine, where he lived in almost abject poverty until Mom went strongly to bat for him with the church and the Veatch fund to give him at least a modest pension. This man, after all, arranged the transfer of the royalty interest which made the Church wealthy beyond belief (it even has at least 3 ministers simultaneously, each earning six figures plus housing allowances, etc.). Yet they were not willing, until swayed by her efforts, to give him the honor and decency of having a livable pension in his retirement. Mom, Pop and the Weary's, including their children, Bill and Kathy, remained friends for the rest of their lives.

When Kay and I married in 1960, we did so in the Unitarian

Church, then located on Plandome Road in Manhasset. (Kay and her parents were Methodist, although she and her father spent several years in the Congregational Church in Manhasset and taught Sunday school there). We asked that Jerry Weary officiate at our wedding. The new minister, Robert Hadley, would not permit it. Mr. Hadley officiated; Kay and I had never met him. Henk and Kathy, however, in 1970 were married by Jerry Weary (not at the Unitarian Church; rather, in an artist/performance studio on Bayview Avenue in Port Washington with a stage where Aida Whedon's daughter performed and arranged puppet shows).

My parents ultimately retired, and happily spent their last score-plus years in Hadley House, an apartment building in Port Washington, built and owned by the Unitarian/Universalist Congregation, and, of course, named after Reverend Hadley, who, together with his wife, Shirley, retired to the same Hadley House and ultimately became close friends of my parents.

My brother and all my male cousins (Hans Warendorf, Robert, Joost and Eric Ullmann and Herman Jacobs) all married non-Jewish (all but one blond) women. Our daughters Laura and Susan, married husbands who were Jewish by birth, but none of them pursued religion after marriage. Valerie married a Catholic young man, and they, too, have not further pursued any religion.

I became devoted to Holocaust remembrance and tolerance education activities. I was active in, and headed, the Anne Frank Center in the U.S. for many years and people always assumed I was Jewish and would wish for me all sorts of things in Hebrew, thinking I would know what they were talking about. I generally answered, "and the same to you and your family," which seemed to work.

In junior high and high school, my Jewish background was never an issue. At Andover, especially through the efforts of a couple of nasty classmates, I was made very much aware of my Jewishness (there were only 7 or so of us in our class of 212). At Sullivan & Cromwell, a very spiffy law firm, I was one of only a group of 2 or 3 associates who were Jewish, and I felt it. Of course, this has all changed, and yet I feel that I'm really missing something in the way of background and culture.

With hindsight, having regard to my Jewish forebears and heritage, and my strong continuing feelings of Jewish ethnic identity, I feel strongly that I have missed learning Hebrew and becoming much more familiar with Jewish religion, history and culture. Yet, much as the choices made early in my life, it remains easier to avoid the efforts and demands. I thus will probably never go to Hebrew School, nor will I be formally Bar Mitzvah'd, although I've been told many times, it's never too late.

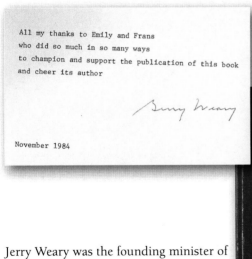

All my thanks to Emily and Frans
who did so much in so many ways
to champion and support the publication of this book
and cheer its author

November 1984

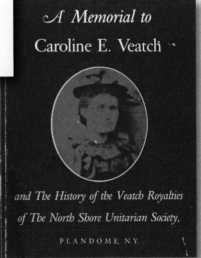

A Memorial to
Caroline E. Veatch

and The History of the Veatch Royalties
of The North Shore Unitarian Society,

PLANDOME, N.Y.

Jerry Weary was the founding minister of the North Shore Unitarian Congregation. The Veatch Fund, created during his tenure, ultimately generated enormous revenues for the congregation and the movement.

The original North Shore Unitarian Church at 8 Murray Avenue in Port Washington (demolished many years ago).

Jerry and Alma Weary, in their retirement.

Aida Whedon, local artist and member of the North Shore Unitarian Church, guided teachers and children for many years in the use of art. Above is a fresco painted by one class studying ancient Egypt. She helped me with the Sphinx. Aida described the church school as "a den of creativity!"

Chapter 26

Finding My Way

Citizenship

Together with my parents and brother, after the requisite 5-year residency and passing a perfunctory test on U.S. history, I was sworn in by a Federal District Court judge as a U.S. citizen in 1953. As important a milestone as that is, and was, after leaving Holland and seeking a new life in America, it left little impression. I had already considered myself American and this was but a seemingly routine legitimation.

Even though we are now fully U.S. citizens, under our U.S. Constitution neither Henk nor I can become President (unlike a natural-born American). I've been hoping since 1953 for an amendment to the Constitution to correct this patent inequity, historically based on perceived risks of loyalties to foreign governments at the birth of our republic hundreds of years ago, but it is unlikely to happen in time for either of us, or even Arnold Schwarzenegger, to be elected.

7th through 10th Grades in Port Washington's Public Schools

The junior high school experience was marked by "tracking," where we were placed in groups based on test metrics, ranging from 1A to 2C (there might have been a 3A for a couple of n'er-do-wells, I don't think it went lower than that). I found myself in group 1B, while some really smart folks were put in 1A. I'd been in the U.S. for 3 years at that point, and thought, but wasn't sure, that I could've, perhaps should've, been in 1A. The problem with tracking, of course, is that you're effectively slotted, basically forever in your own mind, and in the mind of others, in a group where you are immediately aware, or made aware, that you are not as smart as other students in your class. In fact, you are potentially considered either "dumber" than the next person, or absolutely "dumb."

The junior high school also introduced me to the concept of hall police, consisting of peers. I was once skipping stairs and given a "ticket." That same afternoon, I was taken before a jury of peers and a faculty advisor. I decided to plead not guilty, as I thought it was just his word against mine. This was not smart. There was a lesson here that I learned much later in Traffic Court: the judge usually believes the policeman. At any rate, I received a huge dose of after-school detention for being a wise guy, which I took with my by-then-typical sullenness toward the exercise of authority.

A unique institution in our early Junior High (7th grade) days was ("ballroom") dancing school. This was not the girls' ballet or modern dance schools that exist today. Rather, it was an expected part of co-ed social upbringing. While, of course, not mandatory, enrollment was expected. There were two dance schools in those days: Mrs. Powers' and Mrs. Reid's schools. Mrs. Powers' school was generally thought of as the, say, middle class' sanctuary, whereas Mrs. Reid, the mentor of the more upscale school, had, for example, among her pupils, Ronnie Como (son of crooner, Perry Como, one of Sands Point's most renowned residents).[59] Also, Kay Marbut (remember that name) went to Mrs. Reid's school.

Both schools required boys to wear suits and girls to wear dresses, and the two genders lined up on opposite sides of the room. Girls at that age, even without heels, were often taller, and certainly more mature, than the boys. The essential teaching difference between the two schools was that Mrs. Powers taught the "fox trot" (toe-heel, toe-heel, backstep) and Mrs. Reid taught the "Lindy." The functional difference was that Mrs. Powers had no control over the boys and we would disappear for long stretches to the (duck pin) bowling alley in the lower floor of the Masonic Lodge building. Mrs. Reid, whose studio was an appendage to a modest house, could offer no such diversion.

Because of the essential social class differences, we at Mrs. Powers' school sought periodically to start a rumble with the Reid group (the two schools were only a few blocks apart) especially because they had the aforementioned Ronnie Como (who, incidentally, attended private Catholic school), but it never became serious, and, of course, we didn't have either guts or guns (and our Moms were there to pick us up).

We were very late in getting a television and we acquired it only when we moved to the new house (and then only because it was a gift to us kids from Grootmoeder). It was confined to the basement with a "rabbit ear" antenna, and we therefore had mostly snow on the screen. Of course, we had only black and white, whenever we were able to coax a picture on the screen. I therefore looked forward to

---

[59] *Perry Como's weekly television shows and holiday specials over a period of 50 years were immensely popular, and he recorded a zillion songs, such as "Catch a Falling Star," "A Bushel and a Peck," "A-You're Adorable," "Don't Blame Me," "Frosty the Snowman," etc.*

being babysat after school at Juliemarthe's house, where I could watch television for hours, joining cousins Herman, Bertien and Emily.

On TV, I was mesmerized by the Army-McCarthy hearings in 1954 and I watched them for hours on end, rooting for Joseph Welch, the Boston lawyer, against Senator McCarthy and Roy Cohn, and their ruthless witch-hunt of Communists and homosexuals, where one session gave rise to the famous challenge by Welch to McCarthy, "Have you no sense of decency?" He didn't.

In 1954 during my sophomore year in high school, we moved to a new split-level home designed largely by Pop from architectural magazines. The house cost $25,000 to build and featured a special front door with panels carved by my parents' Unitarian friend, Elmer Tangerman, and a door knob in the middle of the door, in a very attractive area of town, with a view of New York,[60] right behind what is now Port Washington's Schreiber High School.

The new house was in another part of town and we all had to make new friends. For me, once again, this happened through basketball with neighboring kids.

Through the very smart and capable son, Kees (Cornelis), of my parents' friends, the Willems's in Holland (Kees attended and lectured at the Harvard Business School), my parents came to learn about Phillips Academy in Andover, Massachusetts, a leading private prep school. He convinced them that I wasn't being challenged sufficiently in the local schools, and I should go there. My parents, of course, had no clue and knew little or nothing about prep schools.

---

[60] *Until the lot across the street was sold, after my parents had the first crack at it, for what-they-believed-to-be, the outrageous price of $5,000, and our view of New York City was lost forever. Typically for my parents, the new owners became life-long friends.*

At a given moment, my parents thus suggested that they wanted me to go to prep school. I, in turn, also knew little or nothing about prep schools. The few kids I knew who had gone off to prep schools were mostly troublemakers who needed discipline. Indeed, this was the very reason in my mind that my parents wanted me to go to prep school; I misbehaved a lot in school and I needed the discipline. I was sure that prep school was a form of punishment and I surely did not want to go.

We eventually took a trip to visit Hotchkiss, Deerfield and Andover. Hotchkiss, with a golf course and all those tennis courts, was clearly much too spiffy for us, though the people there were very nice. Deerfield was great, but Andover was wow, wow, wow. What a campus! Very few colleges have a campus (or endowment) like that! I had no idea as to, and certainly did not fairly appreciate, the sacrifice my parents were willing to undertake to give to me the opportunity to attend Andover.

Andover 11th Grade: '55-'56

I arrived for my Upper Middle year (11th grade) with my parents, scared out of my mind. The school is overwhelming. It is the most gorgeous campus with facilities and amenities beyond comprehension. There's a separate building for most every academic topic, ancient languages, English, physics and chemistry, music, etc. Then there is an archaeology museum (Peabody), a renowned art gallery (Addison), an arboretum, a bell tower with a world class carillon, libraries (Oliver Wendell Holmes), a dining Commons, a huge chapel (Cochran), a (former) Treadway hotel on campus, a little building with ice cream and pool tables (this became a real favorite), etc. In my day there was an enormous (and I'll assert beyond normal) emphasis on sports and, of course, suitable facilities such as the indoor and outdoor ice hockey rinks, an indoor cage for winter track, swimming and diving pools, squash courts, indoor gyms for wrestling, boxing, basketball, etc. and acres upon acres of fields for other sports.

When we arrived at the school, we went immediately to the relatively small dorm, Abbot House, where I was to spend my first year. We were met by our housemaster, Dr. James Grew, head of the French language department, who introduced the then-revolutionary concept of teaching a foreign language, even from the first day, using only the foreign language. My parents, who of course, were fluent in French, loved Dr. Grew immediately. I think I disliked him from the first moment, probably because he lisped.

Academically at Andover that first year, I did really well (much to the consternation of Dr. Grew, who made extraordinary efforts to saddle me with demerits for transgressions like walking on the grass, or not being properly dressed for morning (daily) chapel, to the point where I'd have to leave the school), concentrating in anything but science.

I wound up fifth in the class of some 212 kids and thus became part of the "Junior Eight" in the *Cum Laude* society. This basically meant in those days that I could pick my college, but more importantly at the time, I had my choice of dormitories for the following year, and I thus picked Revere North, where the English teacher and athletic director (and hockey and baseball coach) Ted Harrison, was the housemaster. This was significant in the jock-oriented atmosphere at Andover, and, even more critical, especially in winter, it was just 75 feet from the Commons where we had breakfast, lunch and dinner, whereas most residential dorms were much further away, and the to and fro in winter could be brutal.

Ted and his wife, Marge, became surrogate parents for me and I viciously abused the privilege they accorded to their dorm charges to visit with them nightly if we had done our homework (and if we had straightened our room).[61]

We had to wear jackets to all classes and to daily chapel. We also had mandatory sports every day for 2 hours from 2 to 4 and our varsity sports teams played almost exclusively against freshman teams from primarily New England colleges (Harvard, Dartmouth, Brown, Williams, Bowdoin, Middlebury, etc.) In those days, colleges still had freshmen teams in most sports, and freshmen could not be on college varsity teams. Thus, if you were good in sports you were a hero to your classmates at Andover and if you were spiffy to boot, you could join the a capella singing group, which was really cool because those guys were allowed to go to the girls' schools.

I'd like to mention just two classmates, though I could go on forever.

The guy I (and I believe quite a few others) really disliked, other than one fellow I won't name who used to hurl nasty anti-Semitic slurs at me (especially while I was trying to hit a cue ball in pool or billiards after lunch or dinner), was Ted Forstmann, whose death from brain cancer in 2012 was the subject of worldwide media attention (front page of both *The New York Times* and *Wall Street Journal*). In retrospect this could have been jealousy, because Ted was well to do, he was a star back on the football team, goalie on the hockey team and very good in the spiffy game of tennis (notice the outsized sports focus, certainly on my part). Many of us felt that Ted, who was nearly last in the class (but he nevertheless went to Yale) was probably least likely to succeed after Andover. Irony would have it that Ted became

---

[61] *If we didn't adequately straighten our room, a problem generally not faced more than once, but one certainly faced by my roommate, Ted would come in and literally turn everything, including bed frames and chests of drawers, upside down.*

one of the world's richest men, as head of one of the original leveraged buyout firms, and of IMG (International Management Group), which managed all sorts of famous athletes and media entertainment types. Ted himself never married, but he was linked romantically with Princess Diana and many other high-profile women. He was also immensely charitable for lots of thoughtful causes (other than Andover) (not that giving to Andover was mandatory). In my mind, where would Teddy (or indeed many others of us) have been, but for Andover?

By contrast, a guy clearly guaranteed to succeed, perhaps even become President, the only adult man among us boys, a big guy with hair on his chest, president of the class and of every organization that counted, a brilliant student, fine athlete, and son of the president of one of the most prestigious universities in the country, came back to our 25th reunion as an emaciated divorced Buddhist monk with a shaved head.

Back to Holland for a Summer Internship

For a four- or five-week period the summer between 11th grade and senior year at Andover, I was able to arrange a job at De Bijenkorf department store in Amsterdam, the very store where my father worked before and after he was terminated by the Nazis. De Bijenkorf, as earlier indicated, was co-founded by Arthur Isaac, the father of Aunt Nellie, the wife of Uncle Harry Loeb, who was the brother of my paternal grandmother, Oma Aenni. The store in Amsterdam was run by Hans Isaac, Aunt Nellie's brother; the stores in Rotterdam and The Hague were run by two other brothers, Fritz and Hugo Isaac. The brothers were essentially midgets, perhaps 4 feet tall, if that. In any event, Hans Isaac arranged the job with considerable reluctance. A summer job for a student, much less an American student, in an over-populated, highly-regulated and union-controlled country, was simply unheard of and not done. I therefore had to deal with the company's in-house lawyer, Ms. Charlotte ("Lotje") Aarts, who had worked at De Bijenkorf starting shortly after the War. She managed my way through the immigration difficulties. Amazingly, that same Ms. Aarts would marry Uncle Harry and Aunt Nellie's son, Arthur, later that year.[62] Aunt Nellie, Uncle Harry, Arthur and his brother Otto, were among the relatives who were able to escape to the U.S. via England by fishing boat in 1940.

In 1954, Arthur, who had been working and teaching at M.I.T. in computer science, was retained by the University of Utrecht in Holland for a one-year term to set up a computer program for the University. While there, he attended a choral concert in Amsterdam and was seated next to Ms. Aarts. On their first date they truly made music together (Arthur played the harpsichord and Lotje sang). Two years later they married and Lotje joined Arthur in Cambridge, Massachusetts.

Arthur became a brilliant teacher at Harvard and an early expert in combining art and computer design. He was a close collaborator of both Buckminster Fuller (of geodesic dome fame) and the artist M. C. Escher. Arthur was featured on the cover of *Harvard Magazine* as the "Polyhedral Arthur Loeb." He taught both Burgundian History and Crystallography, for example, while he and Lotje served as house-masters of Dudley House at Harvard.

Uncle Harry and Aunt Nellie, until Harry retired, lived in an apartment just off Harvard Square in Cambridge, Massachusetts, and just a couple of blocks from Arthur and Lotje, whose home, cluttered with

---

[62] *I, in turn, ultimately became a trustee under both Arthur's and Lotje's wills and they remained good friends throughout our lives.*

unbelievable piles of paper everywhere in the basement, kitchen, bathrooms, study, sun porch, etc. was on Shepard Street. Harry and Nellie, upon retirement, concluded that the old-age social welfare benefits were much better in Holland than in the U.S., so they returned to Holland and purchased a home in Laaren, some 15 miles from Amsterdam, right by a large heather field, which, when in bloom, was spectacular.

Upon Arthur's death, I, as trustee under his will, together with his executor (a young lawyer who Lotje and Arthur had met only briefly), ultimately arranged to have his studio transferred basically intact to the Rhode Island School of Design; his baroque musical instrument collection (viola da gambas, recorders, harpsichords, lutes, etc.), which required a climate-controlled atmosphere, went to Holyoke College and a Calder mobile to the National Museum. I wound up with a painting of Arthur made by the well-known Dutch artist, Jan Sluyters, which I surely didn't want, but Pop did. After Pop's passing, I now again have it (in a closet). Neither the Singer Museum in Laaren, nor his brother Otto, wanted it. The Singer Museum, in declining the gift, advised that every rich Dutch Jewish family commissioned Jan Sluyters to paint portraits of their children, and the museum already had a ton of them.

My summer job at De Bijenkorf that summer of '56 was in the "Calculatie," the basement inventory storage area, where I spent most of my time unpacking crates of ceramic tiles and pottery from Italy. I worked my butt off, including nights and overtime plus Saturday mornings, because I didn't want to be an embarrassment to either the United States of America or Hans Isaac, the boss, who came by once or twice to see how I was doing, which in turn impressed my co-workers.

A special treat every morning was the herring cart which rolled into our area and served fresh raw herring with chopped raw onions for the workers. We smelled like hell for the rest of the day, but it was a sweaty job to begin with, and the Dutch folks did not necessarily bathe that often.

At the end of my stay and my weeks of very hard work at De Bijenkorf, I was called in to Hans Isaac's splendid office where he thanked me for my hard work and for the example I set. He then handed me a gift certificate, to be used in the store, for 25 guilders, which I used to buy a small camera. I figured it amounted to compensation of approximately 3 cents per hour.

Senior Year, the Last Year of my Childhood

Junior and senior years in high school these days are fraught with tension and fear, as students and their parents worry about college admission and indeed their entire future. We never had these worries at Andover. More than half the students in the class, 76 plus 35, respectively, went to Yale and Harvard. Another baker's dozen went to Princeton, and a half dozen to Stanford. I have no recollection of PSATs, SATs, APs or anything of the sort. I just knew I was in, and so did everyone else with half-way decent grades. This, of course, included, in classes before and after me, George Bush Sr. and George Bush Jr. It was easy. In those days Harvard and Yale's entering classes were more-than-half-filled with private school grads, and most of those, in turn were WASPs. I often think how unfair it is that I got into Harvard with no effort, largely because of Andover, while my grandkids, for example, who are so much smarter and know so much, and who, as anyone will note, are infinitely more mature and socially accomplished than I was, may never have that chance.

Andover, as a boys school at that time, did not exactly provide much guidance as to dealing with the opposite gender. Unless you were a star in a musical (I only played the cello in the orchestra pit) and got to sing and even kiss a young lady from Bradford Junior College, there was virtually no interaction with the fairer sex. Abbot Academy, a girl's school next to Andover, was completely off limits (it has since merged with Andover in 1973 to create a co-ed Andover). We were confronted with guaranteed demerits if we even walked to town on the Abbot side of the street.

The one chance we had with girls during senior year was the senior prom. This was the chance for each of us, as in 11th grade, to showcase a trophy date. I decided to ask the Port Washington high school queen, cheerleader and all-around popular and attractive Susan Martineau. We were both excited about the event and Susan talked about the invitation to her homeroom friend, Kay Marbut (remember that name) who had the desk next to Susan's. I don't remember much about the dance, but I do remember taking Sue to a Catholic Church service, which was a new and unique experience for me, and I was especially humbled by the number of times that the collection plate came by, and feeling obligated to impress Sue with yet another magnanimous contribution.

A couple of weeks later, after a relatively unmemorable graduation from Andover, Sue was my date back in Port Washington, at the Paul D. Schreiber High School senior prom, the Senior Gambol, and that was a bit of a disaster, as by then she had a new and serious boyfriend, who, believe it or not, was only in 11th grade, but he was the football quarterback. A cello player cannot compete under those circumstances.

I was nervous about my appearance for the Gambol, so that after shaving myself I felt that there was still noticeable stubble. I decided then to go to the barber and get my first and only barber shave ever. The barber could not suppress his giggle, and I came out fairly bloodied. That evening, which was a hot day in June, I appeared in my Harris Tweed that Opa brought for me when I went to Andover, and, had little to do with poor Susie.

The morning after the Gambol, Sue connected with her 11th grade boyfriend and went to Jones Beach, while I went to a pool party at a house in Sands Point, where I met and started chatting up the previously-referenced Kay Marbut. The rest, as they say, is history.

That same Miss Marbut and I married in 1960 between our junior and senior years in college and have been married some 54 years at this writing, with four kids, three sons-in-law and seven grandkids. All are doing well. I can hear Mom now again saying, "We made it; we beat Hitler."

De Bijenkorf department store on Dam Square opposite the Queen's palace and fronted by the War Monument. This store chain was co-founded by Aunt Nellie's father. My father worked there before, during (until terminated) and after the War. I worked there in the summer of '56.

ELLIS ISLAND
1892–1992

The Statue of Liberty–Ellis Island Foundation, Inc.

proudly presents this

Official Certificate of Registration

in

THE AMERICAN IMMIGRANT WALL OF HONOR

to officially certify that

LEO S. ULLMAN

who came to America from

THE NETHERLANDS

is among those courageous men and women who came to this country in search of personal freedom, economic opportunity and a future of hope for their families.

Lee A. Iacocca
The Statue of Liberty–Ellis Island
Foundation, Inc.

LIBERTY
1886–1986

Mr. Iacocca, for a few dollars spent on a brick, confirming my immigrant status.

LEOPOLD ULLMAN

"Luigi" . . . hobby is music . . . likes basketball . . . enjoys English and French . . . outstanding feature is "crazy mixed up hair".

My 9th grade Port Washington Junior High bio. The hair is no longer even the slightest feature.

My certificate of citizenship.

The home at 11 Ridge Drive in Port Washington, designed by Pop, to which we moved in 1954. That house, situated on a lot of less than 10,000 sq. ft. and improved with a couple of dormers, was sold in late 2014 at, believe it or not, $1.19m.

The cover of this book by Elmer Tangerman features one of the 8 panels on the door.

The front door of our home at 11 Ridge Drive with 8 panels carved by Elmer Tangerman.

Port Washington's High School in the '40's.

Carrie P. Weber Middle School now (the same building).

Port Washington's Paul D. Schreiber High School (opened in 1953).

Samuel Phillips Hall, Phillips Academy, Andover.

The Oliver Wendell Holmes Library, Phillips Academy, Andover.

LEO SALOMON ULLMAN
"Luigi"
11 Ridge Drive, Port Washington, N. Y.

Harvard   Upper
July 14, 1939   Paul Revere Hall

Cum Laude   Press Club 4
First Honor Roll (2 terms)   Phillips Society   3
Second Honor Roll (1 term)   Orchestra 4
Vice-President of Orchestra 4   J.V. Football 4

My Andover '57 yearbook bio. Classmates, regrettably, remember me only for the cello. The nickname, luckily, did not stick.

Mom at Andover.

Marianne and Cornelis ("Kees") Willems.

Arthur Loeb - one of the most brilliant men I've ever known, as well as beloved mentor and colleague to the many people he touched (and he's a cousin).

Arthur and Lotje Loeb performing Burgundian medieval music, the sight of which put Mom in uncontrolled laughter.

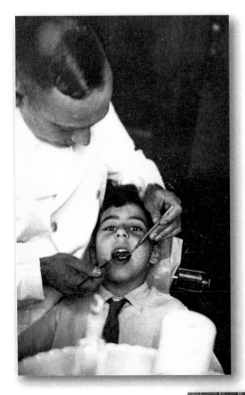

Uncle Harry (Herbert Loeb)
working on some important
teeth.

Hans Isaac (director of De
Bijenkorf) with Uncle Harry
at our home on Ridge Drive.

Mom with Monique and Leontine Van Lent, daughters of Joost Jacobs' brother, Leo (born Jacobs) and Ilse van Lent. Leontine (many years earlier) was my Junior Prom date at Andover.

Sue Martineau, my Andover Senior Prom and Port Washington Senior Gambol date, in her cheerleading outfit.

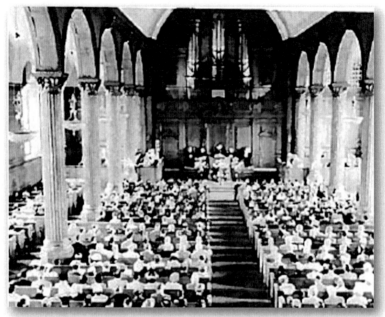

The inside of Cochran Chapel at Andover where we had to attend
Chapel every day before class, with attendance taken and demerits
given for failure to attend. It now houses the Steinway concert grand
piano donated by Kay and me in honor of Frank and Emily Ullman.

"Brigadoon" at Andover with the young ladies from Bradford Junior
College. Regrettably, I was only in the orchestra pit.

Here's a good friend in my dorm smoking in our chimney, a clearly serious demeritorious offense.

Another friend on our bike trip from Andover to Port Washington

Leo at Andover ('57).

Do not let the smile fool you. This man, my first housemaster at Andover, was definitely not a friend.

"Ted" was a wonderful housemaster and, together with his wife, Marge, a powerful personal anchor in my senior year at Andover.

JAMES H. GREW
Harvard, A.B.
Docteur de Lettres
de l'Université de
Paris
Head of the French
Department and
Instructor in French
Appointed 1935

FRED H. HARRISON
Yale, A.B.
Trinity, A.M.
Instructor in English
and Director of Athletics
Appointed 1952

Yale University May 3, 1958

Dear Leo,

" This is what little girls are made of :

95 % water , carbon , phosphorus manganese

Sodium , nitrogen , and a few trace elements .

Whoever started that rumor about sugar and

Spice obviously doesn't know the first

Thing about fundamental biological principles. "

I don't remember where I found this little ditty but it sums up my feelings on the subject perfectly. Some little bitch gave me gas two days ago.

I saw Teeter this morning and he looked rocky as ever. When I went up

A note from my Andover roommate during his first year at Yale fairly describing what the other gender is made of (a discovery after attending Andover, a then boys school)

Epilogue

Mom passed away on October 25 (Pop's birthday), 2000. She had learned of an aggressive brain tumor some three weeks or so beforehand, and rather than any measures to delay or comfort the result, she undertook to say "goodbye" to all her friends and relatives, which, as we'd expect, she did with style and grace.

Her last whispered words to Pop, Henk and me, repeated often through her lifetime, were those of the beloved chanteuse, Edith Piaf, *"Je ne regret rien,"* and she meant it.

When she had taken that last breath, Pop bathed her entire body in lotion before she was taken away.

Pop had always maintained that if Mom predeceased him, he would "slit his wrists." He must have forgotten, as he lived another ten years, and they were very fulfilling years. In addition to his work at the Manhasset Library, he enjoyed the wonderful companionship of the lovely Lilyan Strassman, some 18 years his junior, and looking much younger than that, who shared Pop's love of music and learning. They met at the Unitarian-Universalist Congregation where Lilyan was a member of the choir. She later also obtained an apartment at Hadley House and remained incredibly supportive, even during the last year when Pop's memory and physical abilities rapidly declined.

Fortunately, Henk, my son Frank (Pop's namesake) and I were only minutes away on a daily basis and Pop had the benefit of an extremely thoughtful and caring aide, Dennis Montales.

Young Frank was especially a favorite with Pop. He spent many, many hours with Pop, and joined him in a bridge game for months. Whenever I called Pop to tell him I was coming over, he'd always ask if Frank was coming, and, if not, the disappointment was palpable.

Pop passed away peacefully on July 25, 2010, nearly reaching 97 years of age. Among his last words, a few, too, at that age, were remarkable, such as "I'm too young to die."

Mom and Pop were both cremated and their ashes were buried under a rock to mark the spot at the house they built on Spruce Lake in Vermont, just minutes from the Marlboro Music Festival that Mom and Pop loved so much, and where they spent so many joyful and peaceful days together over a period of 30 years. Henk, Kay and I were joined by Pop and Mom's youngest granddaughter, Valerie (Taylor), and by three Taylor great-grandchildren, Brittany, Leah and Kevin, when we (mostly Henk) buried Pop's ashes next to Mom's. We also left little stones on the rock, under which my parents' ashes are buried, as we do whenever we're at the house in Vermont, to let them know we still think of them.

A matter that I wish to address and it's one often asked of Mom, Pop, Henk and me, is, "what do [we] [now] think of Germans?" I think our answer has always been the same: we cannot blame the next generations for the faults and misdeeds of their forefathers. Yet, somehow, and we acknowledge that it's largely irrational, as we deal, directly or indirectly, with all sorts of German products, persons and entities, we wouldn't dream of buying a Volkswagen , BMW, or, of all things, a Mercedes. Those big ticket items (even though we could hide behind their superior engineering) are still associated in our minds, for better or worse, with the bad times. My parents, for the same reasons, would also not travel to Germany. The foregoing notwithstanding, Pop always had, and loved, his German Leica camera.

On a personal note and somewhat along the lines parallel to the question of our attitude towards Germans, is the question of our attitude toward those Dutchmen, who, as Nazis or Nazi collaborators, were such despots towards Jews and "good" Dutchmen. I can't possibly carry a grudge against people I didn't know and who, as far as I know, never hurt me. Nevertheless, it is probably surprising that I have had a long friendship, arising initially out of a business relationship, with Gimbert Rost van Tonningen, one of the nicest and certainly non-judgmental persons I have ever known. His father and mother were perhaps the most notorious Nazis and Nazi collaborators in the history of Holland in the War. Gimbert's father, Meinoud Rost van Tonningen, was the head of the all-powerful, in allfinancial matters, Netherlands National Bank. He was captured by the Canadians in late-1944 and jailed in Scheveningen where he committed suicide by jumping off a balcony. Many persons say he was pushed. He was never tried for his war crimes. In all, he was responsible for an estimated 14.5 billion Reichmarks in payments to Germany by the Dutch. In U.S. dollars today this would be equivalent to approximately $74 billion!

His widow, Florentine, referred to as the "Black Widow," survived for decades after the War (she died in 2007), continuing to rant and rave pro-Nazi, searing anti-Semitic, creeds and Holocaust denials, which were widely reported in the Dutch media, even long after she may have lost her mind. The Rost van Tonningen name remains among the most hated and vilified in Holland, yet Gimbert wouldn't change it. He is a truly good guy.

I have visited U.S. War memorial cemeteries in Holland (Margraten) and Belgium (Flanders Field) on multiple occasions. Kay and I have now twice visited, most recently with our three youngest grandchildren, the enormously important and emotionally gripping American War cemetery at Coleville-sur-Mer in Normandy where 9,387 military personnel are buried in beautiful peaceful surroundings in rows upon rows of symmetrical white grave markers, most all crosses, with a few Jewish Stars of David. Their families chose to let them be buried there rather than being repatriated to the U.S. It is their truly unbelievable valor in storming the beaches of Normandy on the Western European front together with hundreds of thousands of others among our allies who risked, and ultimately lost, their lives who saved us and preserved freedom for millions of people throughout the world.

In a Jewish tradition, as we do with the rock in Vermont where my parents' ashes are buried, we left a few stones, in this case gathered from Omaha Beach at Normandy, on the Jewish head stones of young soldiers from New York, Ohio, Michigan and elsewhere, to let them know we're thinking of them.

In retrospect, perhaps the most amazing part of our story is how many of our family and close relatives were able to survive the Nazi terror by being in hiding, or, in the case of the Warendorfs, surviving deportation to a concentration camp. Thus, the total number of our closest family and relatives, who survived the German Nazi occupation of Holland, is meaningfully more than two dozen persons. They include, in addition to my parents and myself, my maternal grandmother, my paternal grandparents; a paternal great-grandmother; a paternal great-uncle, his wife, their daughter and son-in-law; Mom's sister Margaret, her husband and three children (whose family story is further chronicled in detail in Chapter 14) as well as husbands (who survived in hiding) of two of those children; Mom's first cousin Bram; two children, Jeannette and Peter of another first cousin (see Chapter 16); Pop's brother Fritz, sister-in-law and their son (see Chapter 13); plus husbands of two cousins. In addition, Mom's sister Juliemarthe and her family, my great-uncle Herbert Loeb, his wife Nellie and their two sons, Mom's cousin Wim, another brother and sister, cousins Philip and Corrie and their two children, Grootmoeder's sister-in-law and a number of other cousins and other relatives of varied degrees of consanguinity, all were able to leave Holland even after the War started, winding up in the U.S. Of course, there were subsequently dozens of offspring in multiple generations who would have never been born had their parents not survived, and many of whom have contributed meaningfully to (American) society. Accordingly, while it is but in small measure, it's worth thinking once again of Mom's motto, "We made it, we beat Hitler."

Appendix

Additional Correspondence

- Letters written to my parents while they were in hiding by relatives, also in hiding in 1943 – 1944, delivered through the intermediacy of Piet Hoogenboom (who arranged the hiding places of all the relatives who wrote the letters) and "Ma" Peyster, the mother in the family who hid my parents in Amsterdam.

- Letters written by my maternal and paternal grandmothers to Piet Hoogenboom's daughter congratulating her on the birth of a grandson (and lamenting the passing of my paternal grandfather, "Opa Sally," whose obituary is printed therewith).

- A letter from Nazi officials in Holland written in 1941 to counsel for the (Aryan) mother of a good friend of my family permitting his mother and the friend to avoid having to have a Jewish ID card, and to wear a Jewish star. The noteworthy paradox evidenced in this letter is the Nazi focus on a narrow, carefully constructed, legal interpretation of statutory provisions in "race laws" relevant to the status of this one applicant, while at the same time millions were being killed by Nazis without even the slightest regard to any law.

1943 UIT DE ONDERDUIK Dinsdag — 27 Juli.

Letter of July 27, 1943 from the hiding place (in Utrecht) written by my paternal grandparents Annemarie Ullmann-Loeb and Salomon Ullmann ("Oma Aenni" and "Opa Sally") to my parents.

Dear children, Frans and Lot: about March 20, 1943

You must have heard by now the tragic news, that my dear mother got
sick. Yesterday our friend, Hoogeboom, came to us to inform us that
she had passed away. I lost my dear, dear, old Mother. Exactly
three weeks after she left us in Amsterdam, she lost her life. Her
kidneys gave way, she lost consciousness, after having contracted
bronchitis.

Oh, how I wish that I could have been with her those last three
weeks. I did not realize, of course, that I would never see her again,
when saying good-bye to her on the steps of your apartment building,
as she descended slowly on the arm of Hoogeboom. You both have given
her a good time those last months at your house. She loved to be
read to, and she loved having your little boy around. This March 19,
on your father's birthday, she closed her eyes forever.

Please, please, try to reach us and write to us. We are so in
need of your words in these trying times. I understand, that Hoogeboom
is coming tonight. I am writing to you hoping that you will have
written to us, and he can give us your letter.

We were extremely unhappy about your last letter. And we still
worry. You wrote about that last razzia in Amsterdam. What tragedy
and what sorrow among your friends and family especially! And how
incredible that Aunt Julie and Uncle Socs were not saved! Hopefully,
their son Bram can still do something for them. And how do you think
Leo is doing?

Translation (by Mom) of letter of "about March 20, 1943" from my paternal
grandmother Annemarie Ullmann-Loeb, ("Oma Aenni") to my parents.

-2-

I dream so often about him, and am walking then with him and my other grandson, Joost, in the park. I cried when I woke up. And I pray now, that I will be able to walk with the two of them, but most of all that your boy will have his own parents with him.

I do not see my daughter-in-law anymore either. We have to live so secretly here. Maybe, if it gets darker, we will be able to get company now and then.

We read a lot and I embroider. My mother would not have believed it, if she could see me embroidering now. I am making large table-cloths with open seams. But it makes me calmer, and life easier. And I finished for our roommate here, Jet van Laer, a large tablecloth. If you want me to make anything for you, just let me know....

Utrecht

Saturday and Sunday

July 13, 1943

Dear Lot and Frans,

Many thanks, for your nice letter, that made me so happy. Now
I feel at ease, because I realize, how well your hiding place is
organised, how practical, and how cozy you have made this so special
stay for all of you.

I hope now, that we soon will be reunited with our parents, with Lot's
Mother, and her sister. Now, that I myself have been the first to bring
you some real good news, by coming back, from the camp, I hope, that
this will be the end of the terrible disaster, and that we all will be
spared from now on, those great and grave disappointments, that we had
to suffer. At any rate, you have to believe, that we will be together
soon, and in our house, to celebrate the liberation of Holland.
We are so lucky to be united, but still, the suffering of so many of
our friends, parents, and others, is darkening our happiness.

I have been able to call Riet by phone, on Sunday, and informed
her, that Pum (Loeb) and I would return from camp, on Monday. And that
she and Bep had to meet us in Amersfoort.
We had to go together to the German office there, where we were supposed
to check-out.

My homecoming, I am sure, was told to you, by Aunt Peyster. It was for
me, something, so great, so incredible, to come back to my little spic-
and-span house, after having been in those dirty, filthy crowded barracks
And to see Joostje, with his blond curly hair, and his two fat little
legs, standing in his playpen, looking with great big astonished eyes,

Translation (by Mom) of letter of July 13, 1943 from Pop's brother, Fritz
Ullmann, sent from the (labor) camp in Amersfoort, Holland where he was
interred, but from which he was ultimately released.

up to that strange Daddy.

First he did not feel at home with me, but now, he stretches out his arms, whenever I enter the room. And he laughs at me, and talks to me in his way.

Riet is so happy, she had such a difficult time. And she has done so much for me. Where would I have been without her? And now, after all the excitement, after all the worries, that she has suffered, because of me, we are looking forward, to enjoy our reunion, till for us all, the liberation has come.

Here in our house, nothing has changed much.

I have the feeling, that I just left for a few days, instead of the year nearly, it took. It seems now like a bad dream, because the same flowers, the same vegetables are on the table, as I left.

But still, time has gone by. Joost, is no baby anymore, but a little fellow. And our dear Oma Mum, is no more. The home in the Dillenburgstraat is gone, many friends have been taken, and no one of our family can share with us now.

It is though real luck, that our parents are so close by, and I hope, that they will be spared till the signal is coming, and if that moment is there, then they will come to us, and you will come to us, in our house. Though it is small, it still is now, the only spot on the earth that is ours, and where we will celebrate the coming back of you all.

Tomorrow is Leo's birthday. It must be a hard day for you, Lot, but we cannot be sentimental, at this moment, and the most important thing must be now, that he is healthy, and safe.

Next year you will be together again, and that is not a fantastic dream. So, I say now, happy birthday. Next year together.

Once though, I was worried about your son, when friends of us, were

caught, and they had played with Leo the day before. As they told me,

in Westerbork. I could tell you so many things about your friends, and

about my time in camp, but I have only time now, to tell you about a

few people, who will interest you most.

First of all, Bram is now back in Amsterdam, and has sound legal

papers, with a good guarantee for a long stay in Amsterdam. He went

back with Pum and me, on the train from Westerbork, and he tries now,

to do for his parents, in Westerbork, what is at all possible, for

them to achieve safe papers.

For the moment, his parents are safe, and sound, in Westerbork, on a

special list, (Putkammer). They even have a chance, to be transferred

to another list, so they might be sent back to Amsterdam.

Especially your Aunt, is brave, and she tries hard, to make the best

of it, laughing, while looking at the incredible mess.

Your Uncle is in the hospital, where he can find more peace, and quiet,

than he can in the large, and filthy and noisy barracks.

And now your sister, and her children. She is always cheerful, despite

the great difficulties, she has to bear. She has a heavy burden, she

works from early in the morning, till late at night, and after that she

has to take care of her children, in all the great mess of life in the

busy barracks.

Fortunately, she heard, that Hans (her husband) is o.k. in London, that

gives her courage. The children are now much better, were weak and

feverish, the first few months.

But they have gotten used to camp life, and especially her little Hans

is a terrific lively completely bald shaven boy, and he looks

Tuesday, 27 July 1943

Dear Lot(je) and Frans, company likely today.   Thus, quickly writing a
message to you and first of all to tell you how happy we were with the
unexpected good reports; the story about our little man has made us very
happy. Finally a bit of a place for him! Playmates and loving step-parents!
I now think with less fear, but with no less longing for him and just hope
further that he will soon have his own daddy and mommy back.

Now three weeks have passed since our son Frits came home. I read
in your letter how happy that made you too. You asked me, Lot, what
I said when our friend Hoogeboom came to tell us that joyous news.
Do you know that for pure happiness, I could not find any words? It
was too good to be true. But still that sad feeling that my dear old
mother never knew that Frits came back.

    Frits writes to us every week. He experiences his great good
fortune so deeply and he loves his little boy. In his warm father's
heart, he sees Joostje as a perfectly beautiful creature. He walked
twice past our house, because he knows, that from 10 to 10:30 our land-
lady cleans our room. And we are allowed to sit in her room, behind
the closed curtains, looking out the window. Frits could not see us
of course, but we saw him walking by, and Riet was with him, the dog

Translation (by Mom and me) of letter of July 27, 1943 from my paternal
grandparents to my parents.

running around the three of them. The little boy in his stroller

looked adorable, with blond curls, and so rolypoly.

Last week they came by again, this time without Riet. Frits

looked so well, clean shaven, well-dressed. They are now very very

careful, of course. It is better that they do not come by too often.

That dark-looking father with his blond little boy, could be something

special to catch the eye, especially because Frits has to wear his

star (of David). I have to be patient, and have to console myself,

that we cannot see them anymore.

In our hiding place, all is still going well, but I have great

difficulties in getting used to this kind of living. We live here

with Jet van Laer, who is my age. She is sometimes difficult to get

along with. We have to learn, both of us, to overlook each others'

shortcomings. That of course, is the big lesson of this way of life.

It promises an easier life in the future, for you, Lot, with your

mother-in-law.

How wonderful that you found your hiding place, living with

such extremely good friends.

It has turned very, very, warm these days. We are so warm here

in the attic. And how difficult it is for us to be unable to leave,

not even in the dark of the night.

I am enclosing six coupons for skimmed milk. You can make cheese

from that milk. We are doing that here also. Just take a handker-

chief, and hang this under your mirror above the washstand. Sally

loves it. Frits wrote, that your Aunt is so brave in Westerbork, and

also writes the same about your sister, Margaret. Love to you two,

and a kiss from Mother and Oma Aenni.

Dear L & F

We are always hoping for good news from you and especially that
Deintje (me) is going well. The last news reports were terrific and
we now hope that it will not last so long and we can all be together!
I am here almost the entire day. For the time being we receive books
from the library and once in a while French ones from Frits. The time
passes relatively quickly! The wound on my leg is still not good, but
much smaller. I have no further problems with it - I wish you the
very best and we hope to hear more soon. Many heartiest wishes - your
father.

February 4, 1944

Dear Lofra, (Lot and Frans)

A long time has passed since we heard a word from each other, but I have the feeling that we know about each other. And it has made us both happy that you sent us your letter telling us the good news that Leo had found a permanent and good home. What a loss for the two of you, to have to do without your sweet little one, whose most lovable years, are just now passing by! But it is not good to be sentimental, the tough reality, has forced us to brace ourselves. Who knows, it might be a blessing for us all, to strengthen our character. Just 7 years ago today we were all together in the Hotel Pays Bas, because on that day my daughter and son-in-law were united, and just at this time, we were giving them a hearty welcome. So much has happened during these seven years, and how many of our guests, I wonder, will we never be able to see again.

The weather is such, that it is just perfect for these thoughts, because it is snowing outside. I hope, that the snow will stay with us, because the Germans will have difficulties with transporting their troops. The latest news from the Eastern frontier is very promising.

I also want to congratulate you on the birth of the second son

Translation (by Mom) of letter dated February 1944 from Fritz Loeb, brother of maternal grandmother, Annemarie Ullmann-Loeb ("Oma Aenni") while he was in hiding, to my parents (in hiding).

-2-

to Frits and Riet. Hoogeboom gave us the announcement in a letter
last night. I hope, that they know how lucky they are, to be able
to live like people - I mean that this child is an official child.
Just like all the people, equal to any other. How long will it be
for us until we can leave these hiding places and be people again???
I hear, that you both are doing fine, and that your host and hostess
are very good to you. Liesje and Hans had to move again, and the
question arises if they can stay where they are now, in hiding.
Their hostess is very active, very busy, which has in their case
caused many complications. Last week, for instance, their hosts went
out for two days, leaving them alone.

We are still at our same address. One cannot have great demands,
of course. After one and a half years, human tolerance has sometimes
been forgotten, but then ... we are still alive. We try to be as good
as possible. And thanks to my optimistic view of life, we can manage,
even when it is hard. We have a good example when we think of your
mother, Lot, because she is so brave, and she has to carry the full
load all by herself. We, and you two, have each other to talk things
over. Unfortunately, we have bad news from my brother and sister-in-
law, Leo and Meta, both in the concentration camp in Westerbork. Leo
is in the hospital, and Meta has a job sorting out batteries. We
cannot send packages any longer, but we were able to send them four of
40 KG each. The rumors are spreading now, that the Germans are emptyin
out the camp. And I pray that they won't go ahead with it, that Meta
and Leo can stay in Westerbork, await their fate there. I am writing
this to you, so matter of fact, but I know, what a great tragedy this
is, for us all. I have read a lot during the last few weeks about

-3-

these pogroms. But I found, that neither in the Middle Ages, nor in
the days of Constantine the Great, nor in Spain, did they try to solve
this problem so drastically. I am sure that you both read a lot too,
these days. The days pass by so quickly that way. Would you like to
know how the two of us keep busy during the day? At 9:30 I get up,
air our beds, light the fire and make breakfast, shave, wash, read the
morning paper, and I clean the room, while Sophie cleans up the porch
(inside). We move slowly, so it is 12:30 by now. I light a cigar,
take a book, till we have our hot midday dinner. We two have our
siesta until 2 o'clock, and then we all listen to the radio, the German
radio, of course. And the afternoon goes by ... we read a book or
write a letter. At 6 o'clock, the evening paper appears. Then we
eat a sandwich, and at 7 our friend, Hoogeboom, arrives. We talk a
bit, and we play some cards together. And the strange part of this
kind of life really is that we do exactly the same the next day. We
have managed 543 days this way.

At least 500 times, I have dusted the desk and the fire place.
If anyone, would have told me that this kind of life could be endured
for two years, I would not have been able to believe him. Now I know,
it will not be long anymore, for sure. Yesterday, the first announcements were posted in the city hall in Utrecht. In case of English
invasion, it said, everyone must stay put. No one is allowed in the
streets.... So, the German masters apparently are considering the
possibility of an invasion. Wait and See, is my belief - do not worry
before it is strictly neccessary.

I have become rather stiff-jointed, and when we get out of this
hiding place, and when we are free to move, we have to get trained to

-4-

use our bodies again. Then we will realize that we did not live

during these years, but that we have just been vegetating. But still,

let us keep faith, and let us hope that we will see you two in ...

let us say ... 90 days.

My love and best wishes.

Frits. *Loeb*

Author's Note

The following are letters written respectively in July 1956 by my maternal and paternal grandmothers, Bertha Konijn-Prins (Grootmoeder) and Annemarie Ullmann-Loeb (Oma Aenni) which both congratulate the Hoogenboom family on the birth of their first grandson while at the same time lamenting the passing of Salomon Ullmann (Opa Sally) with translations thereof by me. They are included here because they illustrate the continuing contacts maintained by both families with Piet Hoogenboom Sr. and his family for many years after the War, and, I believe, fairly evidence the continuing gratitude to Piet and his family for their powerful help during the "darkest days."

Heden overleed na een moedig gedragen lijden, mijn innig geliefde Man, onze lieve Vader, Behuwd- en Grootvader

S. ULLMANN

op de leeftijd van 81 jaren.

    Utrecht,
      M. Ullmann-Loeb
      Dr. F. Ullmann
      M. Ullmann-
               Coebergh
    Joost, Robert, Eric
Port Washington
New York,
      F. L. Ullmann
      E. Ullmann-Konijn
    Leo en Henk
Utrecht, 7 juni 1956
Alb. Neuhuysstraat 17 I.

Liever geen bezoek.

De begrafenis zal plaats hebben maandag 11 juni a.s., des voormiddags 11 uur op de begraafplaats „Den en Rust" te Bilthoven.

Death announcement of paternal grandfather Salomon Ullmann in 1956, referenced in the two immediately following letters.

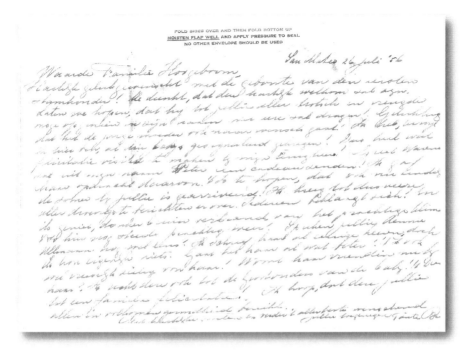

(My translation)

San Mateo, 26 July '56

Valued Hoogenboom family

Heartiest congratulations with the birth of the first male descendant. I trust that this will be greatly welcomed. Let us hope that he will continue to grow and carry his name with honor. Wonderful that the young mother is also doing so well. I have received while I've been here, already three baby announcements. Thus I'll have to make a large number of congratulatory visits when I return. Margaret Warendorf will send Peter a present in her own name. I will take care of giving her orders therefor. I hope in the meantime that summer has arrived. I only received complaints about it. I am enjoying becoming very tanned from the climate here. It is still beautiful weather here. Do you speak to Aenni Ullmann still once in a while? I wrote to her several times, but I have actually heard nothing. Is she doing a little better? It is very sad for her! Does her female friend still live with her? I am directing this also to the grandparents of the baby. It is thus a family congratulations.

I hope this finds you all in good health.

With heartiest greetings and further most sincere best wishes,

your loving Aunt Bertha

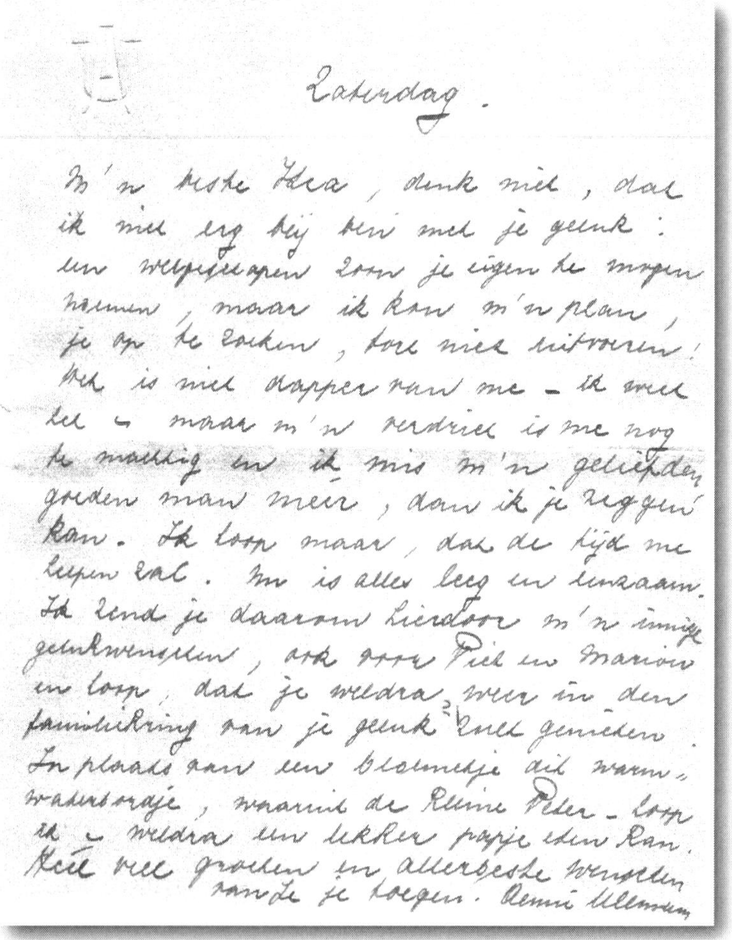

[Handwritten letter in Dutch, beginning "Zaterdag"]

(My translation)

Saturday

My dear Thea, do not think that I am not very happy with your good fortune: a well-formed son that you can call your own, but I cannot yet carry out my plan to come visit you! It is not courageous of me – I know it – but my sadness is still too great and I miss my dear good husband more than I can say. I only hope that time will help me. Now everything is empty and lonely. I am sending you therefore hereby my most sincere best wishes, also for Piet and Marion and hope that you will surely again in your family circle enjoy your good fortune. In lieu of flowers, this warm-water dish, from which little Peter I hope, will have nice hot cereal to eat.
Heartiest greetings and most sincere best wishes from
your loving Aenni Ullmann

A Friend and the Definition of a Jew

The following letter (on page 367) was sent by German authorities to the lawyer for the mother of a close friend, another Dutchman who emigrated to Port Washington, New York from the Netherlands after surviving the Nazi occupation. He, whose identity we need not disclose, and his wife, have been among my parents' (and our) closest friends for some 60 years.

The letter represents an advisory opinion on the application of Jewish race laws in response to a request, prepared and submitted by his mother's lawyer, to the effect that the designations "Sara" and "J" be removed from her passport. The letter in effect provides an interpretation of the Nuremberg laws defining a "Jew" (see page 367) to which the Germans scrupulously and paradoxically adhered.

The letter states that, in spite of her marriage to a Jew, conversion to Judaism, and belonging to a Jewish congregation, she nevertheless remains of "German Blood" since she has four "Aryan" grandparents.

After reviewing the relevant regulations, the Nazi advisory authorities in the Netherlands confirmed in the letter that the designations "Sara" and 'J' on her passport are indeed erroneous. Accordingly, those designations were subsequently removed from her passport and other identification papers and she was thus also exempted from wearing the Jewish Star. The legal conclusions in turn affected her son's status; as his mother and two grandparents were "Aryan," he was thus also able to obtain "clean" (non-Jewish) identification papers and was exempted from wearing the Jewish star.

His father, however, had to continue wearing the star based on his Jewish lineage, but, having an "Aryan" wife, he was exempted from deportation.

By late 1943, as earlier indicated, the mass deportations of Jews from Holland had ceased and Holland, as also earlier indicated, was declared "*Judenrein.*" It was thus presumably inappropriate to have as few remaining persons, including our friend's father, continue to wear the Jewish star while remaining in Holland.

It was in this context that our friend's father and other remaining Jewish males in a mixed marriage were offered the opportunity to avoid having to wear the star by obtaining a certificate from a doctor to the effect that such person was either sterile or had been sterilized. His father and other Jewish males, through friendly doctors, acquired such certificates although in fact they were not sterile and had not been sterilized.

All the foregoing preventive efforts to avoid deportation notwithstanding, the family nevertheless decided to hide in a farm to further protect them from potential harm and they did indeed survive.

Our friend, whose family had a successful consumer products business in the center of Amsterdam, came to this country after the war, served in the U.S. Army, and became a highly successful CEO of a company which designed and distributed consumer products in this country. He and his wife have two fine children. He, too, thus beat Hitler.

DEUTSCHE BERATUNGSSTELLE
IN DEN NIEDERLANDEN
DIENSTSTELLE AMSTERDAM

AMSTERDAM, __26.September__ 1941.
MUSEUMPLEIN 19
TEL. 97101

Frau

A m s t e r d a m

Entscheidung: des Herrn Generalkommissar f. Verwaltung & Justi

Auf Grund Ihrer Beschwerde kann ich Ihnen berichten, dass
Sie nach der ersten Verordnung zum Reichsbürgergesetz v.14.11.3
nicht als Geltungsjüdin anzusehen, obwohl Sie mit einem Juden
verheiratet sind und Sie in Deutschland zur jüdischen Religion
gemeinschaft gehört haben. Wie Sie ausführen haben Sie 4
arische Grosseltern, Sie sind also auch nicht als jüdischer
Mischling anzusehen.- Die Frage der Religionszugehörigkeit bzw.
der Eingehung einer Ehe mit einem Juden ist nur von Bedeutung
bei Mischlingen, ie von zwei volljüdischen Grosseltern abstam-
men, da diese dann als Jude gelten, wenn sie beim Erlass des
Gesetzes mit einem Juden verheiratet sind oder der jüdischen
Religionsgemeinschaft angehören bzw. angehört haben.

Der Paragr. 2 Abs. welcher ausführt, dass als volljüdisch de
Elternteil gilt, der der jüdischen Religionsgemeinschaft ange-
hört hat, hat lediglich für die rassische Einordnung der Enkel
Bedeutung. Der Paragr. 2 Abs. 2 stellt keine Ergänzung des
Paragrf. 5 dar. Ein zum Judentum übergetretener Deutschblütiger
ist hinsichtlich seiner eigenen rassischen Einordnung stets al
deutschblütig anzusehen. Auch die rassische Zugehörigkeit des
Ehegatten ist für die rassische Einordnung ohne jede Bedeutung.
Die deutschblütige Ehefrau eines Juden bleibt also selbst beim
Übertritt zur jüdischen Religionsgemeinschaft ohne Rücksicht
auf die Ehe deutschblütig.-

Die Eintragung des Vornamen "Sara" und der Vermerk "J" im
deutschen Reisepass sind daher im vorliegenden Falle nicht
gerechtfertigt. Dass die Ehe gemäss Paraf. 1 des Gesetzes zum
Schutze des deutschen Blutes und der deutschen Ehre vom 15.9.3
nichtig ist, ist im vorliegenden Falle ohne Einfluss, da zu-
naechst der Staatsanwalt die Nichtigkeitsklage erheben müsste,
sofern die Ehe nach Inkrafttreten des Gesetzes eingegangen war.

Im Auftrage:

Paul & Berthe Hendrix Professorship

On pages 317 and 332 reference is made to Cornelis (Kees) and Marianne Willems, and the critical role played by Kees in my life by steering my parents to Andover. As I've frequently noted, where would I be without Andover?

Some 20-years ago, I met with Kees, who remained a good friend (and client) and Marianne at their home in Amsterdam for breakfast on more than one occasion to discuss the possibility of honoring in an appropriate manner Marianne's parents, who had perished in death camps at the hands of the Nazis during the War while Marianne, like me, survived as a hidden child.

After several meetings, much discussion and correspondence, I suggested to Kees and Marianne (as a suitable opportunity in Holland appeared to be only a remote possibility), that they consider a chair (professorship) at a major U.S. educational institution which would reflect Marianne's extreme interest in/and support of, women's and Jewish causes. Kees agreed to make available $1 million for this purpose. With a virtual $1 million thus in my pocket, I then approached several universities with the thought of establishing a professorship in honor of Marianne's parents devoted to both women's and Holocaust studies.

This proved to be difficult at the outset as we were dealing with two different areas of scholarship at the respective universities.

Walking out of a movie in Port Washington with our good friend Mina Weiner, active as a Director of Alumni Affairs for Cornell University, whose family had also been involved in establishment of an endowed chair in Jewish studies, Mina convinced me that I absolutely had to discuss these matters with David Owen, Professor of Ancient Near Eastern and Judaic Studies at Cornell University, immediately. It is my recollection that either David or someone commandeered by David called me almost every half hour thereafter.

I met David Owen in person in the office at Apollo Plaza in Monticello, New York (an unmitigated disaster of a shopping center adventure for me; Apollo Plaza was one of the very earliest outlet centers in the Country, ravaged by the elements and hooligans prior to our acquisition, and, since the advent of the wondrous and enormous Woodbury Commons outlet center in Harriman, New York, the Galleria at Crystal Run Mall in Middletown, and also Walmart superstore in Monticello, is now again ravaged by the elements and hooligans). At that meeting we agreed that I should write a proposal for a joint professorship involving the women's studies and middle east studies (then called the Department of Semitic Languages and Literature) programs at Cornell University.

The proposal was indeed written and the response was exciting and highly supportive.

A small problem arose just prior to finalization of the arrangements to the effect that the funding for such professorship required a minimum of $2 million rather than $1 million. I, of course, promptly communicated this small wrinkle to Kees and Marianne. Kees, somehow, was able to arrange the additional funding and the professorship/fund was duly established on May 5, 1998, with the title, "Paul and Berthe Hendrix Memorial Professorship in Jewish Studies."

The first course given under the auspices of the newly endowed professorship, and happily reflective of the original intent of the gift, was on the role of women in the Bible. The first professor who held the chair was Gary A. Rendsburg who held it until 2004.

Marianne and Kees and their two children attended the ceremony; Kees was unable to attend but provided a video address.

I will always remember the occasion, attended also by Kay and members of my family, as well as Steven and Mina Weiner, David Owen, and Deans and Directors of the University, as one of the most joyful and uplifting occasions in our lives. It represented, again, in its way, a meaningful contribution to society that somehow survived the Holocaust.

Cornell University
Department of Near Eastern Studies

[A slightly revisionist article, which appeared in the Cornell Chronicle of 9/24/12, on the history of the Paul and Berthe Hendrix Professorship.]

Endowed chair honors Holocaust victims

Endowments are often inspired by fond memories of Cornell, but the Paul and Berthe Hendrix Memorial Professorship in Jewish Studies was birthed in the gas chambers of Auschwitz and Mauthausen-Gusen.

The daughter of Paul and Berthe Hendrix, Marianne Willems-Hendrix, was a sickly 5-year-old when her family was imprisoned in a Dutch transit camp in 1943. Her parents knew she'd never survive the harsh conditions, so they said the blond-haired girl wasn't really Jewish, but the offspring of an extramarital affair by her mother with a non-Jewish man. The lie saved Willems-Hendrix life.

She established the Hendrix chair as a living memorial to her parents and two brothers, all of whom perished in the Holocaust. She wanted the gift to support scholarship at Cornell into the crucial role Jewish women have played throughout history, although she never attended the university.

Willems-Hendrix, who died in 2004, intended the endowed chair for a faculty member who studies women in Jewish studies as well as for supporting curriculum development to encourage faculty to develop and regularly offer Jewish studies courses about women and gender. But a recent agreement allows the chair to also be used for the Jewish studies program director on a per-term basis. [The "recent agreement" to the original terms of the gift was negotiated by Cornell University deans and the author.]

. . .

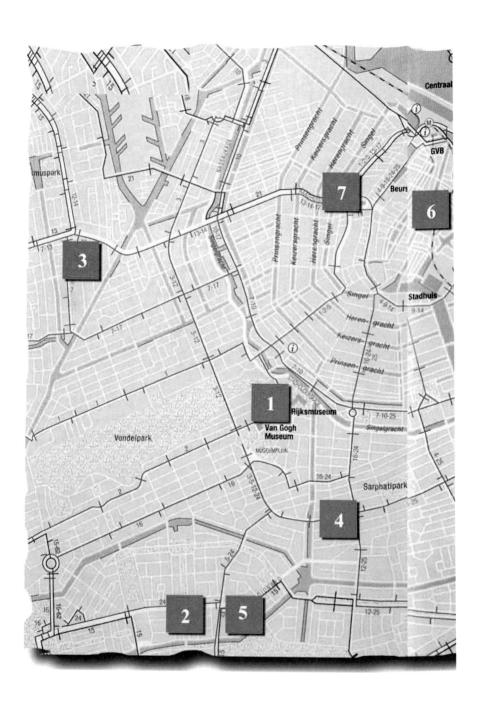

My Amsterdam, 1940's

1 Jan Luijkenstraat Where Mom and her family lived, near the Rijksmuseum

2 Milletstraat 37 In "Old South" where my parents lived just before the War and where many relatives came to live at the beginning of the War

3 Van Speijkstraat 175 My hiding place with the Schimmels

4 Ceintuurbaan 81 My parents' hiding place with the Peysters

5 Velasquezstraat 5 Our family home after the War

6 Dam Square De Bijenkorf department store (Pop worked there), the War Monument and the Queen's Palace

7 Prinsengracht 263-267 The Anne Frank House and Annex

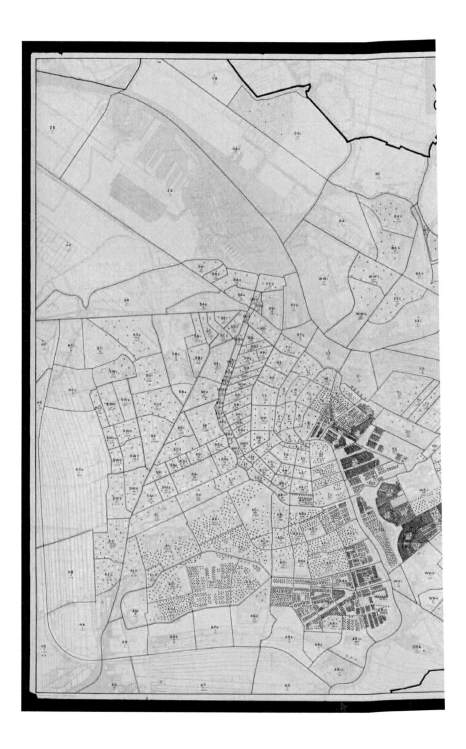

A greatly-reduced, detailed "Dot Map" of the location of Jews in Amsterdam. The original is approximately 39 inches squared. The map was prepared by the Bureau of Statistics of the City of Amsterdam in May 1941 in response to a letter of January 16, 1941 by Seyss-Inquart and its preparation was supervised by Dr. Hans Boemcker, who was referred to as the *"Juden Kommissar."*

Each dot represents 10 Jews. In all, the map, prepared by 20 Dutch officials who went with notebooks and pencils to seek information for the Nazis about the Jewish population, recorded 8,421 Jewish households and 2,221 non-Jewish households in the designated neighborhoods.

The map is re-printed here by permission of NIOD, The Netherlands National Institute for War, Holocaust and Genocide Studies, Amsterdam, the Netherlands.

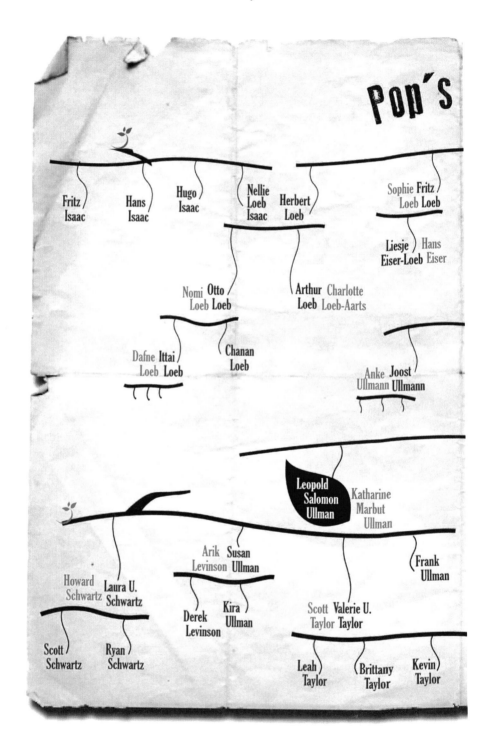

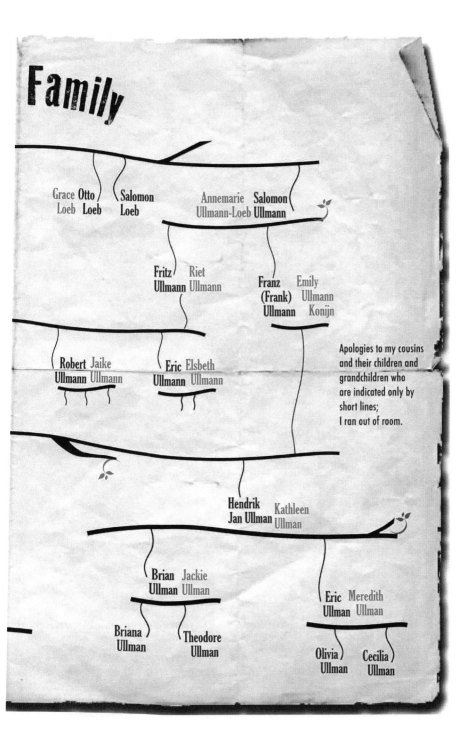

Family

Grace Otto
Loeb Loeb
Salomon
Loeb
Annemarie Salomon
Ullmann-Loeb Ullmann

Fritz Riet
Ullmann Ullmann
Franz Emily
(Frank) Ullmann
Ullmann Konijn

Robert Jaike
Ullmann Ullmann
Eric Elsbeth
Ullmann Ullmann

Apologies to my cousins
and their children and
grandchildren who
are indicated only by
short lines;
I ran out of room.

Hendrik Kathleen
Jan Ullman Ullman

Brian Jackie
Ullman Ullman

Eric Meredith
Ullman Ullman

Briana
Ullman
Theodore
Ullman

Olivia Cecilia
Ullman Ullman

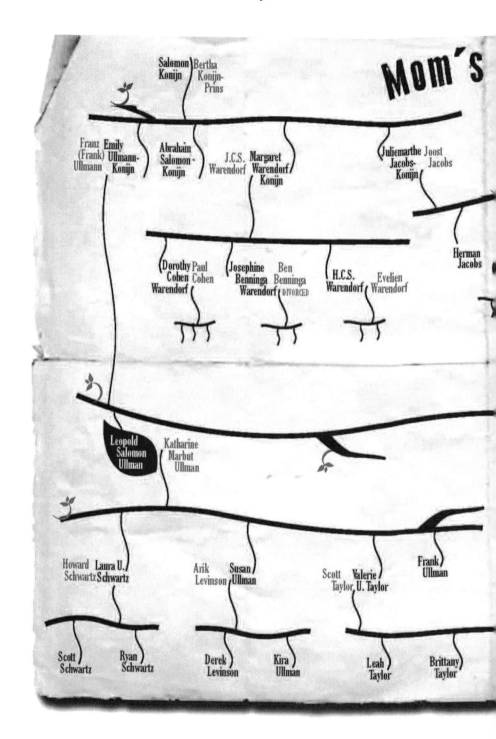

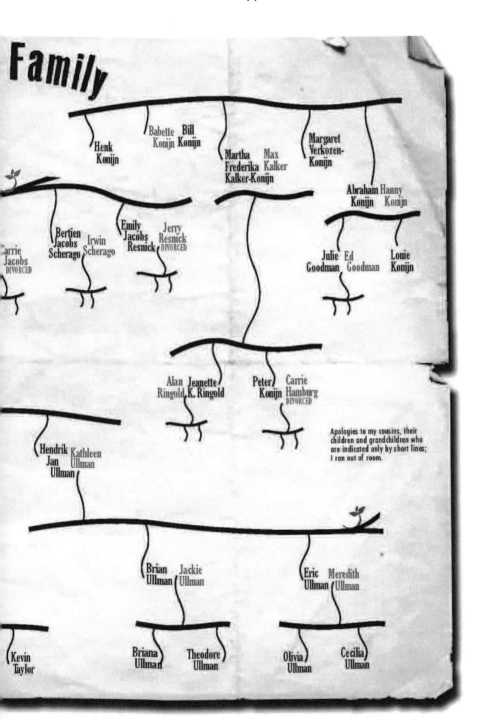

Family

Henk
Konijn

Babette Bill
Konijn Konijn

Martha
Frederika Kalker
Kalker-Konijn

Max
Kalker

Margaret
Verkozen-
Konijn

Abraham Hanny
Konijn Konijn

Carrie
Jacobs
DIVORCED

Bertien
Jacobs Irwin
Scherago Scherago

Emily
Jacobs
Resnick
Resnick

Jerry
Resnick
DIVORCED

Julie Ed
Goodman Goodman

Louie
Konijn

Alan Jeanette
Ringold K. Ringold

Peter Carrie
Konijn Hamburg
DIVORCED

Apologies to my cousins, their
children and grandchildren who
are indicated only by short lines;
I ran out of room.

Hendrik Kathleen
Jan Ullman
Ullman

Brian Jackie
Ullman Ullman

Eric Meredith
Ullman Ullman

Kevin
Taylor

Briana
Ullman

Theodore
Ullman

Olivia
Ullman

Cecilia
Ullman

Timeline

Year / Date	The World
1913	WWI begins
1932	Roosevelt is elected President of U.S.
1933-1935	Hitler is named Chancellor of Germany
1936	Hitler introduces military draft; violates Treaty of Versailles, Nuremberg Race Laws stripping Jews of rights are enacted; Olympic Games in Berlin.
1938	*Kristallnacht (November 6) *Germany annexes Austria and invades Czechoslovakia
1939	*Germany invades Poland *Britain, France, Australia and New Zealand declare war on Germany
1940	*Germany invades Holland, Belgium and France *Battle of Britain
1941	*Japan attacks Pearl Harbor (12/7); Hitler invades the Soviet Union; *U.S. enters the War; *Germany declares War on U.S.

Holland	Leo and His Family
*Holland remains neutral; is not attacked by Germans	*Frank Ullmann is born in Germany *Emily Konijn is born in Holland
	Frank graduates high school; moves to Utrecht, Holland; obtains employment in De Beijenkorf
	Emily and Frank Ullmann marry in Jewish wedding in Amsterdam
	Frank and Emily return to Holland from traineeships in U.S.
Holland declares neutrality; Hitler guarantees Dutch neutrality	Leo Salomon Ullmann is born in Amsterdam 7/14/1939
*Holland is attacked on May 10th and surrenders in 5 days; royal family escapes to England *Parliament is dissolved *All Jewish civil servants dismissed *Jews required to have special ID cards *Jews required to register businesses; ordinance defines "Jew"	A number of relatives escape by boat to England and ultimately the U.S.; Initial ordinances have relatively modest effect on daily life
*All Jews required to register with the Dutch census bureau and to report their assets *Jews attacked by roving Nazi gangs. *National strike (2/25-2/26/41) led by Dockworkers in support of Jews. *March 1941 Jewish Council is formed; first roundups ("Razzias") of Jews commenced. *August – Jews have to surrender gold, silver and other valuables	*While subject to more and more restrictions, life is still tolerable *April 1941 – Pop loses his job at De Beijenkorf; becomes bicycle courier for the Jewish Counsil *My parents deliver certain valuables to employee(s) of De Beijenkorf and bury some silver.

Year / Date	The World
1942	*The "Final Solution" is adopted at the Wannsee Conference. *British bomb Cologne – first attack on German soil.
1943	*Germans lose battle of Stalingrad. *Allies conquer North Africa and land in Sicily.
1944	*June 6 – D-Day. *The Allies land in Normandy. *August – Allied troops land in Nice and move North toward Rhine River. *September – Allies lose a major battle in Arnhem, the Netherlands; part of "Operation Market Garden." *Allied forces liberate most of France, Belgium and Southern Holland.
1945	*Allies invade Germany on Eastern and Western fronts. *March-April – Anne and Margot Frank die in Bergen-Belsen. *Bergen-Belsen is emptied. *April 28-30 – Mussolini is executed and Hitler commits suicide. *May 8 – Unconditional surrender of Germans in Europe. *Japan surrenders; VJ day 9/2. *WWII is over.
1946	
1947	

Holland	Leo and His Family
*All Dutch Jews required to move to Amsterdam. *First major call-up notices. *Increasingly repressive ordinances against Jews. *Accelerated deportation.	*Jews required to have "J" on ID. *Jews required to wear the yellow Star of David. *Great-grandmother, 2 grandparents, and Pop's sister-in-law move to our apartment in Amsterdam.
*All Dutchmen have to turn in radios to the Nazis. *Raids ("Razzias") continue and deportations are accelerated until end of September when Westerbork is emptied. *Last transports to concentration camps. *Nazis declare Holland "Judenrein" (free of Jews).	*Pop hides his radio. *Nazis visit my parents' apartment. *Mom's sister Margaret and 3 children deported to Bergen-Belsen. *Leo, his parents, great-grandmother and 3 grandparents all find hiding places and "disappear"; Leo lands with "War Parents"; his parents in an attic; all in Amsterdam; Leo permitted to play outside for first several months only. *October – Cousin Bram joins Leo's parents in their hiding place.
*Anne Frank and the others in the "back house" are betrayed in August and deported to concentration camps. *War is prolonged in Holland for at least 6-9 months as a result of "A Bridge Too Far" loss. *October 1944–March 1945 – "The Hunger Winter"; Germany places an embargo on food shipments to Western Holland; thousands starved in Holland.	
*March – Dutch Queen lands in Southern Holland. *May 6 – the Germans officially surrender and the War is ended in Holland; celebrations throughout country. *May 7 – A group of armed Germans fire shots into crowd on Dam Square in Amsterdam killing 19 and wounding 117. *May 8 – Canadian Maple Leaf Brigade arrives in Center City Amsterdam.	*March – Leo's "War Parents" sent him to a farm with other children to get food; shortly thereafter his War Father with special permit brings him back. *April – Mom's sister, Margaret and her 3 children leave Bergen-Belsen and land on "Death Train" for 13 days. *May 6 – Leo and his parents are reunited at his War Parents' apartment; Grootmoeder, Opa and Oma Aenni, uncle Fritz, aunt Riet, cousin Joost, great-uncle Fritz, great-aunt Sophie, aunt Liesje and many others survived their hiding and are reunited. *We acquire house in Amsterdam. *Margaret and her 3 children arrive in Amsterdam. *Pop gets his job back.
	*March 23 – Brother Henk (Hendrik Jan) is born.
	*December 8 - Mom, Pop, Henk and Leo land in New York, and move to our home in Port Washington.

Glossary

Arktos *Arktos* was a popular Dutch sorority to which my mother belonged while a student at the University of Amsterdam. The word "arktos" in Greek mythology apparently refers to a centaur who fought against spearmen; in the Greek language it also refers to bears. By decree in 1941 the Germans prohibited Dutch Jews from belonging to sororities or fraternities. My mother never-the-less attended an Arktos "lustrum" (reunion) in 1942. The sorority celebrated its 90th anniversary a few years ago (while the daughter of one of my first cousins was a member). It has since been disbanded. Mom's sorority sisters were critical to our survival. I was weaned away from my parents before I went into hiding by staying for days at a time with the families of sorority sisters. My hiding place was arranged by Mom's sorority sister Aleida Schot (see below). My parents remained close to a number of Mom's sorority sisters and their families to their last days.

Bergen-Belsen   Bergen-Belsen, located in Northwest Germany, was established in 1940 as a prisoner-of-war camp. Most of the camp became a concentration camp in 1943 for Jews, gypsies, homosexuals and others. The camp was intended to be an *Austausch-Lager*, a camp where Jewish prisoners could be exchanged for Germans captured by Allied troops. In fact a small exchange involving 222 Jews for 114 Germans held in Palestine was effected in July 1944. From mid-1944 until the camp was liberated by British soldiers on April 15, 1945, Bergen-Belsen became a collection camp for Jewish prisoners from other camps and the number of prisoners grew from an estimated 7,300 in July 1944 to more than 60,000, while food supplies and available water during that time were substantially diminished.

While Bergen-Belsen never had gas chambers, tens of thousands died there, largely as a result of a scourge of typhus, typhoid fever and dysentery amid such overcrowding; deaths in the first months of 1945 resulting from such conditions are estimated at some 35,000 with another estimated 13,000 deaths after the camp was liberated. Anne Frank's sister, Margot, died in Bergen-Belsen from typhus in March of 1945, followed by Anne in April, just days before the camp was liberated. Mom's sister, Margaret Warendorf, and her three children miraculously survived Bergen-Belsen. The camp was burned down by the British immediately after its liberation to avoid further spread of typhus.

Dam Square   Dam Square is the "heart" of Amsterdam. Its name apparently derives from a dam once located at that spot on the river Amstel. It is flanked primarily by the Royal Palace, the "New" Church (which dates from the 15th century; it is where Kings and Queens are crowned) the flagship store of De Bijenkorf and the Hotel Krasnapolsky. It also features the National War Monument which honors victims of WWII including the victims of brutal killings and machine-gun shootings of hundreds of Dutch people celebrating the end of WWII on Dam Square on May 7th by Nazis firing from the balcony of the private *De Groote Club* (Large Club). Citizens of the Netherlands gather at Dam Square on May 4th of every year, "Remembrance Day"; everything stops and 2 minutes of silence are scrupulously observed in honor of the War dead.

De Bijenkorf   De Bijenkorf (The Beehive) is a chain of large upscale department stores. Its flagship store is on Dam Square in Amsterdam. Other Bijenkorf stores are located in Rotterdam, the Hague, Utrecht, Maastricht and other cities of the Netherlands. The store chain was founded by cousins Simon Goudsmit and Arthur Isaac. Arthur Isaac was the father of my Aunt Nellie Loeb, the spouse of Uncle Harry Loeb, one of my paternal grandmother's brothers. My father was employed there commencing in 1932 when he first arrived in Holland. Because he was a Jew, his employment was terminated in April 1941. He regained his job after the War ended, until we emigrated to the U.S. I worked there during the summer break between 11th grade and my senior year at Andover.

De Hongerwinter (**The Hunger Winter**}   The winter of 1944-1945 was brutal for the Dutch people. Untold numbers (an estimated minimum of 22,000) of Dutch persons starved, in large part because the Germans stopped shipments of food and fuel to Northern and Western Netherlands, including Amsterdam. This Nazi embargo was established in retaliation for a Dutch national railroad strike in September 1944 in support of the Allies, who had by then already liberated the Southern part of the Netherlands.

Dockworkers' Strike   On February 25th and 26th 1941, the Dutch dockworkers led a sympathy strike in support of the Jewish people of the Netherlands, effectively shutting down all transportation and commercial activity in Amsterdam and other cities. This strike, also sometimes referred to as the "February Strike", was the only general strike in support of the Jews in WWII in any country of Europe. Sadly, it led to execution by the Nazis of 450 leaders of the strike and further accelerated deportations and executions of Jews.

Het Parool (The Word)   *Het Parool* (The Word) was an illegal social-democratic underground paper published sporadically throughout the War. It was circulated to an estimated 40,000 persons, making it the most widely distributed of such illegal papers. *Het Parool* was founded by a small group of men including J.C.S. (Hans) Warendorf, the husband of Mom's sister, Margaret. Most members of the founding group were captured and executed by the Nazis. *Het Parool* became a daily national circulation newspaper after the War and still exists today.

Hollandsche Schouwburg (Dutch Theater)   The *Hollandsche Schouwburg*, re-named the *Joodsche Schouwburg* (Jewish Theater) during the War, was a theater built in 1892 in the old Jewish quarter of Amsterdam. It was used in 1942 and 1943 as a holding pen for Jews captured by the Germans before they were sent to the Dutch concentration camp Westerbork (see below) for transit and deportation to concentration and death camps in Germany and Poland. An estimated 15,000 Jews were jammed in at this facility during the War for days, weeks and even months on end. It was finally closed in September 1943. The building is now a war memorial with a wall listing all the Dutch Jews who perished in WWII.

Hoogenboom, Piet   Piet Hoogenboom (b. 1893; d. 1971) was a policeman in Utrecht, and a close friend of my father's family. It was Mr. Hoogenboom, helped by his son, also named Piet Hoogenboom (b. 1918; d. 1984), who was almost certainly more responsible for saving the lives of our extended family than any-one. He arranged the false ID's which permitted us to obtain rations and to avoid jail and deportation. He arranged the hiding places for my great-grandmother, three grandparents, great-uncles and aunts, cousins, and many others, and all of us whom he placed (except my great-grandmother who died basically of old age shortly after going into hiding) survived the War without being deported.

Joodsche Raad (Jewish Council)   The *Joodsche Raad* (Jewish Council) was es-tablished by the Germans in 1941 largely in response to resistance in the *Jordaan*, a Jewish area of Amsterdam, to attacks on Jews by pro-Nazi hooligans. The Council was created essentially to intermediate between German officials gov-erning the Netherlands and the Jewish community in carrying out Nazi orders and decrees. The Council had 19 members and was headed by David Cohen and Abraham Asscher, respectively a professor and head of a diamond-cutting busi-ness in Amsterdam. The Council at its height had as many as 17,500 persons (in-cluding my father as a courier) attached to it. The Council was accused of favoring "elite" Jews in deferring or avoiding deportation when making lists for the Germans, as demanded, to meet quotas for deportation of Dutch Jews. The Council had authority to issue a *Sperre* stamp (see below).

Judenrein   *Judenrein* means generally "free of Jews." In September 1943, at the time of the last deportations from the Dutch concentration camp Westerbork and closing of the *Hollandsche Schouwburg,* the Germans declared Holland *"Judenrein."*

N.S.B. – Nationaal Socialistische Beweging   The Dutch National Socialist Movement (N.S.B.) was a Nazi party in the Netherlands which received 4.2% of the vote in the Dutch general elections of 1937 and several seats in the lower House of Parliament. The party was responsible for much of the collaboration by Dutch citizens with the Nazi occupiers.

Peyster, Gerard and Mrs.   "Ma and Pa" Peyster were the welfare clients who, together with their teenage daughters Ria and Ellie, hid my parents and cousin Bram Konijn, in their attic hiding place, from March 1, 1943 through May 5th, 1945. Even though the relationship, which was wonderful at first, turned sour when times became difficult, they unquestionably saved my parents' lives.

Puls   A. Puls was the name on moving vans used by the Germans to take furniture and belongings of Dutch Jews after they were seized and removed from their homes. The name gave rise to the concept, when referring to a Jewish family who had been taken from their home and their furniture and belongings taken away in a Puls van, that the family had been "Pulsed."

Razzias Razzias were raids frequently conducted by German soldiers and both Dutch and German police, as well as Dutch collaborators, to search for hidden Jews. They generally cordoned off a city block at both ends and proceeded to search house by house for hidden Jews and also, periodically for bicycles to be used by the Germans; dogs were often used during such searches. While such searches took place during the time my parents, others in the family and I were in hiding, we were never discovered or betrayed. The largest *Razzias* took place in Rotterdam where a reported 50,000 persons were rounded up.

Schimmel, Hendrik and Jannigje   The retired policeman, Hendrik Schimmel and his wife, Jannigje Schimmel, known to me as "Oma and Opa Schimmel" (referred to as my "War Parents") together with their adopted daughter Tilly, took me in as a hidden child to be with their family for more than 2 years, when to do so could result in certain death. They cared for me even when there was no food, saved my life without even knowing who I was, and then returned me safely to my parents.

Schot, Aleida   Aleida Schot was Mom's close friend and Arktos sorority sister who made the introduction to the minister of the Dutch Reformed Church who, in turn, placed Jewish children, including, myself, with families throughout the Netherlands. Ms. Schot became a well-known and highly respected professor of language in the Netherlands, specializing in the Slavic languages, and translator of a number of major Russian works into the Dutch language. She passed away in 1969. A prize in her honor is awarded every other year for translations to the Dutch language of works from a Slavic language

Seyss-Inquart, Arthur   Arthur Seyss-Inquart, an Austrian, a vicious anti-semite and a Hitler loyalist, was installed on May 29, 1940 as the *Reichskommissar* of the Occupied Territories. He was thus in charge of the civil administration of the Netherlands. He governed the Netherlands throughout the occupation as a valued Hitler comrade until he signed the surrender documents on May 6th (dated as of May 5, 1945). He was captured on the 7th of May 1945 in Hamburg, Germany by British forces and brought to trial at the Nuremburg trials where he was found guilty of atrocities against the Jews in the Netherlands and sentenced to death by hanging. He was hanged on October 16, 1946. His last words were "I believe in Germany."

Sperre   A *Sperre* (Exemption) was a special stamp placed on an ID indicating that the holder of the document with such stamp was exempt from labor camps. The text in German read *"Inhaber dieses Ausweises ist bis auf Weiteres von Arbeitseinsatz Freigestelt."* My mother and maternal grandmother were able to arrange such *Sperre* for Mom's sister Margaret and her three children after they had been taken in custody and interred at the Dutch concentration/transit camp, Westerbork, by bribing German officials with diamond jewelry. As Margaret's husband was a key figure in the Resistance, the ID cards for Margaret and the children featured the letter "S" for *Straf*, the Dutch word for "punishment," which, absent the *Sperre,* would have resulted in deportation to the killing camp at Sobibor.

Theresienstadt (Terezin)   Theresienstadt, also known as *Terezin* in the Czech language, is a former fortress dating back to the late 1700's located some 45 miles from Prague in the Czech Republic. It was a concentration camp, transit camp, and even a ghetto established by the Germans, among other things, as a collection point for academics, writers, poets, musicians, composers, actors, artists, professors and others in the world of academia, arts and culture, which became an important part of Nazi propaganda to demonstrate to the world the beneficial treatment of such persons in a safe haven during their incarceration by the Nazis. For those who survived in the Camp, many for months even years, the camp in fact had a remarkably rich cultural life with several orchestras, and theaters, for example, while at the same time the camp arranged deportations and killings of thousands. It was there that my parents' friend Jo Spier was ordered to create drawings of captives strolling down streets with caf s while musicians played in gazebos in a park, all intended to deceive the International Red Cross when it came to view conditions at the Camp in June 1944. For weeks the camp was cleaned and beautified, while to avoid the appearance of overcrowding, many prisoners were deported to death camps. Theresienstadt was thus not primarily established as a killing camp, although tens of thousands in fact died there from disease, malnutrition, and other causes and many were deported to death camps, including Auschwitz-Birkenau.

Westerbork   Westerbork, located in the Northeast of the Netherlands, was established by the Dutch government (and in part by the Jewish community) in 1939 as a camp for refugees (*vluchtelingen*) from Nazi Germany. Seyss-Inquart and the German occupation administration took over the camp in July 1942, expanding it and converting it to a concentration and transit camp for deportation of Jews to concentration and death camps in Germany and Poland. An estimated 107,000 persons were deported from Westerbork of whom only an estimated 5,000 survived. Many of our relatives passed through Westerbork before being deported to the killing camps at Sobibor and Auschwitz-Birkenau where substantially all were killed, or to the concentration camps at Bergen-Belsen and Theresienstadt where some survived. While in the camp, Jewish inmates attempted to maintain a sense of normalcy with schools, theater and music performances. The camp was liberated by Canadian troops in April 1945 when there were still nearly 900 inmates. It was demolished in 1970; in its place there is now a museum of remembrance.

Index